MW00477737

# THE SCHOOLING
## OF A
# 21st CENTURY PRINCIPAL

# THE SCHOOLING OF A 21st CENTURY PRINCIPAL

### Connections, Reflections, and Commentaries of an Unwitting School Leader

**A**

**MEMOIR**

From Holocaust Survivors to 9/11
Construction Referendums to Bulldozer Parents
Common Core to Technology Integration
High Stakes Testing to Teacher Evaluation
Bullying Laws to School Shootings
Stressed Kids to 21st Century Innovation

# MICHAEL L. CAHILL

Copyright © 2021 by Michael L. Cahill

Print ISBN: 978-1-66780-8-895
eBook ISBN: 978-1-66780-8-901

All rights reserved. No part of this book may be reproduced or transmitted in any form or by any means, electronic or mechanical, including photocopying, recording, or by any information storage and retrieval system without the written permission of the author, except where permitted by law.

Printed in the United States of America

Disclaimer: None of the names of students used in various scenarios in my book represent any actual students from Millburn Middle School. In fact, names are either "borrowed" from my extended family or fictionalized.

Cover photo by Mike Cahill

Visit my website at www.michaellcahill.com

*In loving memory of my mom, Marie, who passed away in March 2021.*

*This book is dedicated to my family, my wife Lea Natalicchio Cahill and our children, Michael and Caroline. Lea, the love of my life, has been my biggest fan as well as my counselor and editor in this undertaking. For years my family listened to my stories, were sounding boards for my ideas, and helped me through difficult or sad times. My children served as my consultants as I sought to better understand what it was like growing up in the 21st Century and the experience of being a student in their own schools. I survived being a middle school principal and parent, twice.*

*My heart is filled with gratitude for all of the individuals who guided me along my life's journey, especially those who saw something special in me or shaped my principles and the principal inside me:*

*Philip Bruno*
*Lawrence Creedon, Ed.D.*
*Katherine Goerss, Ph.D.*
*Theresa Gonnella*
*Sister Rose Thering, O.P., Ph.D.*
*Charles Tortorella*

*Finally, my book is dedicated to all those who dare to teach and can never turn it off.*

*You know what I mean.*

# CONTENTS

# Preface

BEFORE THE BALLPOINT EVER SCRATCHED THE SURFACE OF paper, or fingertips collided with a keyboard, in my mind I could see scenes from my personal and professional life spliced together like one of my father's 8 millimeter family movies that he would play on the door of our white refrigerator from a clunky brown movie projector. *The Schooling of a 21st Century Principal* picks up where my father and his movie camera left off.

Ubiquitous signs had more than hinted that the time had come for me to shed the mantle of leadership, so I retired after serving sixteen years as a school principal. The question most prominent in my head as a recovering principal was, "What just happened?" Of course, the word "just" did not mean what happened this year, it implied what transpired over the span of a career spent almost exclusively in one school.

So I began to write about my experiences, and I just kept on going. What undoubtedly started as a therapeutic exercise evolved into something deeper, and while I initially conjured a book along the lines of "a year in the life of a middle school principal," I realized that all the details captured in my notes as well as those hard-wired in my brain served to illustrate or illuminate greater movements and moments, themes, transitions, and epiphanies since the time I was in high school and already knew I wanted to be a teacher.

As the framework of a book emerged, I pondered my purpose for writing. For starters, everyone has a story to tell, and the tale of triumphs and trials of my leadership roles in Millburn Township - an affluent, complex, and demanding New Jersey suburb - is also the sharing of the story of my school, the school where I had worked for more than half of my life, a life that revolved around my school. For those of us who have spent significant time in our careers in one place, our stories, milestones, challenges, achievements - our lives - are interwoven. It occurred to me that a memoir - seemingly about myself *and* my school - was most fitting.

Ultimately, as I thought about the people who influenced me, events that had a profound effect on me, and the opportunities to learn and to lead, I saw the connectedness of how I came to do what I did and where. It also became evident to me that the reasons and purposes - the "why" - of my leadership came with a timestamp and an expiration date.

But my book is not just about me. It's also about the changing dynamics of teaching and learning in 21st Century schools. The times we live in. Rising expectations for students, teachers, and schools. The health of our kids. Leadership in response to sometimes overwhelming reform. The domination of technology. More aggressive parents. Teachers under attack. School shootings. The principalship.

It is no wonder school districts face a dwindling pool of candidates to fill principal vacancies. Indeed, why would anyone want to do this job, considering its never-ending expansion of mandates, stresses, and liabilities? I hope to enlighten readers about how these factors have upped the ante for school leaders everywhere and in unexpected ways in this new millennium.

It is also important to me to shine a light on the rising levels of stress and myriad mental health challenges that middle school and high school students face today. If a school is indeed a microcosm of society, then we should all be concerned. The state of our children's health, especially mental health, deserves and demands a broader social policy response than just how stretched school personnel are able to help kids in crisis while they are still of school age.

My book conveys my journey, including the detours and doubts, to become a teacher and an administrator. The examination of my roles as principal exposes the nitty-gritty of what it means to be a part of the universe of middle schoolers, and specifically in a high-achieving pressure cooker environment. The culminating chapters are about leading in a culture of change as well as in a changing culture.

As I chronicled the events and the internal and external forces that impacted me, my leadership, and my building, I realized that educators across the country also weathered a transformation unlike any other during the last decade.

Though I never set out to be a school administrator, I was destined to serve in several leadership capacities at the Millburn Middle School, the other place I called home for three decades, an experience I found at times exhilarating, exasperating, and enervating.

# 1. First Day Jitters

THE HUM OF HUNDREDS OF SIXTH GRADERS REACHED A crescendo before silence settled over the masses. These seekers of truth and light had crossed over the abyss from their comfy neighborhood elementary schools where, like seedlings, they were watered and nurtured every day. Today was a milestone most of them had anticipated and some had dreaded. It was not only their first day in a new school, it also signaled their arrival at the precipice of pubescence with all of the rights and privileges pertaining to an imminent and unprecedented growth cycle not seen since their early days of teething. On this day we welcomed them to the hallowed hallways of the hormone highway, otherwise known as middle school.

Today was my first day as well, even though I had spent the last fourteen years here at the Millburn Middle School. As I approached the lectern, all eyes were on me. Not just the anxious eyes of these kindred spirits, but also the battle-scarred eyes of my teacher colleagues.

How did I get here?

I never wanted to be a principal, here or anywhere else. At least not throughout most of my twelve years as a classroom teacher. Along my journey came the influencers and guides whom I alternately blessed and cursed for coaxing me out of my own comfort zone. I was on the precipice of something, too, of proving myself worthy. Now it was showtime.

My suit betrayed my position. It said to everyone else, "He's in charge." This costume, sporting a red power tie designed to fabricate confidence, masked the doubt that welled up within. What will this day be like? What can go wrong? Will the master schedule work? How do I balance encouragement with expectation in my words of welcome? Today was a day of first impressions. Today was the only day to get an entire school and a whole year off to a good start.

No pressure. Easy peasy.

While I was aware that I was lacking in the wisdom and experience of those who had walked in my wingtips before, I have always had a streak of independence in me, of wanting to figure things out for myself. So I relied on my teacher instincts to prepare in every way possible to make this day successful. I comforted myself that I knew all about middle level learners, my building, the district and the community. I had a leg up in knowing the teachers. I had the benefit of learning from a gifted mentor. I had a reputation of taking things - and myself - seriously.

Still, I was distracted. And for good reason. I remembered when, as assistant principal, all of the information I had entered for the new school year schedule muddled together on the monitor and then suddenly and inexplicably vanished before my very eyes. And not only my eyes. I had someone else come in to witness this phenomenon when I attempted to start over so that others would not think I was crazy, or completely inept with technology.

Was the cause malfunctioning machinery? An algorithm gone awry? A data-destroying virus? Had another seventh grader hacked into the system? Our tech consultant had never experienced an anomaly like this in any of the number of districts that used his services. No, this was some unmistakable bad juju, a familiar yet unwelcome energy at work here, the scapegoat for all of the unforetold and unexplained calamities in our school.

Karma redeeming a receipt for some past life transgression. Or the haunting of unreleased souls, like at Hogwarts, of past principals trolling hallways shouting to students to walk, reminding them to stay to the right, and picking up errant pencils, erasers, notes, and gum wrappers, hazing newbies like me with their warning, "Don't think you are going to have it any easier than I did!" Or a hex by some haters who did not want to see me succeed. Forces within the universe test our mettle as they rattle us with the unexpected, undermine us with the uncontrollable, confront us with resistance.

The disappearing data episode had chipped away at an already fragile sense of security when it came to technology. It was the dawn of the twenty-first century, only one year after surviving the prospect of millennial mayhem from the much-ballyhooed Y2K threat. Schools were on the verge of becoming utterly reliant upon the tools of technology, now our enabler in this codependent relationship.

Other questions that loitered in my head as I prepared for opening day had to do with the more operational realities of school life. Will messy summer renovations be completed, and will the building be cleaned in time? Were the lockers coded accurately with their combinations? How many of those old dilapidated locker doors just won't budge in September?

As if all of this were not enough, our school was undertaking a major construction project, adding a new wing of classrooms. My primary concern, and additional focus, was the safety and welfare of our students and staff.

The best way to describe opening day in middle school is "managed chaos." A building dormant for the summer suddenly transforms into a hub of motion and sound as kids pour in, like bees to a hive. When more than a thousand middle schoolers show up on the first day, or any other day for that matter, a healthy percentage of them will not know where they are supposed to be, or what they are supposed to be doing, at any given moment.

Because we did not want sixth graders to fret about finding classrooms on their first day in an unfamiliar, intimidatingly larger, and at times bewildering building, they were corralled into the auditorium as soon as they stepped over the threshold. Seventh and eighth graders, seasoned survivors of the middle school way of life, were instructed to report to their homerooms to receive a copy of their schedules and locker assignments.

That, at least, was the goal.

What really happened was that kids from all grades forgot where they were supposed to be, with not a clue about their schedule or homeroom, and were unable to open their lockers. A few neurotic sixth grade parents hid in the shadows of the hallway stalking their children while new families showed up without an appointment to register for school. The office was inundated by students, teachers, and parents with a ton of questions.

During the sixth grade assembly I was one of a cadre of administrators, a guidance counselor, and a team leader who welcomed our new class and kicked off the day's orientation activities. We did not want to overwhelm them, and we knew sixth graders were nervous and antsy, so it would be important for our newcomers to move around and discover their new surroundings for themselves.

As the first official speaker, I seized upon the significance of the moment, the consolidation of all students from five elementary schools. "Look around this room. These are the peers you will be with through middle school and high school. It is important for you to make new friends because today you begin this big journey together as you form the Millburn High School Class of 2008."

I continued, "You spend six years in your elementary schools and four years in high school, but you are all going to do the most growing and changing in the school where you will spend the least amount of time. Believe me when I say these next three years will go by quickly!"

In my mind's eye I could still see the dignified Eighth Grade Move-Up Ceremony held barely two months ago in this very auditorium, a cathedral of gilded chandeliers, golden crisscross ceiling lattice, and gold-leafed Corinthian columns that consecrated beginnings and endings. We marveled at how our students had sprouted and evolved even as we were filled with wonder at how swiftly the years seemed to pass.

Our regal auditorium where we welcomed students and bade them farewell.

I often prepared to speak about someone in the news or on student radar - an athlete, author, hero, leader, or model citizen - such as Michael Phelps, Nelson Mandela, J.K. Rowling, who could serve up some inspiration on opening day.

I chatted about the differences between elementary school and middle school and unpacked our school motto: Respect, Responsibility, and Excellence.

I deemed it important to declare war on bullying on the first day of school. "We do not tolerate bullies at the middle school. If you had a conflict, or just could not get along with someone at your elementary school, then stay away from that person. There is no reason to continue any feud since you have so many other people you can be friends with."

Hinting toward my goal of developing character and good manners, I said, "If you see me in the hall, say 'hello.' I will say 'hello' to you, too. Say 'please,' 'thank you,' and 'good morning.' Hold the door for others. Help people who drop something or who are struggling. These actions are expected in our community."

I said what I felt I had to say, to set a tone on the first day of the school year about how we interact with others. I kept my remarks brief, ending on a sweet note, "Don't forget about the ice cream party!"

After the assembly, sixth graders were released to their homeroom teachers. Pandemonium soon broke out in the hallways as I watched pupils practice their locker combinations, tour the building, and wander around the school in hordes to complete their treasure hunt. This enterprise led them on a safari searching for answers, such as the names and locations of the principals, guidance counselor, nurse, and secretaries as well as details about our school found on banners, signs, and displays. Over the years tearful students would lose their way and seek my help to reconnect them with their group. Teachers and hapless substitutes would also somehow lose their entire class of students.

The best part for me was that the kids were smiling.

I strolled into the sixth grade lunch to answer questions and mingle with students. I was on bended knee many times at dismissal to assist sixth graders with opening those infernal lower lockers. And one of the first things I learned to ask was, "What is your locker number?" because it was amazing how many times children were trying to open the wrong locker.

Of course, opening day assemblies were scheduled for seventh and eighth graders, too. I framed my messages to the upper grades around the themes of setting goals and using all of the resources available to achieve those goals. I forewarned seventh graders about the "bump it up" challenges of the curriculum and explained the placement process for eighth grade. My focus in the eighth grade meeting was on readiness for high school and the important role that eighth graders embodied for our younger students by their model behavior and contributions to the life of our school as its leaders.

My own goals for the first day were to welcome everyone, communicate a message of expectation and support, and tend to the essential details.

When I returned to my office periodically in between all of the assemblies and activities, I observed a growing pile of phone messages, emails, notes and folders. The red message light on my phone, like my tie, blazed with determination. Parents eager to petition the principal for team switches, teacher changes, and higher level placements impatiently awaited a fateful return call. The folders contained transcripts and information about new registrants that required my review fairly quickly for them to become active students.

Administratively, it is a day where you have to be everywhere at once.

The first day of school is also the culmination of a summer of planning and gearing up for the opening. If this day was successful, and every indicator suggested it was, it was largely because preparation commenced well before the prior school year ended. People do not realize how much work there is to do, and over the years parents have said, "I thought you were off the entire summer."

I wish.

All of the groundwork was behind me now. So, at the beginning of this, my first year as principal, I held my breath.

By all counts it had been a "normal" and relatively smooth opening. It was against this backdrop of relief and the growing confidence of smooth sailing into a new school term at the helm that made me start to think, "I can do this!"

Until the fourth day of school of my first year as principal.

# 2. Baptism by Fire

THE SKY WAS BLUE, THE AIR COOL, AND THE SUN BRIGHT ON this glorious waning day of summer. It was Tuesday, September 11, 2001, and I was engaged in a telephone conversation with a parent regarding her son's reading progress. The time was about a quarter to nine in the morning, and I could detect morning news show banter in the background.

Suddenly the woman shrieked, "A plane crashed into the World Trade Center!"

Somehow in my mind I pictured a small plane that lost control and accidentally struck one of the towers. But then this news evoked a foreboding memory of the bombing of the World Trade Center several years earlier.

I immediately thought about my younger cousin, Richard L. Salinardi, Jr., employed as the general manager for Aramark food service at the observation deck of the World Trade Center.

No one could have anticipated that a large commercial airplane was intentionally flown into the North Tower by militants of an Islamic extremist group, or that it would happen again about twenty minutes later to its companion, the South Tower.

I watched these "twin towers" rise on the Lower Manhattan skyline as a kid growing up across the Hudson River in Hoboken, New Jersey. The towers were a sight to behold from our vantage point and for all of the people on cruise ships and boats that sailed around the lower tip of Manhattan between the towers on one side and the Statue of Liberty on the other. For several months I traveled through the towers every morning on my way to work during a "gap year" between teaching jobs. I also escorted summer exchange students from Mexico on field trips to the observation deck. My wife and I had our second date there, lingering over the luminescent spires of classic older skyscrapers, the twinkling lights spanning the bridges of the East River, and the majesty of the Lady of the Harbor on a clear summer evening. It was inconceivable that literally in less than one hour and forty-five minutes these beloved iconic New York City structures and symbols of American prosperity and ingenuity would crumble.

Photo of the Twin Towers taken by my aunt, Joan Cahill, on September 9, 2001, from Hoboken, N.J. Two days later she captured graphic images of their destruction.

No one in school or anywhere else could really understand the scale of what was later determined to be an attack, a *jihad* on America intended to cripple our government, military and financial institutions. No one could have expected that those two behemoth edifices would collapse and take with them thousands of employees who worked in commercial, legal and investment companies, the very people who lived in surrounding communities and whose children attended suburban schools like mine. Stories were later published about the many unclaimed automobiles sitting in the parking lots of the suburban train stations that dotted the New Jersey Transit railroad tracks. Millburn, New Jersey, is located only about 20 miles outside of the city. Eight individuals from Millburn Township perished in this massacre, as did my 32-year-old cousin, still known in our family as "Little Richie."

News about two more hijacked planes, one flown into the Pentagon and United Airlines Flight 93 that crashed in a Pennsylvania field, heightened everyone's anxiety about further terrorist attacks and left a feeling of panic, disorientation, and even helplessness. Inside it felt as if we were suddenly at war, but what was unfamiliar and shocking was the realization that the fighting was happening *right here*, only miles away. We were on the battlefield. We asked ourselves, What was next? Do we need to defend ourselves? What were our country's leaders doing? We longed for reassurance that the attacks were over, and we banked on our government to restore some semblance of leadership, order, and security.

As the principal of the school, I sensed these were things everyone also needed from me.

Principals have to be a presence in their buildings on a normal day; on a day like this it is imperative to be everywhere. It was a two-way street; staff and students want to see you when all is not well, and as principal I wanted to be as responsive as I could.

Ominously, a police officer had been posted at our front entrance. Frequent communications started coming from central office. Parents trickled in to retrieve their children. Of course, teachers began to find out, and their emotional reactions, worried looks about their loved ones who worked at the World Trade Center or in the surrounding area of Lower Manhattan, and conversations made it inevitable that the news would seep out. With no script to follow, no preparation or plan for a national emergency, I wondered what, if anything, I should tell the children while they were here in school.

I tried to stick my head into the teachers' room to glance at what was happening on the news. The information and images on the screen were disturbing and horrific, unimaginable and impossible to comprehend, yet it was difficult to pull away. But watching wasn't helpful to the tasks at hand. My goals were to remain calm, think, and take care of the people in my building.

Board of Education members soon arrived to offer assistance, and discussions ensued about closing school early. Regardless of the time of dismissal, the concern became one of making sure that every child had an adult at home since so many of our parents worked in the city. The Midtown Direct commuter train barreled past our school, literally only yards away from our classrooms, all day long. But now the tracks were eerily quiet, and no one knew yet how shattering the loss of life would be to this community and others nearby.

The peace of the morning's bright sunny skies was broken by the *whoosh* of fighter planes circling the metropolitan area. Smoke from the inferno permeated the air, and people were glued to their television screens and uncharacteristically emotional news anchors. The area near our school had local look-out points where residents could view the skyscrapers of Manhattan, and they now could see for themselves that the two tallest buildings had so incredulously disappeared, leaving plumes of black smoke rising from the ashes.

The skyline, like the lives of so many families, had been forever altered.

Our administrative team decided that it was important first to make sure all of the teachers knew what was happening, but without using the public address system. I composed a concise factual statement that was delivered to every classroom by a teacher's hand (a method of communication used in critical times referred to as "the pony express"). In my message I asked teachers to try to keep quiet about it, and to continue teaching, in order to allow students the opportunity to reckon with the enormity and the details at home with their loved ones. Of course this news would be traumatic and difficult for adults to handle, too, much less try to act as though everything was fine. It was especially hard when one teacher was worried about her son, who turned out to be okay, and another one was concerned about her soon-to-be son-in-law, whose life would be lost. The wedding, scheduled for October, became a repast.

I did speak with our students during their lunch time. I provided basic information, immediately after which I was surrounded by anxious children. "Mr. Cahill, do you know which tower was hit? Do you know if this was an

accident? My dad works...my uncle...Do you have any more information?"
Their worried expressions and palpable concern tested my own composure.

Shock, for adults and children. Unanswered questions. The need to
know. Fear. Already a sense of loss, even if we did not yet know who, or
understand what, was lost. Brimming emotion.

Keep it together, Mr. Principal. Focus on what you have to do.

We had to establish an orderly and secure way to handle the barrage of
parents who were now descending on our school demanding their children.
Teachers scrambled to help along with board members, other parents, and
administrators. We had a responsibility to release children only to their
parents, guardians, or other individuals authorized by parents as emergency
contacts. We aimed to make sure that each child was safe and accounted for,
so we established a sign-out procedure, first confirming the identity of the
adults requesting to take their own kids as well as the children of relatives,
friends or neighbors.

It was not until the next morning that an African American mother
came forward to express her anger at what she described as the racism of one
of my administrators during the commotion of the mass exodus from school.
A rookie assistant principal had inquired if the mother was the student's
nanny instead of just asking what her relationship was to the as yet unseen
pupil she was requesting to sign out. The child was also African-American.
A Jewish parent presented herself to warn me of her belief that Short Hills
was probably the next prime target for an attack by Muslims because so many
affluent Jews lived in the community, and crippling rail service at the township's train stations would make strategic sense in what now seemed like a war
zone. And a Muslim parent, a medical doctor who worked for the military in
the city, came in to convey her concern that her children would be subjected
to reprisals in this white and heavily Jewish community. World conflict
landed in the principal's office in a blur of shock, confusion and uncertainty.

It was actually this doctor who conveyed to me that no more survivors
would be recovered from the rubble of the towers. I appreciated her candor,
but she had no idea how devastating that news was to me personally. Despite
all the flyers with missing people's faces and the ongoing futile searches of

hospitals and shelters for unaccounted-for loved ones like my cousin, who did not want to push into an already crowded elevator and instead would wait for the next one, now any flicker of hope still alive from yesterday was snuffed out.

Six years earlier I had flown to St. Louis to attend Richie and Brittley's wedding. Though Richie was also born in Hoboken, he had moved with his family to St. Louis at a young age. My warm and loving cousin's fate, reminiscent of a tragic Greek figure, was ironically and fatally sealed when he returned to live in Hoboken, the home of his immigrant ancestors and extended families and a short subway ride away from his new job at the World Trade Center.

Richie was about to embark on a trip to Ecuador the next day to visit the parents of the friend who waited alongside him for another elevator. The people on that first elevator managed to escape before the tower collapsed.

Other stories came to light about how individuals on this work day were either saved or lost. One mom in my school was running late to work and was on the ferry crossing the Hudson River when the first plane struck the North Tower. The ferry turned around. Other people decided not to stop at the office first, or to take advantage of the idyllic weather and call in a vacation day.

Many families had to wait to see if their loved ones who lived or worked anywhere in the city were okay, for it was difficult to flee the city because all transit systems were shut down amidst fear of further attacks, and communication was nearly impossible due to equipment damage and because phone lines could not handle the volume of callers.

Students remaining in the building at dismissal were either going to board a bus or walk home. An adult spoke with all of the children to ascertain if a parent was at home or where else - a friend, neighbor, relative - they could go. Anyone who had nowhere to go stayed with us in school. I remember when the last parent arrived around 6:30 in the evening, a dad who worked in the city who looked as if he had been to hell and back, covered with ash and grief. I had no words.

On my drive home I thought about how my daughter, barely four months old, was born into a very different world. Underneath all of the emotion, grief, worry, and weight of responsibility, what lurked in my brain was the utter shock and anger that an act of war could be perpetrated upon our people on our soil. And how the United States, world power and champion of freedom, did not protect its citizens. No one ever imagined this could happen here, and now that it had, it seemed to change everything, including the prospect of it happening again.

As a principal, I never could have foreseen that I would be leading a school during what was an unprecedented invasion of our country's mainland. It was a giant wake-up call for schools to have multiple emergency contact numbers and crisis management plans precisely for cataclysmic events like this one as well as the unthinkable and tragic shooting sprees that were becoming a part of the school landscape.

Ultimately, our job became to pick up the pieces and "normalize" the experience of students, whatever that meant. Our school cabinet meetings developed a blueprint focused on identifying students who lost parents or other relatives and connecting with them to provide support, planning presentations about grief to the general parent community, and monitoring all students for signs of stress, anxiety, and depression. And it also meant being fully prepared with a communications and dismissal plan should something like this ever happen again.

Not everyone was happy with our approach, but there was no playbook or perfect plan. Some parents lobbied for student assemblies about grief. I believe we all grieve in different ways, and over the years I have seen the contagious and destabilizing effects of overwhelming emotion in larger groups of young adolescents. Our plan was to move forward, honoring the right of way for each student, preserving an environment for learning, and maintaining school as a structured, dependable, and safe place for students to feel as though this aspect of their life had not changed.

Halfway into the school year, we experienced something that had never happened before, and never happened again, during my time at Millburn Middle School. Someone had set off a fire alarm. We have had other occasions where dust or an insect in a smoke detector triggered an unexpected alarm, but when I discovered that someone had purposely pulled the lever on a fire alarm box I was stunned. Having two brothers who were active duty police officers just across the river from Ground Zero during this time of heightened alert also brought this stunt closer to home for me. It was highly unusual for me to convene an impromptu assembly, but we needed to deal with this immediately as I was hell-bent on finding the wrongdoer and sending a clear message that this kind of behavior would not be tolerated. This is what I said:

"Today's fire alarm was not a drill. In fact, it is the first time our school has ever had someone pull a false fire alarm. This was shocking to me also for the reason that only months ago we watched as so many first responders lost their lives at the World Trade Center.

Every time an emergency call comes in, our police, fire and emergency personnel put their lives at risk. We cannot tolerate allowing individuals to make a game out of a fire alarm. The student or students responsible caused the evacuation of our school, put firefighters and police in danger, and also took them away from what could have been real emergencies.

I want the names of the individuals responsible for today's fire alarm, and I want them by the end of the lunch periods. If you did it, you need to come to the office and tell me. If you know who did it, you need to tell me because it is the right thing to do, especially in light of what happened on September 11th."

I appealed to our students' sense of right and wrong, as individuals mature enough to understand. I could see that my words resonated with the kids. It was not long before I had four separate visits from individuals and pairs of students, all of whom came to my office bearing the same name of the alleged culprit. I had faith in my students, and I was proud of them. I also knew that middle schoolers never stop talking and that no one would dare to do this without hoping to reap the glory.

Through the next fifteen years several students in my school were children from families who suffered the loss of a parent, including some who were not yet born when 9/11 occurred. I was honored to be able to provide any accommodation when a parent wanted to meet or discuss the children. Coming to know them and internalizing their immense loss influenced my thinking and decision-making when it came to future 9/11 anniversary dates. For years I sided with the survivor families by not holding public ceremonies or moments of silence on 9/11 so that their children would be able to come to school and make it through a day that was already too difficult to bear.

It was easier to integrate the needs and wants of everyone once the anniversary was officially dubbed "Patriot's Day" and we could pay tribute to the ongoing contributions of first responders. We started a tradition of having our sixth graders plant small flags into the ground on the lawn in front of the school. Of course, the assistant principal would reset them so that the flags would be in straight lines. This was a nice optic for the community as our school was located on a very busy county road, across the street from a regional theater called the Paper Mill Playhouse, near the town center, and only a block away from the train station.

Photo by Theresa Gonnella

As a school we knew we had to conduct more than an annual commemoration of the terrible tragedy that reeled America. While we already had a peer leadership program and a new course entitled "Leadership for a Peaceful School," we decided that we had to continue to thread the topics of leadership, character, and tolerance in our curriculum in all grade levels.

Like so many other organizations and institutions, momentum was building in our school to dedicate a physical space, not just in remembrance of 9/11, but also using art and messages as a powerful way of turning grief into hope. Peer leadership advisor and art teacher Claudia Sohr, in concert with other teachers, parents, and peer leader students, and with the help of local landscaper Chris Chiaramonte, an alumnus of our school, constructed a 9/11 Peace Garden on the front lawn.

Moms and dads, teachers and students gathered on a Saturday in our school cafeteria. Using an assembly line approach, cement was poured into pizza boxes to fashion fifty steps. Each step was bordered on the top and bottom by four blue rectangular ceramic tiles so that all of the steps had a common pattern between which the participants, mostly students, decorated them by embedding the cement with various fragments of scrap metal, colored glass, and symbols. Each step was endowed with a word, a theme considered an important ingredient for cultivating peace, such as love, tolerance, empathy, and hope.

My son Michael and I also designed a step. After the cement was poured, I selected a key as a symbol and Michael picked out some plastic cows (he was five years old). We created a mosaic from sky blue ceramic fragments, beige and cream-colored stones, coin-shaped shiny pieces of metal, and the rotating dial of a combination lock to decorate our step, the theme of which was "believe."

These steps were laid out on the front lawn right outside my office windows, adjacent to the front door, in an interlocking spiral shape. Anyone could walk the path of peace on a journey around these stepping stones, in the middle of which was a wooden post inscribed on all four sides with our wish "May Peace Prevail on Earth" in English, Chinese, Hindi, and Hebrew.

The spirals were eventually lengthened, enriching the garden with more themes.

This artistic endeavor engaged our community in a process of sculpting something beautiful and meaningful, a pathway that became a teaching tool for classes - or for wandering students, or visitors to our school, or attendees at our concerts and programs - and a visible symbol of what our school stood for. It was a reminder not only of what happened but of the many ideals to which we should all aspire in order to be better human beings. My personal hope was that visitors could also find a measure of comfort and healing.

Image of Millburn Middle School Peace Garden, 6/29/2006
The Item of Millburn and Short Hills - Now named NorthJersey.com.
© Adam Anik – USA TODAY NETWORK

At the end of the school year I found myself registered for a summer institute on arts education at Lincoln Center in New York City. I was not your typical participant in arts programs, especially ones that might require some public expression or interpretation of the "touchy-feely" type. After persevering through some morning hands-on creative activities, the group attended a lecture by the late Dr. Maxine Greene, known as the Philosopher-in-Residence of the Lincoln Center Institute for the Arts in Education. It was then that I knew why I was there.

I was surprised that at this event Dr. Greene's presentation was about 9/11, and it seemed as though she was speaking directly to me. Dr. Greene acknowledged the courage, commitment, and sense of responsibility exhibited by educators on the day of the attacks, especially by those teachers who taught near the World Trade Center complex. She spoke teacher-to-teacher to the audience about the importance of taking the time necessary to process and integrate all of what had happened in order to heal. Educators would continue to shoulder responsibility for traumatized children who needed us, their teachers and administrators, to deal with our grief first if we were going to help them move forward.

Every year on the anniversary of these attacks people commonly post the expression "Never forget!" I don't need a reminder. This day was a defining moment in my life and profession. I know I speak for many others, including my own family, when I say I lost a part of myself that day. Loved ones were taken from us - nearly 3,000 - including the first responders who sacrificed their lives in the line of duty. A piece of the city we loved went with them, and so did a peace of mind we may have taken for granted. It is a hurt that does not heal.

No one could have predicted the scope of tragedy and heartbreak that transpired on 9/11, and no textbook or course could have prepared school leaders for that dark day or what followed. An epiphany for me was that principals have to expect the unexpected, so I created my own template of a crisis management plan, and henceforth it went everywhere I did.

9/11 strengthened my resolve to lead and take care of my school in the best way I could.

I learned that leading in a crisis of this magnitude demands common sense and clear thinking; decision-making based on priorities; and compassion, communication and collaboration. While the organizational and technological details of running a school matter, they pale in comparison to when truly unimaginable events impact the security and well-being of the children in our charge and their families. Meeting these needs constitutes the foremost challenge of leadership. I was blessed to have the right people all around me as we stepped forward together in a grieving community and a very different world than when the school year had opened less than a week before.

# 3. Suspend Reality

LAKE WOBEGON IS A FICTIONAL TOWN IN GARRISON Keillor's canon of Prairie Home Companion tall tales. Keillor characterizes his utopian setting as a place "where all the women are strong, all the men are good-looking, and all the children are above average." Whenever I listened to Keillor spin his yarns, this description always reminded me of the place where I worked.

Millburn Township, comprising Millburn and Short Hills, is indeed an affluent suburb. In a March 5, 2018, *Bloomberg* internet article by Shelly Hagan and Wei Lu entitled "America's 100 Richest Places," Short Hills was ranked #5 in the nation with an average annual household income, based on 2016 U.S. Census data, of $354,500. By comparison, 2018 census data determined median U.S. household income to be $63,179. Real estate websites in 2018 listed median home values in Short Hills at more than 1.4 million and in Millburn at over $820,000.

Families in the district travel far and often, and venture into Manhattan to attend Broadway shows, concerts, and museum exhibits. Many have vacation homes, not just at the Jersey Shore but in the Hamptons, Nantucket, Telluride or Jackson Hole. Some students have a nanny or au pair and a housekeeper. Other students commute to school via a car service. Children are involved in a wide variety of school-sponsored extracurricular activities and team sports, as well as extended after-school learning in music, acting, languages, and religion and, for some, taxing training for professional, competitive or even Olympic aspirations in swimming, tennis, skating, and horseback riding.

While only 30% of the nation's residents have acquired a bachelor's degree or higher, 84.4% of the township earned at least an undergraduate degree.

It is fair to say that the reality of living in and growing up in the township is starkly different from most other communities in New Jersey or the country, for that matter. But for so many people it is not just about living in an affluent leafy bedroom community, it is also about sending their children to the best schools. And the statistics pertaining to the high school graduation rate, college attendance, selective college acceptances, National Merit Scholars, average SAT scores and other evaluative data indicate that Millburn is a community engaged in fostering effective schools.

During the twenty-one years I spent as an administrator at Millburn Middle School, our enrollment soared from 513 and peaked, at least until I retired, at just under 1200 students. Our growth was due to a convergence of several developments in the 1990's, including direct train service to Manhattan from Millburn and Short Hills, construction of 481 new residential units, and the implementation of full-day kindergarten. Births in the township in 1998 hit a 28-year high while residents over age 55 declined by 25% and accounted for only 22% of the population, leaving the door wide open, literally, for an influx of young families.

People come to Millburn with expectations. Children are sent to school from homes where often both parents are professionals. Residents have careers as Wall Street brokers, doctors, judges, attorneys, movie and literary critics, *New York Times* journalists, business owners, professional sports team owners, corporate executives and entrepreneurs. They are successful, well-educated, and cultured. Over the years I have sat around the table with P.T.O. moms who had Ph.D.'s, M.D.'s and M.B.A.'s. Parents are ambitious, accomplished, and achievement-oriented, and that is what they yearn for their children to be as well. Families from all over the globe come here to buy a house and pay the taxes because they want their kids to attend premier public schools and often expect them to be admitted to the finest colleges and universities.

Millburn has earned a reputation as a leading school district at the state and national levels. In its biennial rankings, *New Jersey Monthly* magazine named Millburn High School to the #1 slot for two times in a row, 2008 and 2010. The high school, also a National Blue Ribbon School of Excellence, continued to place near the top of the state's more than 300 high schools.

In 2018 *U.S. News & World Reports* ranked Millburn High School as #380 in the nation, awarding it gold medal status as one of America's top 500 public high schools. Niche.com ranked Millburn High School as #68 out of 17,867 high schools.

Niche.com also named Millburn Middle School the best public middle school in the nation, New Jersey, and the Metro New York area in 2016, comparing data from 15,656 schools in the country.

During the early 2000's the New Jersey state business community teamed up with education officials to identify "Benchmark Schools," largely based on how students performed on the Grade Eight Proficiency Test (GEPA), the state standardized test at that time. Millburn Middle School was honored during each of the four consecutive years the awards program existed, and my interviews with NJ News reporter Tony Caputo were broadcast on News 12 New Jersey.

Sharing a banner of recognition with Board President Dr. Mary Litterman and Superintendent Dr. Richard Brodow.

Our middle school playwright program consistently won awards from the NJ Young Playwrights organization, which sponsored equity actors to perform our students' plays on a local college stage. Our math teams invariably returned home with medals and trophies, as did our pupils who participated in world language competitions and our music students who competed in regional contests. The district has also been recognized as one of the 100 Best Communities for Music Education in the nation.

From an educator's point of view, teaching in a place like Millburn was, mostly, living the dream. Students perceived the importance of learning and achieving. While middle schoolers were still kids - impulsive, distracted, energetic, and highly social - our teachers could usually eradicate behavior issues with a conversation or a call home or, if necessary, with an email to a guidance counselor or a drop-in to the assistant principal's office. Kids also knew their parents would usually back up the school. In fact, most of our students were polite and could often be heard thanking teachers, not for doing something specifically for them, but for just teaching them. Unlike schools where teachers are worn down by how much they have to manage behaviors and muster parent support, our faculty could and did focus on teaching and learning.

We have had families, including those whose children transferred from private schools, tell us that it felt like we offered a private school education in our public schools.

Parents generously supported the educational system beyond what they already paid in taxes. Millburn Township is located in Essex County, the county with the highest average property taxes in New Jersey and one of the highest in the country, according to a *NJ101.5* internet article (4/5/18) entitled "4 Counties in New Jersey Have Highest Property Taxes in Nation" by Dino Flammia. Millburn Township also topped the list of towns that paid the highest average property tax bill of any community in New Jersey, according to a *NJ.com* internet article (3/9/2020) by Sarah Marcus captioned "Here are the 30 New Jersey Towns with the Highest Property Taxes." Despite the high cost of purchasing a home and residing in the township, the Education

Foundation of Millburn-Short Hills over the years raised more than $3 million to support school initiatives.

Prior to my final year at the middle school, the Ed Foundation had granted my request for $40,000, without which it would not have been possible to add three exciting new S.T.E.M cycle courses: TechConnect, Inventions and Innovations, and Design and Engineering. The Ed Foundation also funneled grants from a corporate donor, Dun & Bradstreet Credibility Corp., in a total amount of over $30,000 for the middle school to create S.T.E.M. courses, including robotics, animatronics, and coding. Over the years the Ed Foundation contributed SmartBoards and LCD projectors to reach our goal of equipping every classroom as well as funding a dedicated broadcast lab. The truth of the matter is that state-imposed budget caps, high property taxes, and scarce state aid forced districts like Millburn to depend on the fundraising and support of parents and the community to advance its technology and innovation agenda.

The middle school P.T.O. also fundraised to amass an annual balance sheet of close to $100,000 to fund mini-grants throughout the year for magazine subscriptions, teaching materials, library books and databases, teacher stipends for robotics club, peer leader activities, shirts and supplies, resources for guidance as well as larger sums for LCD projectors, Smart Boards, document cameras, photography equipment, fitness machines, computers for a broadcast lab, and an electronic sign on the front lawn - an incomplete list at best. In addition, the P.T.O. sponsored cultural arts events, after school clubs, after school homework support, teacher appreciation luncheons and TGIF (Thank God It's Friday recreation nights with a DJ and dancing, games, open gyms, and pizza). Cultural arts programs included grade-level residencies in poetry, short story writing, political cartooning, dance, and playwriting as well as assemblies on science, Shakespeare, various authors and composers, and music. In 2004, the PTO Cultural Arts Committee funded a memorable visit from Princess Heng Yi AiXinJueLuo, the granddaughter of the last emperor of China, who demonstrated painting techniques in the classic Chinese tradition for our sixth graders.

No doubt parental aspirations, resources, and a collective "can do" attitude fueled the district's ability to stay current with technology developments, cultural enrichment, underfunded curricular initiatives, and opportunities for parent education.

Beneath the veneer of the perception of the township as a perfect place in which to live and work lurked a culture of comparison and competition. While for some that might have just been considered a given, like "keeping up with the Joneses," one must consider the compounding effect of the expectations of opportunistic and often pushy parents within a homogenous, high-density concentration in the fifth wealthiest community in the nation. School leaders and staff had a front row seat to see how that played out in classrooms and in schools in a variety of ways every day.

One significant overt example of the competitiveness of this community could be seen at what was the middle school's annual science fair. Our upper gymnasium was packed with what were supposed to be displays of student work whose obvious sophistication and professionalism far exceeded expectations for students who were 12 or 13 years old. If it was not already clear that there was often more than mere influence or assistance by parents in the design, research and presentation of the submissions, it was confirmed after the judges - a panel of district and out-of-district teachers, supervisors, and superintendents - awarded prizes for the best projects. Parents argued with the judges, and with each other, about the merits of their work as compared with the winners. It spelled doom for what was supposed to be a fun, inquiry-based activity based on a question or an area of interest or the curiosity of a pupil.

The election of class officers, another long-ago abandoned student activity, generated stress because of the way parents interfered in what was primarily a popularity contest. After the election results had been tabulated, I announced the names of the winners at the end of the day over the public address system. Parents would follow up with phone calls demanding to know the vote count. I never shared the tally because I did not want anybody to feel bad. It was not important for students to know how many votes they received or won or lost by. Yet, parents persisted, even calling central office. One parent angrily declared that her daughter lost because I mispronounced her child's name when I called her to the podium to deliver her campaign speech.

As our school evolved, students acquired more meaningful roles in school governance and leadership through our peer leadership program.

I learned early on as a building administrator in Millburn that any award, honor, recognition or selection of a student resulted in questions from parents of other pupils about why their child was not chosen. Whether it was a peer leader group assignment, or a public speaking role at a school or district event, or the lead role in the play, or a special presentation, parents often wanted what someone else's child was having.

When I was first hired to teach at Millburn Middle School, I wondered why the teams at each grade level were identified simply by what initially seemed like random letters of the alphabet. Only two teams per grade existed then, and students and their teachers were either on Team B or Team L. I learned that the B and L represented two of the ingredients of the "great sandwich," bacon, lettuce and tomato, after which the teams were named. I further discovered the reason to be that in this district there could be no hierarchical naming system, like 1-2-3 or A-B-C, conveying a pecking order. As our school expanded, we added the T and later dressed the sandwich with the M for mayonnaise.

Ever since I started working in Millburn, the township had a divided feel to it. The municipality shares two zip codes, which is in and of itself a divide, indicative of different towns. Short Hills was a land purchase of 1500 acres in Millburn Township acquired by Stewart Hartshorn, who had a vision of what has been referred to as an "ideal town," a place "where natural beauty would not be destroyed by real estate developments, and where people of congenial tastes could dwell together. Mr. Hartshorn once in his later life said, in describing his attitude toward his chosen village, that his sole purpose was to create a harmonious community for people who appreciated nature, for he had found them to be people of taste and initiative." (Meisner, *A History of Millburn Township,* 2002). According to this account, Hartshorn selected his tenants or purchasers carefully, and he insisted that no two houses look alike.

Everything about these homes built in the late 1800's was large, including the staff of servants to care for the household, grounds and stables.

And so today larger estates and greater affluence can be found in the Short Hills section of the Township, and a "better than" attitude has reared its head in school over the generations in the words and spats that kids and even parents sometimes had. There is a certain cachet about Short Hills, including the name of its upscale shopping center, "The Mall at Short Hills." When I first started working in Millburn, a student organization's fundraiser sold T-shirts printed with a knockoff logo of the *Beverly Hills 90210* television series, substituting the name on the T-shirt logo with "Short Hills 07078," making Short Hills its rich East Coast equivalent.

Some Millburn parents had a "chip on the shoulder" attitude, like the ones who, after an incident in which their middle schooler was injured in a fall at school, accusingly said that their child would have received better first aid treatment from school personnel had the youngster lived in Short Hills.

Over the years I have known Millburn parents who would have sold their souls to say they lived in Short Hills, but I have also seen families relocate from Short Hills to Millburn, although a move in that direction raised questions. On one occasion, I was speaking with a parent outside the building after dismissal when another mom interrupted our conversation, saying, "I heard you moved to Millburn. Are you okay? Are you having money problems?"

Both sections of the township boast expensive real estate and high property taxes.

The polarity of the township generated political fall-out as well. Board and administrative decisions delicately considered the zip code ramifications as they sorted out personnel, programming, standardized test score results, and budgets for the elementary schools in the Millburn section.

Over the years I have received countless calls from parents regarding their child's team assignment or placement level for the purpose of being with the "right" peers. Sometimes, it was because parents encouraged the positive influence of specific individuals, or to continue a friendship from elementary school, a neighborhood, or team sports, and at other times it was, as they explained to me, "to get the right invitations," to be a part of the social elite.

Seventh grade is bar and bat mitzvah season, and this cherished rite of passage could be expected to be held almost every weekend given the proportion of our Jewish population. Whenever there are celebratory occasions, starting in elementary school, decisions about which peers will be invited can cause social ripples in school. The scale of the middle school is far greater than that of smaller elementary schools, so ripples become rip tides. It became fashionable for Jewish families to purchase a garment, generally a shirt of some kind, printed with the name of the bar/bat mitzvah and the date of the event. The celebrations ranged from humble family-oriented gatherings to grand parties at catering halls to flying invitees to vacation destinations. No matter the scale or the venue, attendees were expected to wear the garment together upon return to school. Just about every Monday the staff and the entire student body could see the sea of same colored shirts of the lucky kids who were included and the shadow cast upon those who had been passed over.

I decided to write about this every September in the P.T.O. Newsletter:

*Something to Think About… It's Monday morning and you are 13 years old and you walk into school, homeroom, the lunchroom, or the auditorium and everywhere you see a group of your peers wearing the same color sweatshirt or pants marking the occasion of a student's bar or bat mitzvah from the past weekend. And the scene repeats itself virtually every Monday throughout the year. It is a practice that divides and hurts…repeatedly. It fosters a culture of exclusivity and a competition for the greatest number of friends. It is a way of saying who is "in" and who is "out." Wear the shirts and the pants, but not as a group on the same day. When the group intentionally wears the clothing on the same day, it sends a statement about who was invited and who was not. As a school we hope to create a culture of inclusivity, tolerance, and acceptance at a critical time in the development of our students, but we need the support of parents to change this practice.*

I had a small band of parents who agreed with me and applauded my efforts. These parents would commend me at a PTO meeting or send me an email thanking me for confronting this issue. If nothing else, they could use my article as leverage against their child's pining to be a part of the pack on Monday.

The widest band of parents were those whose typical response was, "I agree with you, but when I spoke with my child his/her reaction was that *everyone else* who was there would be wearing the hoodie on Monday." The kids just stopped short of explicitly saying, "Wasn't that the point?"

Then came a solo dissenting opinion in a voicemail: "Mr. Cahill? I read your article in the newsletter, and here's how I see it. You don't run the whole world. Not everyone is invited to everything. Kids just have to learn to get over it."

Some parents countered that I should just ban the wearing of bar/bat mitzvah clothing. While that certainly would have made it easier for parents who agreed with me but were unwilling to play the heavy at home, wearing the clothing was not a breach of our dress code.

Working in a community with a large Jewish population, and also with staff members of Jewish heritage, I began to incorporate some Yiddish expressions that flew out of this second generation Irish-Italian American principal's mouth so naturally that others would smirk in surprise. My favorite was *mishegoss*, as it aptly described the chaos of most days in middle school and the often anticipated results of district decisions. *Nosh* was what the administrators and secretaries in the office did all day. A *noodge* characterized seventh graders. A *yenta* used to have to tell everyone everything in person but could now post it for the masses on social media. *Chutzpah* was what it took for those seventh grade students to hack into the school's database. *Farmisht* was the result of trying to understand a memo from the NJ State Department of Education. *Verklempt* was how I felt when the chocolate basket was empty. *Oy* just about became a daily exclamation. *Farkakte* means "messed up," to be polite.

On the scale of farkakte events, a scandal at Millburn High School while I was the middle school principal rocked our world. In 2009, it was revealed that senior girls had created a "slut list" of freshmen girls as part of an annual hazing ritual that had endured for a decade. The *New York Times* (9/18/09) wrote about these embarrassing events at "New Jersey's top-ranked high school." The details of this "vulgar" rite of initiation became fodder for television news networks and talk shows as well as newspapers, websites, and social media.

The incident impacted me in two ways. The first was a report, soon after the breaking news, that some girls at the middle school were trying to strong-arm other middle school girls into wearing a specific color of clothing. Whether or not this was true, it was reported to me by a parent, and trying to circumvent a copycat bullying incident at the middle school, I immediately alerted parents via a broadcast email.

The second way was how I was caught off guard when parents, moms to be precise, told other administrators, and me, that they hoped their daughters' names would be ON that list the next year. Likewise, The *New York Times* reporter Tina Kelley quoted the high school principal as saying that there were "girls who were upset that they didn't make the list." I was shocked to hear moms of the rising freshman class wishing their daughters would be included in what apparently was the "in" group. It was an extreme take on what I said before about the critical friendships, associations, and inner circles that confer status or street cred and garner attention, at any cost.

The township had another more alternate reality, one that was often not in the spotlight. While all students and their families lived in an affluent township, not everyone who dwelled in the township was wealthy. According to the New Jersey State Department of Education website for the school year 2018 - 2019, based on 2016 Census data, Millburn Township had 292 children, or 5.7% of the student population, who fell within poverty guidelines. This demographic in a township whose overall population exceeded 20,000 residents qualified one of the wealthiest suburban school districts in America to receive Federal Title One grant money.

The funding was put to good use as the number of our school's supplemental support teachers (what used to be called "basic skills") had increased from one to three full-time staff members over the last five years of my tenure.

And we could have used even more remedial classes because the class sizes in our supplemental instructional reading, math and study skills sections were not conducive to individualized learning. Of the eighteen students in one replacement math class, fourteen had transferred from other districts, mostly urban settings, within the prior two or three years. Students from other districts often had wide gaps in learning that rendered them functionally discrepant when compared to Millburn peers, and even though their parents struggled to live in the township, it was because they wanted their kids to attend better schools. This was a sign of our changing population and evolving educational needs.

Title One funds also allowed us to plan afterschool and summer programs under the name "PowerSkills." Courses were offered in reading, writing, study skills, and English Language Learners. In the two-week summer course teachers would tackle the assigned summer reading novel so that pupils could start the new school year having read the book and completed the assignments, prepared for the conversations and follow-up assessments in September.

The demographics of the Millburn community had been changing at a rapid pace in another way as well. A 2018 summer glimpse at a *Sunday Star-Ledger* list of real estate sales transactions demonstrated that of the 15 homes sold in the township, 13 of the new residents had either Indian or Asian surnames. This supported a trend about which my administrative colleagues and I had been cognizant over the last several years as we watched the number of Asian students at the middle school soar from single digits to over 20%. Census data confirmed that the Asian demographic in the township had doubled between 2000 and 2010, and my guess is that additional growth will be captured in the 2020 Census, significantly diversifying what was a predominantly Caucasion community. Over the last couple of years, these expanding ethnic groups have galvanized to advocate at board meetings for the observance of Diwali and Chinese New Year on the school year calendar.

The Millburn Public Schools District was one to which other schools, districts, and colleges, as well as journalists, often looked as a leader in the field of education. Which world languages are available to Millburn students?

Why did Millburn select the Connected Math curriculum over other instructional approaches? What exploratory classes does Millburn offer? School systems called or visited to learn about our school organization, catalog of courses and levels, and the particulars of scheduling, fueling the swagger of a district distinguished by its reputation for excellence.

In general, as a district we tended to be more traditional than trendy. Change was achieved through a carefully guided process that ultimately resulted in improved opportunities and greater learning for our students. When other schools turned to block scheduling, creating classes 60-90 minutes in length that did not meet every day, questions would come up as to why we were not following suit. The answer was because our students were better served by our traditional schedule.

It is not possible, when scheduling fewer and longer blocks of time daily, to offer the exact same program of a traditional school day, especially when it comes to non-academic classes such as music, special education, remedial instruction, grade level lunches, and team study halls. Block scheduling could limit pupil participation in performance ensembles while our students were able to enroll in all three: band, chorus, and orchestra. Block schedules could force pupils to choose between ensembles and hands-on exploratory cycle classes, such as art, leadership, technology, and S.T.E.M, or pull students from physical education for band. I knew of a school that programmed remedial courses during a time when most students attended classes like art and robotics. Every scheduling option has trade-offs, but I would never agree to a configuration that denied any child access to what were often the only non-academic and most innovative classes.

A pure block schedule offers no alternative to having all grades eat lunch at the same time, compelling pupils to eat in classrooms or hallways, raising questions regarding safety, supervision, potential bullying, allergens, and cleanliness.

Finally, I have always believed that very long blocks of time, such as 90 minutes, are not suitable for middle level learners, especially without the curriculum modifications and teacher training necessary to accommodate a very different paradigm of instruction. And that belief was fortified by the experiences of my own children in their middle school block schedule.

Millburn's tradition of excellence was predicated on programming that worked. If our students achieved such heights in their academic careers that they were accepted into the most competitive colleges, then it was my opinion, when it came to educational reform, that we had to evaluate those trending changes in light of their impact on our district's goals and ultimately our students. It also seemed that we would let other districts try something out first so we could learn from their experience.

In summary, the Township of Millburn was a fascinating and complex place in which to work. It was a community blessed with abundance yet still with a sufficient number of families earning below the federal poverty guidelines to qualify for subsidies. Some of our students were the children of parents who lived on the properties of the affluent homeowners by whom their parents were employed. Both the property owners' children and their employees' offspring attended the same public school.

Some folks let me know that they were not among the wealthiest of residents, but they worked hard to pay their mortgages and taxes, or rent, so their kids could benefit from the school system.

In juxtaposition, other parents referred to themselves as "rich" in conversations with me such as one individual who proclaimed, "My family is just like *Leave It to Beaver* (television series popular in the 1960's), except we are rich!" or with members of my staff, "As a teacher, you are probably not used to dealing with rich and powerful people." My jaw would drop at these comments.

Some of the most affluent families were the most grounded who did not make excuses for their children while others lawyered up at the hint of a student harassment investigation and demanded that no administrator speak to their child without a parent or attorney present. Of course, these latter individuals were but a small minority of people who lost sight of the fact that we were a school system and our job was to educate all different kinds of learners and teach them life lessons, too, regardless of their zip code.

Middle school is where kids should make mistakes as mistakes foster learning. This understanding was a teaching component in our disciplinary approach with students and parents because, depending on the level of transgression or bullying, even being a little bit older at the high school could result in more serious legal jeopardy for students as well as an abiding threat to their future endeavors.

As our guidance team used to say, middle school is the "figure it out years."

For those of us who were a part of the Millburn district for a long time, the saying "You have crossed into Millburn, now suspend reality" became an internal way of helping new personnel, and ourselves, better understand and finesse the otherworldly affluence, attitudes and idiosyncrasies that accompanied working in such a driven place. Like Dorothy and Toto, we weren't in Kansas, or Hoboken, anymore.

Millburn was a coveted "lighthouse district" for aspiring and experienced educators alike, but the idea of teaching and leading in a district the caliber of Millburn seemed literally as far away as a kid from Hoboken could get. But the road to Millburn, and my career in education, was not without its twists and turns.

# 4. I Don't Belong Here

IT WAS HARD TO TURN DOWN, EVEN IF I KNEW IN MY HEART it was not what I really wanted. A free ride to a prominent private engineering school, two short blocks away from my home. I wanted to please my parents. I wanted to have an open mind. Maybe I wanted to share that same sense of achievement and satisfaction that would make my parents proud.

The Stevens Institute of Technology in Hoboken, New Jersey, gave life to Hoboken in more ways than one, its presence inextricably woven into the founding and fabric of the city. The school employed locals as secretaries, custodians, security guards and, like my mom, as food service workers. Residents of the Mile Square City escaped the urban grid of blocks of houses on top of houses, cars crammed into parking spaces on both sides of the streets, and the noise from sirens, car horns, alarms, and buses by hiking up the campus hill to the Stevens Center to gaze at a breathtaking view of the Manhattan skyline. Hoboken kids, aka "street urchins," explored the campus, played touch football on the fields until they were banished by campus security, and sneaked behind the dorms and along the Palisades that led down to the Hudson River, chasing the lore of a "dead man's cave."

The college, perched on the city's highest bluff overlooking the Hudson River, generously offered full-ride scholarships to graduates of Hoboken High School, a chance for children of residents who were economically and educationally disadvantaged to achieve in a way unattainable for many in their parents' generation. This was the opportunity of a lifetime for street urchins who, in the pursuit of enlightenment, could climb up "Murder Hill" to take their place as legitimate denizens of campus.

My parents, like me, grew up in Hoboken in the shadow of Stevens. They were first generation offspring of immigrants from Ireland and Italy, neither of whom went to college. No one in our family, or anyone else we knew, had actually attended Stevens.

I would be a first.

Hoboken High School did not provide opportunities for career exploration, and the school lacked an effective guidance program for its minority of students who were college-bound. Even then, I sensed the ineptitude of my guidance counselor and the lack of any cultivation of discernment about career goals, or conversations about preparation for college, or college searches beyond local post secondary schools. We were on our own.

I could make the argument that I was ill-prepared for any engineering school, some of that my own fault when it came to the selection of courses that would have immersed me in more rigorous preparation and perhaps led, ultimately, to a more informed college and career choice. But I did not choose those courses because, well, I was not a math and science person. I always knew I wanted to be a teacher, and my interests resided more in the humanities.

Yet, here I was, at Stevens, cowering in the back of a crowded calculus class from a professor who flaunted a frenetic teaching style. It did not feel like he was teaching at all as he bantered with students in a language unrecognizable to me while solving problems and scribbling gibberish on the board. And just like in the physics lecture hall, all those mathematical abstractions were missiles flying over my head. When I worked up the courage to meet privately with the calculus professor for help, this stocky man with dark features, thick eye glasses and a booming voice became agitated, barking at me, "It is not my job to teach you what you should have already learned."

Physics lectures, chemistry labs, calculus, computer science projects. I felt disconnected.

Amidst the tumult of that sole semester at Stevens I met with a staff member of the college's career development center who administered a career profile survey, and it pointed me to a field that was more people-oriented.

When the professor of my humanities class, the one class in which I excelled in a schedule dominated by math and science, asked me to stay after class one day, she was more blunt: "What are you doing here?"

It was not just the classes and teachers but also the students I found unrelatable, their backgrounds more suburban and already accustomed to collegiate level content and expectations while in high school. Ironically, they were typical of the students I would later teach in competitive high-achieving districts. It was difficult to build relationships with people with whom I had nothing in common, including a future as an engineer.

My mother felt hard work was enough to overcome any obstacle. I, too, wanted to believe that. But who I was and what I aspired to be, a choice I intuitively made while I was middle school age, complicated, even negated, this struggle to fit in and pursue a career in a field in which I held no interest.

I don't belong here.

Of course, guilt and second-guessing became my companions on this bumpy offroad venture. What I call "the enough" questions sabotaged the reality and the clarity of thinking in the moment. Was I smart enough? Determined enough? Working hard enough? Good enough? These questions had a way of dogging me since my Catholic elementary school days.

My parents hoped for an engineer, a son who graduated from Stevens, the recipient of a four-year scholarship. While they had high regard for educators, my parents also felt that teachers were not respected and were poorly compensated. Still hopeful, my mother said, "You are smart. You will ask for help. You will figure it out."

In my own coming-of-age moment what I figured out was that it was time to call off the charade and follow my passion for becoming a teacher. When I contacted Seton Hall University, the admissions office reinstated the partial academic scholarship they had originally offered and welcomed me back into the fold.

Everything happens for a reason. I grew up a lot during that semester. I went from trying to please others to taking charge of my own future. And that led me to the people, learning, and opportunities that would prepare me well for my various roles in education in that "ideal town" not far from my new campus.

When you are on the right path for you, everything tends to line up perfectly.

# 5. Lessons from the Holocaust

THE RUMBLE OF TRAINS ENTERING THE HOBOKEN STATION echoed like the thunderous rolling of giant bowling balls accompanied by the belching of hissing steam and the rhythmic clanking of metal wheels. Fluorescent lights cast shadows of people scrambling for their track or the stairwell to the subway inside this cavernous hub where the masses were arriving from the suburbs to board PATH trains, what locals called "the tubes," enroute to New York City. The dank air inside the station was a potpourri of steam, cigarette smoke and the musty smell of the Hudson River right outside.

Hoboken's Erie-Lackawanna Terminal was a magical, action-filled destination of my childhood, a perfect place for my dad or my grandfather to escort four young boys and their baby sister to watch the trains come and go or board a ferry to The Battery in Lower Manhattan. The elegantly appointed waiting room with long wooden benches and twin grand staircases under a Tiffany stained-glass skylight became a playground for running, jumping, and climbing. Up one side of the stairs to go down the other side. And again. A perfect way to release the bottomless energy of children and simultaneously get them out of their mother's hair for a while.

Now, no longer a child, the time had come to climb aboard, for this was a place where journeys began, too. It was still dark on this chilly January morning, the start of the spring semester and my very first class at Seton Hall. Instead of a short uphill stroll to campus, I hoofed it about ten blocks to the train station. The 6:35 AM New Jersey Transit train would deliver me to the Village of South Orange, New Jersey, where I faced another uphill trek of several blocks with just enough time to make it to my 8 AM class.

With her brisk stride and business-like demeanor, the professor entered the classroom, seemingly intent on enlightening us about the Foundations of Education. Sister Rose Thering, O.P., Ph.D., a Dominican nun and professor of education at the School of Education, immediately shared her syllabus. Her first assignment was for us to read *Night* by Elie Wiesel. The second was to read *Day* by the same esteemed author and survivor of the Holocaust.

After a cursory review, I was taken aback by the appearance of these books on the course syllabus. What did these selections about the Holocaust have to do with the history of public and private education? What place did the Holocaust have in a Catholic university course?

And who was this nun who sprinted into class donning a pantsuit, an uncovered head, and a silver cross intertwined with the Star of David? She certainly did not look like the Sisters of St. Dominic of Caldwell, New Jersey, my grade school teachers, even after modifications to their habits following the Second Vatican Council of the 1960's.

It did not take long to find out the answers to all my questions. Sister Rose's doctoral dissertation had generated research in support of a new Vatican Council document known as "Nostra Aetate" (In our Age) which proclaimed to the faithful of the Catholic Church that Jews were not responsible for the death of Christ, a tenet she found embedded in catechism texts being used to teach religion to children. Her life-long work of building bridges of understanding between Jews and Christians would later be captured in a documentary film, "Sister Rose's Passion," which was subsequently nominated for an Academy Award. Sister Rose was a force to be reckoned with.

Sister Rose knew that the most effective way to change perceptions and beliefs was through educating teachers. What schools refer to today as "character education," including instruction about prejudice, tolerance, and empathy, was what Sister Rose was teaching future teachers using Wiesel's seminal accounts about life and death in Hitler's camps.

In my background combination of Catholic parochial elementary school and public high school education, I never formally learned about the Holocaust. Or other religions. Or much about other cultures. It was a parochial education in the narrowest sense of the term. Even the American history class I had in high school did not extend to studying the Second World War. Sister Rose, along with other proponents, would successfully lobby for a new law in New Jersey requiring all high school students to enroll in a course about the Holocaust.

Another observation about my ignorance regarding this historical era is the fact that this "greatest generation" of individuals, among whom were my parents and aunts and uncles, who prevailed during some of the most trying times in history, including the Great Depression, World War II, and the Holocaust, did not talk about their ordeals, even with their families. They often at least appeared to have put these experiences behind them. Alas, as this generation began to age and others broke their silence, more and more Holocaust survivors became afraid that if they did not speak their truth, these events would be erased from history. There were already people who denied the Holocaust had ever happened.

Stories have been used to transmit our history, culture, and learning since the beginning of time. The more personal the experience shared through speeches and writings, the more powerful the tool for others to understand the context of human striving and struggles. I could not have surmised as I sat in Sister Rose's class in the spring semester of 1979 that I would have the opportunity to be in the presence of numerous Holocaust survivors, including Elie Wiesel, to hear their stories and read their memoirs. Or that my middle school would embark on several projects that would connect children to survivors so that their testimony, a first-person narration about the Holocaust, could be preserved for future generations.

Sister Rose did indeed establish a "foundation of education" that prepared me for my future professional life. Already a teacher during the summer of 1987, and weeks prior to my start date as a middle school language arts teacher in Millburn, I would spend time at the Anne Frank House in Amsterdam (while almost everyone else in my travel group went to the Heineken Brewery) to gain a better understanding of the annex in which the Frank family and their friends had become hidden fugitives of Nazi aggression. I wanted to acquire resources and artifacts and use my visit to add a personal dimension to teaching "The Diary of Anne Frank" play with my eighth graders.

My photograph of the Anne Frank House and a brochure from the museum that opened into a poster displayed in my classroom.

In the years leading up to "The Prom of Your Dreams," the late Mary Vazquez, a teacher at Millburn Middle School, suggested that our school offer a course about the Holocaust in response to the principal's invitation for elective course proposals. Mary learned of student interest in this area from her incorporation of multicultural literature in her reading classes. She also saw the need for children to be educated about this historical and horrific event while many of the survivors were still alive. Families in our community had relatives and friends who were survivors, and the MetroWest Jewish Community Center and Seton Hall University, among other schools and organizations, also served as valuable resources.

For me, it was at the college level that I was introduced to Elie Wiesel's autobiographical works; now these publications were a part of the reading requirements in Mrs. Vazquez's eighth grade class known as "Lessons from the Holocaust."

Mary invited many Holocaust survivors to share their personal experiences both in her classes and during assemblies. She used the narratives they wrote to give life to the reading, viewing, and historical research her students were conducting.

I observed Holocaust survivors speaking with our students, and I was moved by their stoic recounts of terribly painful memories. Speakers recalled events and details - the persecution, the separation from family, the torment, the sorrow and the good people who helped or hid Jews - as though they were reliving them in the moment, seeing it all play out in their minds.

And they welcomed the kinds of questions middle level learners were prone to ask, usually related to their own transitions and challenges. For example, a youngster who had significant physical challenges asked Ruth Millman, a Holocaust survivor whose grandchildren attended our school, "What did you do to fit in? How did you make friends?" when she explained how she attended public school after arriving in New York City, even though she could not speak English and found herself in a culture that was entirely foreign to her at the tender age of ten.

My belief is that these survivors were destined to live and become witnesses and transmitters of history. An important message for our students was the encouragement to move forward and live one's life despite the trials of the past. The inspiration to be resilient was the ultimate gift from speakers who lost their families, homes, country, culture, and language, but not their will to live, adapt or succeed.

In 2004, Mary's classes at Millburn Middle School decided to sponsor a prom for survivors of the Holocaust who had missed out on this teen rite of passage. The catalyst for this idea was Holocaust survivor Marsha Kreuzman's account of unimaginable loss, of her family and her childhood.

The visionary teacher of this course raised some money to hold a dance right in our own school, but some middle school parents and members of the local community generously transformed this event into a classy, posh, and memorable gala well beyond anyone's wildest imagination. What started out as a traditional dance in a school cafeteria quickly evolved into a sophisticated prom at The Crystal Plaza in Livingston, New Jersey, an elegant catering hall owned by middle school parents Allan and Debbie Janoff. This affair was a feast for the senses hosted in a palatial room with tall gold leaf Corinthian columns and crystal chandeliers, tables set with fine china and bouquets of red roses, festive music from a live orchestra, and the aroma of Chateaubriand.

*The Prom of your dreams... A gift from the children.*

Other people in the community also donated their services and time to create what felt like a surreal storybook experience, including the crowning of Marsha Kreuzman as our prom queen. The two hundred Holocaust survivors attending the prom, many of whom were advanced in age, were incredulous that this celebration was for them. It was such a happy occasion with survivors smiling, laughing and dancing. Our students were our school's ambassadors, taking care to provide whatever assistance and service they could. They escorted and danced with survivors, and our guests were so appreciative of our students' sincerity and hospitality. My hope was that this generation who endured insufferable losses experienced a glimmer of hope in our students and in the future.

When I offered some brief remarks as principal during the festivities, I acknowledged Mary Vazquez by saying, "Where there are inspired students, so too is there an inspiring teacher."

News about a prom sponsored by Millburn Middle School students for Holocaust survivors was broadcast and reported on by major New York television networks and in national and international journals.

In 2006, another dinner event followed, also at the Crystal Plaza, in order to include more survivors in a celebration. "The Wedding of Your Dreams" feted Holocaust survivors who married other survivors. Inspiration for this affair came after students compiled a booklet about the chronologies of how these survivors met and married.

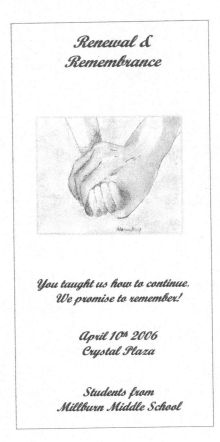

*Renewal &*
*Remembrance*

*You taught us how to continue.*
*We promise to remember!*

*April 10th 2006*
*Crystal Plaza*

*Students from*
*Millburn Middle School*

Mary Vazquez continued to develop myriad creative ways to engage her pupils with survivors in learning about the Holocaust. Students participated in an Adopt-A-Survivor program where they paired with survivors to chronicle their personal sagas and pledged to present these transcripts of eyewitness events to others in the future. A mapping project to track the history of survivors led to an exhibit at the MetroWest Jewish Community Center. In addition, Mary arranged for her classes to collaborate with eighth graders in Israel, via technology, in an International Book Sharing Project on titles about the Holocaust.

The class was so popular that not everyone who wanted to participate was able to do so.

It was serendipitous that Mary Vazquez enrolled in coursework offered by The Sister Rose Thering Scholarship Fund for Education in Jewish-Christian Studies, begun in 1993 to honor my former long-time professor's scholarship and advocacy. The fund continues to promote the mission of Sister Rose, who died in 2006, by providing financial assistance for public and private elementary and secondary teachers to matriculate in a community-outreach arm of the Jewish-Christian Studies graduate program at Seton Hall University. Mary Vazquez was a perfect example of Sister Rose's belief in the power of teachers to effect change.

Sister Rose wrote to me after I sent a letter recommending Mary for admission, saying, "I am pleased to learn that students that I had many years ago will also be involved in the teaching of the Holocaust...I am sure you will support Mary in her teaching of the Holocaust once she has completed her courses here at Seton Hall...."

It was inevitable that Mary Vazquez would later become a trustee of the Sister Rose Thering Fund and recruit more teachers to attend courses. Mary's ongoing work with survivors also connected her with the greater Jewish community, and representatives from the state Department of Education asked for her assistance with another major project connecting tragedy and intolerance: the formation of a curriculum to teach school-age children about the attacks of September 11th.

On a personal note, I came to know Sister Rose well not only as one of my undergraduate professors but also because I was a work-study student in the School of Education. Later, I became a graduate assistant owing to her encouragement and support. When I returned to school in the fall of my junior year, she cried with me over the sudden and unexpected death of my father during the summer of 1980.

"Sister Rose's Passion" featured her visit to Millburn Middle School to speak with Mary's students. Sister Rose remembered me when I welcomed her even though much time had gone by. I was invited to attend a screening of her documentary in 2005 where Dr. Elie Wiesel was a guest speaker, coincidentally in the same banquet hall that held our "Prom of Your Dreams." When I suggested to Sister Rose that her documentary should have won the Oscar, she heartily agreed.

Mary Vazquez continued her own education by attending workshops and lectures and visiting a concentration camp. Each semester she escorted her classes to the United States Holocaust Memorial Museum in Washington, D.C., as well as the Holocaust Museum in New York City.

In 2006, Mary Vazquez was honored at the Pierre Hotel in Manhattan with a Korczak Teaching Award presented by the American Friends of the Ghetto Fighters' Museum. Mary invited me to join her and her family in traveling to Manhattan in a limousine to attend this elegant awards banquet. At the conclusion of her acceptance speech, Mary directly addressed survivors of the Holocaust, "...you are our conscience of yesterday and my students our promise of tomorrow."

Mary Vazquez flanked by her husband, The Honorable Peter Vazquez and her mother, Dolores Dopart, and surrounded by her family, friends, and myself.

A humorous aside is that during the cocktail hour I recognized Dr. Ruth Westheimer, a Holocaust survivor who claimed fame as a radio show sex therapist in the early 1980's, surrounded by a group of admirers and shaking hands. When I extended my hand, she returned with a plate. Fearing that she might miss out on the appetizers, she implored, "Be a dear and get some hors d'oeuvres for me."

Mary's work was recognized by other organizations, community supporters, and admirers, but words cannot express how much Mrs. Vazquez meant to her students and their families. Mary also had personal relationships with many survivors, and they appreciated her efforts in making sure their individual and collective stories of the Shoah would not be forgotten. In return, they generously gave of their time to relate to our students what happened to them during the Holocaust when they themselves were about the age of our students. Mary Vazquez's mission, indeed her legacy, was uniting survivors with our students to teach them - and us - not only about the

Holocaust but also about life, family, faith, and perseverance. Their life stories and lessons about humanity linked the past, present and future, transcending history, generations, and time.

Mary retired in 2010 so she could spend more time with her growing number of grandchildren. She was honored at our eighth grade move-up ceremony, and my personal gift to her was a pendant that combined the Star of David with a cross, a replica of the one Sister Rose wore. It seemed to me that Mary Vazquez continued the work of Sister Rose by educating the next generation of children and supporting Holocaust education for the next generation of teachers.

Our school eventually replaced the Holocaust elective with a Human Rights course which continued to study the Holocaust as well as other genocides as a part of a three-year strand of leadership courses for *all* students.

Mary Vazquez passed away in October 2015 at the age of 65 from cancer, two weeks after the loss of her 92-year-old mother for whom Mary had provided care for many years and who was a former substitute secretary in our school. I had a final opportunity to see and speak with Mary at her mother's funeral.

Mary's funeral Mass was attended by Millburn parents, community members, and former students, several of whom went on to become teachers because of Mary's influence. I will never forget, after the service, the image of grief-stricken Marsha Kreuzman, the Holocaust survivor who was crowned queen of the prom, now in her nineties, frail, and struggling to fathom why God would take Mary instead of her.

It was not until I was nearing the completion of my first draft that I read about Marsha Kreuzman's passing on September 12, 2018. Her terse obituary did not mention that she was our prom queen or that she was a hero, like so many other survivors, for sharing her story so that students everywhere could witness the deadly consequences of intolerance, hatred, and bigotry. Marsha had been the sole survivor of her immediate family in the Holocaust.

Mary Vazquez's contributions served as a reminder to me of the impactful role of teachers and their formidable capacity to help children embrace diversity and differences.

What I also learned early on in my career was that often the best ideas for curriculum writing, for community-building, and for staff development emanate from teachers.

And just like sometimes what we learn sticks with us forever, so too does the visage of consequential teachers like Sister Rose and Mary Vazquez and so, so many others.

As for me, I don't believe in coincidences. Preparation for my role as a leader at the school where I spent the bulk of my career started when I returned to my goal of becoming a teacher and transferred to Seton Hall. What I learned there, under the influence of a powerful change agent, helped me to fulfill my destiny of ministering in supportive ways in a Jewish community so that survivors and their families could trust that their suffering and heartache were neither in vain nor lost forever.

# 6. Way Leads On to Way

MY EXPERIENCE AT SETON HALL WAS SO DIFFERENT FROM
my short stint at Stevens. I fit in right away and developed friendships with
peers, professors, and even priests in the college community. I loved what I
was studying and started working as a student assistant in the alumni office,
that is until Sister Rose found out and requested that I transfer to the School
of Education. This was a great move because I came to know the professors
and staff in a more intimate way. I made the Dean's List every semester
and graduated *magna cum laude*. The School of Education's chapter of the
Kappa Delta Pi International Honor Society selected me as the recipient of
its Outstanding Undergraduate Award.

Kappa Delta Pi Award presented by School of Education Assistant Dean Dr.
Claire R. Barrett and Seton Hall President Dr. Edward R. D'Alessio.

At Seton Hall, education majors had to set aside three hours per week per education course to complete practicums in schools. This usually meant scheduling classes in a way that left one day a week "free" to spend time observing classes and working with students. For my first practicum I returned to my own parochial school, Saints Peter and Paul "Grammar School" in Hoboken, where I had the good fortune to continue learning from one of the first teachers who inspired my own vocation to be a teacher, Sister Lauretta Timothy Healy, O.P., who was now the principal. "LT" had prayed that I would become a priest, but that call never came. Sister was nonetheless pleased that I aspired to be a teacher.

I took summer classes and extra credits to make up for the lost semester at Stevens. Though I technically completed my coursework in the spring of 1982, I had not yet fulfilled the student teaching requirement, which I did during the May-June intersession at Oratory Prep in Summit, New Jersey. I marched with my peers at the graduation ceremony anyway, and then marched again for the official graduation in 1983 when President Ronald Reagan was the commencement speaker. I actually marched a third time the following year because I had completed a master's degree program.

My decision to attend Seton Hall and how what I learned there shaped the practice of my teaching and leadership at Millburn Middle School was powerful, but the last chapter was a detour off the chronology of my journey. I did not commence my teaching career in Millburn; I actually started next door in the Summit Public Schools.

I can remember nervously driving west on Route 78 to interview for a language arts position at the Summit Junior High School. This was my very first interview for a "real job," and now it was time to put to work, literally, my preparation over the last several years that had made possible this opportunity to realize my dream of becoming a teacher.

His office was a windowless cave, dimly lit and worn, and the principal had an energy level to match. He was pleasant enough, but businesslike, which made it all the more surprising that he offered me the job at the conclusion of the interview, confiding, "The last applicant sitting in that chair had a degree from Harvard, but he lacked the ability to communicate." Even if I was offered the job by default, I figured I was in the right place at the right time.

LOOKING AHEAD TO A GOOD YEAR - Meeting at a reception for new administrative and faculty members, Superintendent of Schools Dr. Richard L. Fiander, left, confers with Dr. Diane Grannon, new curriculum constultant-coordinator for the Summit schools, and Michael Cahill, new Junior High School English teacher.

My time in Summit was the perfect launch to a teaching career. Without a doubt, I would have stayed in Summit for the long-term if the opportunity had presented itself. I was supported by my department colleagues and chairperson and had access to volumes of materials to deepen my understanding of the content and assist me in hatching lesson plans.

I connected with teachers and staff across the school and looked forward to our lunches together in a smaller faculty room on the second floor. Some fond memories from this room include how one teacher roasted hot dogs for everyone on a Hibachi grill just outside the window on the rooftop of the first floor, and another time a staff member ignited the rum topping, the final detail of our Bananas Foster dessert. Ironically, my department chairperson had warned me to steer clear of the perils of the more frequented and roomier first floor faculty room, a "den of iniquity," where I bet they weren't lighting fires in school.

The lunch crew embarked on many outings together, including dinners at a Portuguese restaurant in the Ironbound section of Newark and concerts at Madison Square Garden. I was 23 years old and included in a group of warm, friendly colleagues. It felt like family.

I also struck up a friendship with the man who was the school's office manager and so much more within the Summit community. We would meet for dinner at Marco Polo's or drive "down the shore" to grab a bite and trade tales about our respective summer beach rentals. Many years later I got to see him again when I attended the ceremony that renamed the school in his honor: the Lawton C. Johnson Summit Middle School. Inscribing his name over the entrance of "his school" cemented his legacy of 52 years of service.

Professionally, I had grown up as a teacher. I could see how my performance had improved over the three years I spent there. My evaluations reflected my hard work. I also coordinated the writing submissions to the regional Teen Arts Festival, advised the school newspaper, and performed in the school play.

*December 1984*

**Photo with Santa at Holiday Dance.**

Rehearsing to be a G-Man in "You Can't Take It With You." Yearbook portrait 1986.

I could not have asked for better students, and I can fondly recall the names of so many individuals whom I had the privilege of teaching for two years when we migrated together from eighth grade to ninth grade. These wonderful "Hilltoppers" left an indelible impression on me as a new teacher.

No job opening existed at the junior high school after my third year, apparently due to teachers returning from maternity leaves or other leaves of absence, though I was surprised and suddenly unclear about the status of my employment. Had I been a long-term substitute, or a tenure track teacher? Whatever the true answer, I realized two things. First, I was told there was no longer a position for me at the junior high. Second, I was bypassed for a one-year leave replacement at the high school for the next year, which may or may not have resulted in tenure. I will never know.

It was disheartening not to be able to continue. And the gloomy countenance of my students reflected their disappointment as well during the final months of the school year. On the last day of school, during one of those half-days that lasts an eternity, a gathering of students came to school just to hang with me. They asked questions about my future and joked about the funny things that happened and signed my yearbook. The gang helped me clear out my belongings and fooled around a bit, but their antics were not enough to mask their sadness. When it was time to say good-bye, one boy was so upset that he left the room. I went out into the hall to find him, and then I made a beeline for my car. I did not want to see anyone else. I still could not believe this was happening.

Some parents had offered to fight for me at a board of education meeting, but I felt the die had been cast and did not want to draw that kind of attention to myself. So, instead, one family, the Dunnings, hosted a farewell party at their home for me along with another teacher who had also lost her job. I was gifted with a silver keychain engraved with "M.K.Hill," which in addition to "Special K" was what my student fan club took to calling me.

Years later, as an administrator, I acquired a more nuanced perspective about personnel decisions. A determination about a teacher's employment can incorporate many factors, including one's versatility of job skills and range of experience within a broader context of timing and staffing needs, yielding more of a district game plan and not necessarily a personal statement about a staff member. But as the teacher affected by the decision, it sure did feel personal and, in some ways, political. For me, it was the lack of communication that this ending was even a possibility that came as a shock. The vibe from the tenured folk was that it was just very difficult to attain tenure, the perpetual right to a teaching job guaranteed by state statute, granted on the first day of a teacher's fourth year in the district. I was so close, or so I thought.

Was I smart enough? Determined enough? Working hard enough? Good enough?

Perhaps the timing was not right. Maybe this one was not meant to be. Possibly I would have a different career after all. So, hearing the echo of my parents' reservations about a teaching career in my head, I would consider finding another kind of job.

My mom offered to pay for law school.

I collected unemployment compensation for a couple of months, after prevailing in an appeal by the Summit Public Schools who poured salt in the wound by contesting my eligibility for benefits. In the mid-1980's there was a dearth of teaching jobs available, and I was hesitant about starting over just anywhere else after working in such a positive, connected environment. Discouraged by this experience and about the lack of prospects, I spent the next year employed in a corporate environment in two different positions in New York City.

I was first hired by a service organization to write articles in an industry newsletter about pertinent state and national changes regarding insurance laws, procedures, and practices. I knew next to nothing about the insurance industry, and I had as my guide a younger department secretary, Maggie, who was quite capable of doing my job but was unqualified because she did not have a college degree. You might sense some resentment.

If I thought an office job was going to be devoid of politics, I was in for a rude awakening. I soon learned about the turnover of people who were hired to do my job as well as the office cliques and rivalries and union workplace issues. There was little actual supervision and no support for someone new in the field. Just Maggie. It was not long before I felt trapped, then targeted, on an upper floor of an airless metallic prison overlooking South Street Seaport.

Maggie set me up good. Our section supervisor, a curmudgeon named Walter, assigned me a project through Maggie. Even though Maggie knew that the clock was ticking, she piled on other tasks. When Walter asked her for a status report on my progress in front of me, she simply shrugged her shoulders. I was called into a conference room with the two of them in which I explained that I ran out of time because Maggie prioritized the other work. Walter replied, "Maybe I will run out of time to give you your next paycheck." I asked about the chain of command. Did I report to Maggie, or to him? Maggie, to my surprise, piped up and wanted to know the answer to that question, too. Walter turned on her, his face reddening, muttering her name and shaking his jowls from side to side, shutting her down. I was not supposed to ask questions, it seemed. Maybe nobody was.

Where was the creativity, the engagement, the meaning, the rapport, the inspiration, the connections - to kids, the world, life - that were a part of teaching?

I don't belong here.

I set out to apply for teaching positions. I knew I had to bide my time before teacher vacancies for the next school year were posted in the spring, so I took a temp job in Midtown Manhattan in the accounting office of a new weight-loss company. It had a small office staff who were a more collegial group of employees than in my prior workplace.

From time to time we enjoyed a laugh as letters written by customers demanding a product refund contained humorous anecdotes about lackluster results. It was not their struggle to lose weight that was amusing; I knew from my own experience all about that uphill battle as I had dropped eighty pounds in my college and post-college years. Rather, it was the funny phrasing and the unreasonable assumptions and expectations.

The firm was growing and relocating from an apartment in a residential building to newly renovated office space in a corporate highrise. I was offered a salary and a raise to stay on, but I needed to get back to my first love.

I didn't belong here, either.

# 7. On the Job Again

AMIDST ALL THE HUSTLE AND BUSTLE OF VISITORS COMING and going and flocks of chatty students meeting up with their harried chaperones, I waited and wondered what I was getting myself into. Just beyond the periphery of the glass-enclosed lobby of the New York Museum of Modern Art, I was aware of the busyness of Manhattan, the cacophony of honking horns, revving motors and screeching brakes, and pedestrians scurrying by at lunchtime on a promising spring day. It was, without a doubt, an unconventional and chaotic place to rendezvous for a job interview.

When I was contacted by the Millburn Township Public Schools English Supervisor regarding my application for a teaching position, and I told her I was working in the vicinity of Rockefeller Center, she informed me that she was chaperoning a field trip to the Museum of Modern Art and would interview me in the lobby. If she liked me, she continued, I would be accompanying her back to Millburn for a second round interview with other administrators.

I guess she liked me.

It wasn't long before I was boarding a bus back to Jersey to meet with the middle school principal and the assistant superintendent of curriculum and instruction whose countenance, she had forewarned, was the likeness of Richard Nixon. She was so spot-on about the Nixon resemblance that I almost guffawed when I met him. After the interview in Millburn I hopped on the same train line that used to transport me home to Hoboken from Seton Hall.

I was elated when I was offered the position, and now with employment lined up for September I signed on for a summer trip to Europe. I had never journeyed across the Atlantic, and I realized in my teaching career that so many of my students had traveled to, or lived in, sundry parts of the world. I had some catching up to do, so I embarked on a 26-day tour of England, France, Italy, Austria, Germany, Switzerland, and the aforementioned Holland with a friend as well as the novels I was expected to teach beginning in September.

I spent the rest of my career at Millburn Middle School where I was a teacher for nine years, the fifth grade coordinator for one and a half years, assistant principal for three and a half years, and principal for sixteen years. A second chance at a long and fulfilling career in education had its auspicious launch in a life-changing interview in the lobby of an art museum in Manhattan.

When I was hired in Millburn I became a member of a team of teachers, whereas my former junior high school was not organized to accommodate teaming in the upper grades. I did not know what a team was. Teaming created a smaller community within the larger school where all the students on a team shared the same teachers. This made it so much easier to discuss students and brainstorm strategies. It enabled teachers to identify common curriculum intersections for co-teaching or interdisciplinary activities. It was also an opportunity for the team of teachers to schedule programs, events and trips, update the academic calendar, and meet with parents all together. When I arrived in Millburn, administrators were also embedded in this network of teachers and guidance counselors, all working together on behalf of students. I felt welcomed and supported in my chosen profession from the beginning in Millburn.

Working the crowd in a team activity.

My team leader, Tom Perry, was this Pied Piper for kids and colleagues alike. Tom had a great sense of humor and knew how to render challenging social studies content about cultures and religions comprehendible for pre-adolescents. Tom and I co-taught units, like my language arts novel *The Good Earth* by Pearl S. Buck with his social studies unit on Chinese dynasties. We showed content-related movies like *The Good Earth* and *The Forbidden City*, even if it required us to assemble a labyrinth of cables that snaked down a corridor to connect five classrooms to a VCR because the auditorium was unavailable. For one of the movies Tom even picked up 95 eggrolls for the entire team, the aroma of which lingered in his truck, and our classrooms, for some time.

For this unit on China, our classes visited the New York Metropolitan Museum of Art and the Pearl S. Buck House in Bucks County, Pennsylvania. On one rainy field trip to the Pearl S. Buck House, the bus driver could have parked anywhere in the empty paved lot but somehow the bus came to rest on a muddy patch and a tow truck had to be summoned to extricate us. Wouldn't you know that one of our students was expected to board a plane in New York that very afternoon? This was a memorable Murphy's Law moment as the first tow truck to arrive was unable to budge the bus, eating up more time waiting for the mother of all tow trucks to rescue us.

Tom was always up for a project or adventure or new ways to use technology and other resources. He would come into class dressed as Mohammed, wearing robes and a head covering while carrying a walking stick, explaining to his pupils, "Mr. Perry couldn't come today. I am here in his place and I want to talk to you about Mecca and how I discovered Islam." He videotaped himself speaking in the voice of other prominent figures from history. We embarked on research projects, spending days in the library together helping all of our students locate information.

In the 1990's eighth grade teams conducted what I remember as extraordinary interdisciplinary projects on the topic of AIDS and HIV. AIDS had reached the pinnacle of its pandemic, and we felt a responsibility to educate our students in its prevention. We utilized a cooperative learning approach in which groups of students chose their "specialty" topic, such as transmission, risk factors, reflections in art or music, myths, political response, pharma-ceuticals, statistics, or discrimination, among many others. Cohorts had options to present their research to the entire team: role-playing, pamphlet design, poetry, videotape of a dramatization, debate, songs, artwork, a test of knowledge, etc. While what we all learned was enlightening, two other factors made this experience unique in my mind. The first was that we as teachers afforded our students a great deal of freedom to make choices, and we were rewarded by their commitment and zeal to understand and teach others about this potentially deadly virus. The second was that the inherent nature of this topic presented tricky questions about human behavior and sexuality to which I never thought I would have to respond in an eighth grade language arts class.

Another meaningful interdisciplinary project called "Profiles in Heritage" complemented the social studies theme "The Peopling of America" and engaged students - and their families - in the study of how they or their ancestors came to live in America and their cultures and traditions. We visited Ellis Island and students learned about genetics in science class and studied their families to understand the genesis of their own unique traits and talents. In this pre-*Ancestory.com* era, one had to shake his or her own family tree to see what kinds of nuts would fall out.

Tom and I were invited by Spanish teacher extraordinaire Judy Fredman to chaperone an eighth grade spring vacation trip to Costa Rica. Despite some setbacks, such as the airline sending our luggage to Florida (translation: no clean underwear), frequent loss of power in the lodges of the national parks, and a flat bus tire on an unpaved highway in the scorching Central American afternoon heat, it was the adventure of a lifetime - enough so that I later accompanied other student trips to Spain and England.

As our team leader, Tom sponsored annual fundraisers in order to maximize the number of holiday gifts our team hoped to purchase for area children whose families were struggling. No one could forget Mr. Perry the auctioneer who sold the stuffed animals, games, and gadgets donated by our students back to their peers. "Do I hear 10 dollars? How about 12? Going once, going twice, SOLD!" Tom was hoarse by the end of a very profitable morning. Moms came in to help with the afternoon "pig-out" to divide up all of the donated pans of cupcakes, brownies, cookies, etc., so that students could inhale a pre-purchased plate heaped with their favorite confections.

Tom and his wife, Jeanne, also a middle school teacher in a different district, would drive to out-of-state outlet stores to take advantage of lower retail prices in order to stretch the money for as many kids as possible.

The versatile Mr. Perry as auctioneer, administering the National Geography Bee; captivating his students while squatting on top of his desk; changing a bus tire in Costa Rica.

Tom was a master teacher and mentor, but when he retired there was no engraved plaque or gold watch. He got a goat - a Boer goat to be exact - a special breed we knew he wanted for his little farm. The aforementioned 9/11 Peace Garden was also dedicated in his honor, though we did not disclose this detail until he was done digging holes and laying heavy concrete tiles in the shape of a spiral.

It did not take long for me to become known as "the kid from Hoboken," and I was happy to import Hoboken's finest foods. For field trip lunches I would make a trip to Biancamano's to buy mammoth home-made milky mozzarella sandwiches for all the adults. Other times it was to share Lepore's homemade chocolates or Italian bread from Marie's Bakery. On occasion the administrators had me pick up enough Italian pastries - cream puffs, napoleons, eclairs, cannoli, and sfogliatelle - from Carlo's Bakery for the entire staff.

It was during my third year in Millburn that my fiance Lea and I were married. Tom Perry offered a blessing at our wedding reception which Ellie Prach, long-time secretary at MMS, inscribed with her exquisite calligraphy in a framed work of art that hangs above our bed. Vice Principal Phil Bruno and his wife June also attended. Ellie, guidance counselor Mary Pedicini, and other members of my team were also present at the church. Phil, who loved to take pictures, assembled a professional-level quality photo album for us. Barbara Jonas, our then librarian, lent her technical and artistic skills to help me design the program for our nuptials.

The school's organizational template maximized our ability to do our jobs. And it did something else, too. It provided a collegial network of support and trust, generating common experiences, professional sharing, opportunities for growth, and camaraderie in the workplace. This was a special place with special people, and I had found a new family and home for my craft.

# 8. I Never Wanted to Be a Principal

I NEVER WANTED TO BE A PRINCIPAL. THERE, I SAID IT. IT'S a good starting point. And we all know where this is going.

Three years after earning a master's degree I decided to return to school for additional graduate credits. Teachers increase their compensation by continuing their education, and our district incentivized teacher learning by paying the tuition. Earning 30 additional credits meant that I would leap to the next column on the salary guide and earn what had the potential of being almost $10,000 more a year. I was all in for completing 30 credits, *nothing more.*

At this point in my life, in addition to my full-time job in Millburn, I was teaching an English class to inner-city high school students enrolled in the Stevens Technical Enrichment Program (STEP) on Saturdays. I was also an adjunct writing instructor at Hudson County Community College in Jersey City one night a week. And I spent at least two Friday nights every month chaperoning the middle school's TGIF socials.

I decided to attend the state college closest to our apartment in North Bergen for the sake of convenience. To be honest, I did not have high expectations and considered this more of an exercise, a means to an end. But I came to the right place at the right time. What is now known as New Jersey City University had recently added new faculty to its graduate education department, and I was fortunate to meet some very talented and experienced teachers. The courses required a tremendous amount of reading, analysis, writing, and application in weekly summaries, research papers, class discussions and cohort projects, and I was energized by the challenge.

In my first semester a professor gave me a C on a paper. Unaccustomed to getting anything less than an A, and thinking these classes would be a breeze, I was mortified and went to see him. The professor reviewed my paper and suggested how I could improve, and he invited me to try again. I was successful in my second attempt, and when the semester was over, he hired me to teach summer seminars on learning styles and study skills in public and private schools in the metropolitan area for his private company.

Another professor, Dr. Lawrence Creedon, became a guru of sorts. A veteran superintendent of a large urban district in Massachusetts, not a theorist from an ivory tower, he had seen and done a thing or two. He remained passionate about his work by reinforcing key educational leadership concepts, such as inclusive decision-making, reflective practices, and quality assurance, in his future school leaders. This professor repeated the following democratic mantra so many times that it stuck in my head (and wasn't that his objective?): "Those affected by a decision ought to be involved in the making of the decision." Reflective practices evaluated how well school culture and programming fulfilled the school's mission statement. Quality assurance, a fancy term, boiled down to creating the right conditions for each child to receive what he or she needed in order to learn.

He placed a great deal of emphasis on collegiality, and so while there were always going to be building management demands and administrative tasks, Dr. Creedon seemed to offer a leadership paradigm that was more congruent with my comfort level in working within a team framework. This was the opening of a window in which I could view the principalship as something different, a more inviting model of leadership than what I had observed.

I never set out with the intention of becoming a principal, though, or a school administrator of any species, for that matter. I perceived principals to be authoritarian figures who conducted investigations and evaluations, unilaterally made what seemed like life-and-death decisions, and dealt with a never-ending array of situations. Traditionally, it was the principal's school, a model according to Dr. Creedon known as "command, control, comply."

In my experience, principals were often unseen unless there was a problem, and the position of principal looked like one burdened with responsibility, detached from teaching and learning, and lonely, too.

It dawned on me later, as the principal of my school, that shared decision-making, collaborative leading, and inclusivity conferred upon the work of our administrators the same approach we already had in place everywhere else in our school. Students and teachers were on a *team*. We had a child study *team*. Guidance counselors were a *team*. So, as principal I created, and fostered, an administrative *team*. And I established one more team, a school leadership *team*, which included parents, PTO, teachers, guidance, and myself. This was a vehicle for us to educate each other on our viewpoints and study current educational trends and school-based issues.

On a personal level, Dr. Creedon complimented me on my reflection papers and encouraged me to write for publication. Unlike an undergraduate professor who never wrote anything other than a letter grade on every paper, Dr. Creedon injected comments practically on every line, scrawling in his signature black felt tip looping cursive penmanship, agreeing or disagreeing with my statements, acknowledging a "good point," or posing a question. Feedback and rambling editorials continued on the back sides of the pages. He was especially keen on a paper in which I analyzed supervisory personnel in my school vis-a-vis their personalities. He encouraged me to publish it. Dr. Creedon visited my school and convinced me that I possessed leadership qualities and should finish a second master's degree in educational leadership to earn the principal certification. He also encouraged me to pursue a doctoral degree.

When Dr. Creedon visited my school, he said he knew that Millburn was a hoity-toity place as soon as he drove by Saks Fifth Avenue and Priscilla of Boston, both of which were located on the main drag, Millburn Avenue. He acknowledged there were many things that our school district got right, but he was also aware, through my writing, of Millburn's central office stance that leadership styles such as shared decision-making belonged more in those urban districts that needed fixing.

During my matriculation in post-master's graduate work, the enrollment in my district was concurrently ballooning so rapidly at the elementary level that there was no longer any room for the fifth graders at their respective neighborhood schools. The district's plan was to jettison all fifth graders to the middle school, which until this time had housed grades 6, 7, and 8. The fifth graders alone numbered nearly 220 when they arrived, approximately 50 additional students in a grade level. This jump in enrollment was, in and of itself, worthy of a raised brow, but little could anyone have anticipated future grade level ranges of 360 to 440.

Needless to say, parents viewed moving fifth graders to the middle school as leading lambs to the slaughter.

It would be four years before the fifth graders could return to their elementary schools, but in the interim this nomadic grade level needed a coordinator at the middle school. This was my segue into educational leadership and the world of fifth graders.

Phil Bruno, our middle school's legendary long-time vice principal who was about to retire, was instrumental in recommending me for the fifth grade coordinator position as a "try on" opportunity in administration. Because I knew how much Phil cared about "his" school, I sensed the trust he placed in me to do a good job, perhaps to continue his people-centered legacy of service. Once again, it seemed like I was in the right place at the right time. It would be an invaluable chance not only to experience a leadership role, but also to expand my understanding of the continuum of childhood development and elementary versus middle level learning, structures, and expectations. This would serve me well in planning future transitions to our middle school.

The administrator who had been the first fifth grade coordinator was appointed to replace Phil Bruno. It would now become my job to introduce fourth graders, and their nervous parents, to the middle school. "Will they still be able to have a fifth grade program? How can you expect them to wake up so early? Will they be able to dress up for Halloween and go on field trips? Will they have to be with the older students on the buses? In the cafeteria?" Parents were concerned that the bigger kids would gobble up the little ones.

Ironically, later when the fifth grade classes were slated to return to their elementary schools, parents clamored for a way to maintain the fifth grade at the middle school. This was a testament to the programming that provided their children an appropriate elementary setting while at the same time transitioning them to middle school.

I really had little experience with students younger than middle school age since my twelve years as a teacher were spent primarily in eighth grade. I discovered that fifth graders were not very different from sixth graders in stature or maturity, and I could understand why some districts included fifth grade in their middle school configuration. For the most part, our fifth grade organization and curriculum replicated what pupils would have had at their elementary schools. I could easily see the bond that developed between teachers and students who were together most of the day every day. Fifth graders still put the teacher, and the principal, on a pedestal. They seemed to love their new environment and were eager to please. As I observed classes and interacted with them I found these kids to be inquisitive, creative, interactive and funny, and they had huge hearts.

In the one and a half years in my role as coordinator of this "fifth grade school within a school," I quickly learned that people - teachers, parents, kids - needed all kinds of attention related to academics, learning, professional, or personal matters. I was their pseudo-guidance counselor (God help them), curriculum supervisor, teacher evaluator, field trip planner, scheduler, communicator, disciplinarian, and general go-to person for any reason. If anyone needed a mop or a fly swatter, I was their guy. I was responsible for creating class groups, dealing with classroom issues and parent concerns, and coordinating special events and activities. I was the liaison to special education. In essence, this was ground zero for administrative training. And I was also assigned student supervision responsibilities and teacher observations in the greater middle school as well as special projects by the superintendent.

Behind the desk in charge of fifth grade

An incident that happened while I was supervising fifth grade was one that foreshadowed what I would learn about the competitive nature of places like Millburn where students begin to think about likewise competitive colleges starting from a young age. I was called to a fifth grade classroom to comfort a student who was clearly in distress. I escorted him to my office to find out that the teacher had just returned a spelling quiz on which he had scored an 80. The fifth grader, sobbing, informed me that with grades like this he would not get into Princeton.

It was while I was the coordinator of fifth grade that I became a dad for the first time. I was surprised, and moved, by the baby gifts and creative projects the teachers and students made for my wife, myself and our son. The fifth grade teachers colluded with other middle school staff to plan a surprise baby shower. Unbeknownst to me, they smuggled my very pregnant wife, Lea, into the school. Over the public address system I heard, "Mr. Cahill, please report to the library" after students had been dismissed. I did not know what to expect, but I can tell you that administrators being paged to go somewhere is usually not a good thing, so I was truly surprised when I arrived.

After my son Michael was born, fifth grade classes and their teachers constructed cards, composed a chronicle of current events, and compiled two volumes of advice books such as "Everything You Need to Know About Being a Father From a Kid's Point of View" and another that contained suggestions about how not to embarrass my son in public (I should have read that one again), when to reward him, how to play games, the art of telling jokes, what to read together, and even baby name suggestions. There were stuffed animals and a hardbound anthology of personalized childhood tales. We were also gifted with a magnificent quilt embroidered with his name and birth date.

It was a new day in many ways. I had a leadership position and was learning and growing on the job. I had the opportunity to meet teachers whom I would have never known, and our connections lasted long after the fifth grade classes returned to their elementary schools. And my family was expanding. It was an exciting time at work and at home. The teachers would check in about MJ's sleeping patterns, and kids passing in the hallway would congratulate me or inquire how my son was.

And when people ask me when my hair started to turn white, I am ready with a response: it was the year that I simultaneously became an administrator and a parent.

# 9. Trouble in Paradise

INSTANT INSTABILITY. THAT'S WHAT IT FELT LIKE JUST AS I
was transitioning from the classroom to my new administrative post. Vice
Principal Phil Bruno was set to retire at the end of June before my new
position started in August, but at the last minute the principal unexpectedly
exited as well.

The former fifth grade coordinator was ready to take up her new role as
the vice principal, and the district appointed an interim principal, ironically
a former central office administrator from Summit who had interviewed
me years earlier, while the board embarked on a nationwide search for a
permanent middle school principal.

Now there were three new kids on the block, so to speak, one of them
temporary and two with no experience in their new positions, during a time
of rapid growth after thirteen years of stable building leadership. Phil Bruno
had actually been a vice principal for twenty-six years in our school. A second
vice principal position had been phased out earlier.

Midway through the year the search netted a new principal from
another state who had some years of middle school principal experience.
When she arrived, there continued to be a necessary sorting out of job tasks,
personalities, and leadership styles and a rift quickly developed between the
new principal and the new vice principal, a well-regarded member of the
school community.

The new principal also began making changes - personnel decisions,
team switches and room assignments - that generated much concern from
the faculty. The decisions did not make sense to the staff who wondered if this
amounted to change for the sake of change, a general shake-it-up approach,

or something more sinister. Staff members were not included in conversations, or provided reasons, about these and other decisions that would affect them, so teachers felt as targeted as they perceived their vice principal to be.

I learned some important lessons from being in the middle of this quagmire. Individuals in a new leadership role would do well to invest some time in understanding the history and culture of a building, to speak with people about what they value and what concerns them, and to see how things work before attempting any significant change. A former superintendent for curriculum and instruction, Maryann Doyle, said it this way: "You have to let your garden grow a little before you pick the weeds." Newcomers also have to wade, slowly, into the politics of the organization and get to know all the players.

Leaders cannot do what they want with impunity. Effective leaders have to be able to listen to stakeholders and see the bigger picture. If the time had come for the school tableau to be re-imagined, a necessary albeit challenging task of the leader, then it was the job of the principal over time to make the case for change through the communications and conversations that engendered support and understanding with the very people who would carry out the mission, beginning with teacher leaders. It was the principal's role to tie together rationale and strategies in a plan for gradual implementation, answering the questions, Where are we going? How will we get there? Why is this important? It's called "cultivating buy-in."

We are all works in progress. Looking back on my own practice, I have owned up to making mistakes and have changed directions at times, enlightened by new information or perspectives or an updated cost-benefit analysis. Leaders do not know everything there is to know, and listening is a crucial component of forging ahead with the best plan to accomplish a reboot.

School leaders must tend the fire of relationships with all staff, from teachers, union representatives, paraprofessionals, secretaries, and custodians to everybody else who gives life to their vision and values. Open and honest conversations do happen when staff members trust that administrators respect and value their opinions, regardless of whether everyone is in agreement.

When there is a rift between leaders who have to work together, much like when there is a falling-out between parents, it is difficult to disguise. The new principal was determined to oust her second-in-command within a very short period of time of her arrival, and by doing so beleaguered herself from parents, teachers, and board members.

I saw the writing on the wall and tried to talk to the principal about the teachers' concerns. I wanted to support her, and I considered myself a part, even if unfledged, of the school administration, but I also did not want my colleagues to think I was on board with her decision-making.

At a tense faculty meeting, teachers spoke openly and with obvious emotion, exhorting the principal to declare her support for the staff. Right after the meeting, in her office, I tried to convey to her what the faculty was feeling. I will never forget what she said: "It was a good thing this district hired somebody like me who has experience because someone new to the position, like you, would never survive."

But at a rancorous public board meeting teeming with supporters of the vice principal, the superintendent reversed course and renewed the vice principal's contract. In effect, this outcome preordained that these two individuals would continue working together as the administrators at the middle school.

Our school was described by a teacher as "a rudderless ship on a turbulent sea."

Incidentally, the superintendent and board spent good money to have a university come in to conduct a culture study to find out why so many staff members were unhappy at the middle school. The study included surveys and interviews. The investigation yielded three recommendations: (1) achieve consensus on a clear mission statement for the school (2) the administrative team needs to demonstrate a commonly held vision for the school based on the mission statement, and lead the staff in implementing this vision, and (3) the staff needs to be recognized as a group of professionals whose views will be considered when decisions are being made which affect them. To my great satisfaction, these steps were all in line with the course objectives and preaching of one Professor Creedon.

In terms of my new job as an administrator, it was the beginning of the beginning, and I have to admit that the job began to grow on me. As a teacher my role was to provide instruction for my students. In my leadership position I was not only learning the ropes but also seeing how all of the pieces came together to make a school.

Unbeknownst to me, though, I was already on a path to becoming principal of my school.

# 10. Replacing the "Vice"

I DIDN'T LIKE THE WORD "VICE." ONE COULD EASILY ASSUME that the term accurately depicts the work of "vice" principals because of the inappropriate, disrespectful, or sometimes illegal student behaviors with which they have to deal, reminiscent of a vice squad. Phil Bruno was the consummate traditional vice principal disciplinarian. With his military posture, eagle eyes, and commanding voice, he intimidated students and teachers alike. I would never be able to emulate that, nor did I want to. Of course, the real meaning of the term is something altogether different. *Merriam Webster* defines "vice" as meaning "in the place of," like a substitute or next in rank. Later on when our next principal arrived, she referred to me as her "assistant," and it stuck.

Halfway through the second year of my role in fifth grade, the vice principal transferred to a director's position at central office. This was an opportunity for me to advance, though I was unsure what the future had in store for me by working more closely with this lame duck principal. Within a few months of my becoming vice principal, however, the community learned that the principal's position would once again be vacant.

It made sense to apply for the vice principal position. I was learning so much about fifth grade, but I knew the job would not last forever. Though it seemed a Divine hand was opening a door, I naively waited to see if the superintendent was going to reach out. When I finally contacted him, of course he said he had been waiting to hear from me. We had an interview, and it seemed that he was intent on hiring me from the get-go.

An assistant principal's job is expansive, largely defined by managerial tasks, primarily the supervision of students. I spent time in hallways during the change of classes and refereed the lunch periods. I opened assembly programs and kept a watchful eye. I was outside with the buses in the afternoons. It's an on-your-feet job.

I met with children about peer hostilities or disciplinary concerns and contacted parents. A common parent response, after I identified myself as the assistant principal, was "Uh-Oh."

Conflicts and shenanigans occurred most often in less-structured settings like the cafeteria. In middle school, you could have 16 students at a table (even though there were supposed to be no more than 12) and hear 16 different versions about what did, or did not, transpire. An example of a more innocent middle school caper resembles the exchange I had with seventh grade boys in an investigation:

> *Andrew reported that someone poured Skittles down the back of his shirt. It happened so fast and he didn't see who did it, but he accused Max because he and Max aren't really friends.*
>
> *Max said he can't stand Andrew, but he didn't do it. The only reason Max sits at the table is because he's best friends with Teddy.*
>
> *Teddy said that it couldn't be Max because Max was sitting next to him and Max never got up.*
>
> *Jerry said, "Whoa, somebody poured Skittles down his back. I wish I had seen that!"*
>
> *Doug, who went to buy cookies, said, "I didn't see nothin'."*
>
> *Dylan said that Ron had done things like that to other kids, but Ron never purchased Skittles.*
>
> *Ron proclaimed his innocence and quickly fingered Gabe whom he saw eating Skittles.*
>
> *Gabe purchased Skittles, but said, "I wouldn't be dumb enough to waste them!"*
>
> *Ken said that Andrew isn't a nice kid and there's probably a lot of kids who would do that.*
>
> *Paul, a future defense attorney, said, "It could have been someone from another table."*
>
> *Jimmy said Max was sitting next to Gabe and probably stole some of Gabe's Skittles when Gabe turned to talk to Ryan to play a joke on Chris while Teddy was buying M&Ms.*

Anyone else need a scorecard? Or access to a polygraph?

A sixth grade scenario about a girl who was accepted into a group of new friends but wants to cut ties with a former friend, played out like this:

Samantha, why did you tell your friends to ignore Gina and not let her sit at your table in the cafeteria?

*I don't know.*

Aren't the two of you friends?

*Not really.*

You attended the same elementary school where your fifth grade teacher said you were best friends last year.

*Sometimes we hung out. That was a long time ago.*

Why do you not get along?

*She is interfering with my life. She wants to be friends with my friends.*

Is that so bad?

*They like ME. She really needs to get her own life.*

Do you understand how someone might feel if you were good friends and then suddenly you're not?

*She should talk to the guidance counselor about that. Maybe he could help her find someone who actually likes her.*

Isolating someone is a form of bullying. You don't have the right to say where people can sit.

*Well, she is harassing me.*

How is that?

*She won't leave me alone. She follows me.*

Well, this has to stop.

*I agree. She should stop.*

Untangling these types of situations or far more serious ones, and addressing their underlying issues, when they are even discoverable, demand patience and prudence of middle school assistant principals everywhere. But it's sometimes like living in the Abbott and Costello comedy routine "Who's on First?"

Assistant principals enforce the rules in a school. I dealt with kids cutting classes and students chronically tardy to school. I met with pupils about their classroom comportment or cheating on assignments and assessments. There were locker room thefts, misbehavior on the bus and infractions to the dress code. As technologies advanced, assistant principals had to deal with transgressions of the computer/internet user agreement and cell phones, cell phones, and cell phones.

Administering the school's code of conduct was a way for me to maintain an orderly learning environment, but it was much more than about deciding disciplinary measures, it was also an opportunity to teach. Often (but not always) the significant time that building administrators spend counseling, processing and connecting with students eventually results in better behavior or some learned strategies to de-escalate a confrontation with a student or a teacher. Former students, or their parents, have thanked me years later "for caring and not giving up." Some even apologized for the way they acted. Assistant principals play an important parental role in schools by providing structure, grounding, and consistency, especially for the kids who are often the most marginalized or for those acutely affected by ADHD (attention-deficit/hyperactivity disorder) or other behavioral challenges.

With regard to violations of the dress code, I tried to reinforce the now apparently Victorian concept of "under-wear" to mean that bra straps, boxer shorts, and thongs (yes, even in middle school) were supposed to be hidden from view behind an outer layer of clothing. Moms have told me that stores just don't sell clothes like that anymore.

Lockers are the property of the school and the province of assistant principals with regard to their maintenance and school safety. I scheduled quarterly clean-outs and advised students to toss foods that reeked, wiggled, bloomed or fizzed. If reports of contraband or a pocket knife or a stolen item reached my ears, I would wait for the halls to clear and take a witness. Just like the vice principal in *Ferris Bueller's Day Off*, we tried to look calm and cool run-walking past classroom doors as we hurried to examine the contents of a locker, but anyone who saw two administrators traveling together knew something, or someone, was going down.

Other more behind-the-scenes components of the job are planning and scheduling, including presiding over the master calendar for every school activity, fire/emergency drill, meeting, and facility rental. It became my job to schedule students into all of their classes. Much of this involved the use of technology, also vital to generating numerous state reports, an oft-dreaded task. Assistant principals not only need to be tech savvy, but also able to train and support the staff, too.

For me, using technology to schedule the school presented a major learning curve. For years I watched as Phil Bruno hand-scheduled students into classrooms on charts, creating first a paper mock-up that served as his back-up before inputting the data into the computer. Phil did the schedule, not the technology. This not-so-21st-century process had been my model before it became a paperless enterprise. It also served a much smaller school population without the added constraints of many more special education classes, especially in-class supports.

I was the assistant principal during the 1999-2000 school year when news outlets filled the airways with panic about Y2K, the Armageddon of the turn-of-the-century if the prediction came true that all computers would crash when the calendar year started with the numeral "2." Already a world, and a school, entrenched in technology, the fear was that when the crystal ball dropped in Times Square, computers would implode and schedules, grades, and contact information would vanish. For that reason, printers and copiers were put to the test so that we had paper access to all of our data, just in case.

And, of course, running a building meant dealing with the day-to-day and often unexpected situations that arose, like sewage backing up, the elevator stuck between floors, Wi-Fi problems (which interfere with all of the technology-based learning now happening in classrooms), children and teacher trapped in a classroom, and an invasion of skunks that tunneled under a science lab. I have had to find missing substitutes and wake a few up, too.

Later, during my time as principal I watched as an assistant principal scooped food onto plates in the cafeteria, rode a Zamboni-like machine slurping up water on the floor, babysat twelve classes at a time in the auditorium because 30 teachers were absent, used a net to catch a bird in the auditorium, nabbed the neighborhood labrador that slipped in with the kids, and drove around town in a police car searching for a lovesick preadolescent boy who decided to skip last period so he could hike to the next town to walk his girlfriend home. It's all a part of the pledge to do the job, whatever that means on a given day.

Everyone has to pitch in once in a while.

In recent times vice principals inherited additional and considerable time-consuming tasks, such as investigating allegations of harassment per the new New Jersey HIB (Harassment, Intimidation, Bullying) laws and conducting all the extra teacher observations required by new teacher evaluation legislation.

Aspiring principals receive invaluable on-the-job training as an assistant principal, though not every assistant principal wants to be a principal. While these two positions overlap, there are distinct differences as well.

Principals are the public face of the school and its overall program, attending PTO, district, board, and sometimes regional meetings. I have often spoken and written about the middle level philosophical beliefs that were the underpinnings of the curriculum and instructional practices in my school. And I had to be up-to-date about the goings-on in my building because principals can be blindsided at meetings about rumors, incidents, teacher actions, alleged policy transgressions, and curriculum content under scrutiny. Grace under fire is an acquired skill, especially when fake news or gossip can be based on a kernel of truth, in dealing with a public not entitled to know confidential information.

It was my duty as principal to advocate for funding for staffing and supplies and a well-maintained facility. It was my responsibility to maintain communications with all stakeholders and to respond to concerns about the budget, personnel allocations, program changes, technology, and resources in a variety of venues and media. It was my place to develop the master schedule, paint the bigger picture, and even dream a little. I was simultaneously the steward and the visionary, responsible and accountable for the quality of education and adaptations necessary to remain a viable and relevant institution of learning while meeting the developmental needs of young adults "in progress."

For me, the principalship was a 24/7 job. I never stopped thinking about my school.

Of course, the major difference between a principal and an assistant principal is that the buck stops with the principal concerning all decisions as well as the general conduct and performance of the school and all its inhabitants in every regard.

A principal is also an "influencer." His or her values, leadership style, and personality determine a lot about relationships between all of the stakeholders. The kind of school a building becomes, its learning environment, is also a reflection of its leader.

When I was appointed to the assistant principal post, I became more interested in what we were creating and achieving collectively, centered on the essential question: How do all of us create a middle level environment that promotes learning and growth for all students?

Since I had taught in this school for nine years, I had an understanding of the culture and the staff and felt them rooting for me. But it was at times awkward, and then some, to become a supervisor of my colleagues and friends.

For the most part, I was proud of our staff and our tradition of excellence. However, the faculty consisted of a hodgepodge of teachers, some of whom were leftovers from the junior high school model (translation: teach like a high school for shorter students) or forced transfers from either the high school or elementary levels. Others were breathing remnants of the Dark Ages whose teaching methods or interactions with kids made me cringe. For example, teachers who sat behind their desk the entire time or who stood and lectured for a whole period, indifferent to diverse learning styles or active learning techniques. Or the use of belittling sarcasm, yelling or humiliation tactics. An occasional throwing of chalk or an eraser, or slamming a book.

Though we had changed the sign outside over the front door from "Junior High School" to "Middle School," we had a ways to go toward establishing a more authentic middle school on the inside. While teaming was the perfect middle school organizational construct, teams required the right teachers to create the environment and pathways to learning that breathe life into the middle school concept.

This reality opened my eyes to the importance of leadership and effective supervision in defining and refining the vision of what a middle school is, and what practices are encouraged and which have no place in any classroom.

The person selected to be the next principal had to be exactly who and what we needed at this point in time, a middle level expert and a leader who could unite us in a common mission.

So, to recap, in the last three years our school had had as many principals. Our school was in a state of flux as enrollment was rising so fast that the fifth graders had to return to their respective elementary schools, and not a moment too soon, in order to make room for more middle schoolers coming our way.

As the only assistant principal and building administrator, it was nerve-wracking for me as we headed into summer that we did not have a new principal on board yet. I was also concerned about how, as the second-in-charge, our personalities and styles would mesh. I was hoping for someone with whom I could "click" and who could be a mentor.

According to the stars, my lot in life was going to improve. My horoscope for August 11, 1998, read, "An important person captures your attention - by this time next week, you are drawn in! New management will show more appreciation for your work than the others did. Enjoy the change." My wife, who knew my school was still without a principal, or even a mention of a new principal, read my horoscope and decided to clip it for me to see when I arrived home. I found it among my papers as I was writing this book.

Mum was the word from central office until there was an announcement about a new principal, seemingly at the last minute.

# 11. Destiny Came Calling

THE NEWLY APPOINTED PRINCIPAL HAD YEARS OF EXPERI-
ence as a teacher, supervisor, and middle school principal. She had also
served for a brief time as a superintendent. Much of her professional practice
had taken place right here in New Jersey in similar school districts. And it
turned out that she used to work for our superintendent in neighboring
West Orange.

Dr. Katherine Goerss, known as "Kay," was another force to be reckoned
with. She was super bright with strong interpersonal and social skills. Kay
was unafraid to take on the challenges of the job, which were considerable.
A vacuum of leadership in a school building invites others - board members,
PTO, parents - to stake their claim both on how a school should be run in
general and specifically with regard to matters pertaining to their own children. But now it was clear who was in the driver's seat. However, from the
beginning Kay created an inclusive culture and built a process, predicated on
research, study, and collegial review, to make informed decisions. Kay had
the personality and the paradigm, combining the two aspects of leadership
I had reflected on in my graduate studies.

Kay Goerss, Ph. D.

Kay told us, upon her arrival, that she would play the part of the archae-ologist to learn what she needed to know about our school. Kay talked to people all the time, even venturing into the hornet's nest to have coffee with the queen bees in the morning.

Her approach was such a juxtaposition to her predecessor's.

Leaders who are really in charge carry themselves in a certain way. They do not have to remind people. They do not have to threaten anyone. They have a job to do, and as long as they are good listeners and have integrity, and their actions are rooted in reason, even those who disagree can respect the person and the process and live with a decision.

Our new principal immediately formed a partnership with her assistant principal. Her values and thought process permeated our conversations for planning and managing the miscellaneous matters of "life in the middle." Kay took her leadership roles to heart, often reflecting back on decisions, always seeking to do the right thing as guided by her conscience and beliefs.

I could not have hoped for a better mentor.

Kay quickly established a motto for our school: Respect, Responsibility, and Excellence. She also determined that once every month our school would host a nighttime event for the community. Three new events included Evening of Excellence, Dialogue Night, and Parent Academy.

Evening of Excellence invited parents to experience their child's learning environment by viewing curriculum projects in their child's classrooms. Teachers displayed Japanese calligraphy, interdisciplinary research projects, and science experiments while others planned technology presentations or world language skits. In language arts classes students read their stories and poems. The orchestra and band performed selections in the hallway, and a preview of the upcoming spring musical was staged in the auditorium. Physical education teachers set up dance lesson demonstrations while the art teachers assembled remarkable exhibits of student artwork along the main corridor. Peer Leadership played movies of the student-faculty basketball or volleyball games. STEM cycle classes featured a specially themed engineering design for this showcase along with samples of their classwork.

Dialogue Night was sponsored by Peer Leaders and the Guidance Team and focused on intergenerational communication. Parent Academy invited parents to sign up for workshops taught by administrators, child study team, and guidance counselors.

Kay's focal point was middle level education, a common thread in her conversations, staff meetings, professional development, and her own writing. Her book entitled *Letters from the Middle* was published in 1993. Kay also authored educational articles and essays, such as "Who's Afraid of Heterogeneous Teaching?" for the National Middle School Association.

In fact, Kay championed the middle school movement in her various supervisory and administrative roles and by founding the New Jersey Association for Middle Level Education and serving on the National Board of the National Middle School Association. To honor her vision and zeal for promoting authentic middle school programming, NJAMLE created the *Dr. Katherine Goerss Leadership Award* to recognize middle school practitioners who "promulgated the tenets of middle level education as found in *This We*

*Believe* and *Turning Points 2000"* and "encouraged exemplary practices" in their schools.

Kay designed activities to bring teachers together. One of her goals was to have teachers meet colleagues with whom they might never have spoken because they worked in a different department or wing of the building. She asked for staff input and invited everyone in to speak with her.

A firm believer in heterogeneous grouping, Kay tackled the problem of having way too many accelerated classes beginning in sixth grade. Kay understood that differentiating the kids instead of the instruction was antithetical to middle level philosophy, especially for sixth graders.

The transition to middle school, and preadolescence, is huge. The middle level philosophy is about this journey that all kids have to take, leaving behind their elementary, contained-class experience where primarily one teacher provided the structures, supports, and communications for all of the children in his or her class. At the middle school students are challenged to navigate a 9-period day with different instructors who have their own unique organizational requirements, teaching styles, and personalities.

It simply did not make sense that fifth grade teachers, who did not know the expectations of sixth grade instructors or the curriculum, made decisions about which pupils were ready for accelerated learning in sixth grade. The elementary grading system was not compatible with the middle school report card, and parental influence in the placement process meant that most students would be pushed into accelerated classes.

After presenting her rationale to parents, Kay eliminated learning levels in sixth grade. She believed that students should be allowed time to transition through sixth grade and be assessed by middle school teachers. In a sense, removing tracking labels in the sixth grade was intended to "let kids be kids" in a nurturing as well as preparatory, adaptive, and transitional setting, preventing the gestation of peer-to-peer competitiveness before pupils even reached middle school. Teachers were expected to differentiate instruction, especially in math, for truly exceptional children.

Her next step was to establish a middle school committee for the purpose of defining who or what an accelerated learner was. This was necessary because Kay inherited a mess after a prior principal eliminated the "basic level" of instructional learning, the lowest of three performance groups. Basic students were blended into the middle strand, known as "standard," inciting an uprising by parents of standard level students that their children did not belong in a class "with those basic kids" and therefore demanded that their children were a better fit in the accelerated class. With this migration of students, in effect, teachers instructed four accelerated classes a day and one basic class that saw its name changed to "standard." So it was not the basic grouping that went away, it was the middle standard group that disappeared. And the honors classes were not honors at all.

Kay recommended reading the research on giftedness by Dr. Joseph Renzulli and also canvassing how other schools, including colleges, defined readiness for their advanced classes. She led a consensus-seeking process to identify the characteristics of accelerated learners, and the product of this collaborative study was a "characteristics checklist," a tool for teachers to assess readiness consisting of objective measures of student learning as well as observed benchmarks of student behavior and development. The data on the checklists would not only augment borderline grades in consideration for placement, but also serve as a profile, or snapshot, of a learner for parents, teachers, and guidance counselors and even at times as a source of feedback for students.

In the seventh and eighth grades, our objective was to reestablish the integrity of our curriculum offerings. If we were going to continue sponsoring accelerated classes, then the accelerated level had to deliver different content and greater depth and rigor than the regular level for students who were "ready, willing, and able." By definition, the performance level of students in accelerated classes would have to be relative to an already high-achieving norm group.

Kay's final step was to codify these revisions and share the criteria, checklist, and process with the community.

Kay disarmed parents and teachers with her openness and honesty and sense of humor, and she had no problem agreeing or disagreeing or bluntly pointing out something. Her personality, and therefore her delivery, made all the difference.

It was obvious she had done this before. In New Jersey. In a place not unlike Millburn.

When a parent left a message, Kay could not return the call fast enough. Whether she wanted to nip a situation in the bud or confront a problem, she knew that time and communication were of the essence. Kay was also an outside-of-the-box thinker, unafraid to brainstorm ideas to better our school or find solutions that treated children as the unique individuals we believed they were.

Kay began a tradition I also continued: keeping a stash of chocolate in the principal's office. The first time I saw her emptying jumbo-sized bags of miniature chocolate bars into a basket, she answered my nonverbal question by saying, "It's better to feed the teachers so they don't eat the kids." She kept a picture of her cockapoo, Lady (short for Lady Snowden, named for the lane in Princeton over which Lady presided), on her desk. A foodie like me, Kay often paid for our lunch if I went to get it from the amazing Millburn Deli. A Sloppy Joe, fresh sliced rye bread with turkey, swiss cheese, homemade creamy coleslaw and topped with Russian dressing for Kay, and the Gobbler for me with turkey, warm stuffing, cranberry sauce, lettuce and mayo also on rye. You have to live a little!

Needless to say, Kay was a breath of fresh air, full of confidence, competence, and charisma. She was energetic, outgoing, funny and so sensible, and as her assistant I not only found refuge in such a positive role model, I also made a life-long friend. Kay's vision and leadership were exactly what our school needed to come together and to be able to move forward.

After a first year together in which I learned so much and our school became a much happier place, Kay informed me when we returned to the second year that she had been diagnosed with invasive breast cancer. The outlook seemed grim.

Kay was in for the battle of her life, and she needed time to take care of all of the surgeries, treatments, and side-effects. Kay was absent for most of the year.

In our quickly growing school I was the only building administrator. For a couple of months the board of education hired a retired middle school principal from a nearby district as an interim. While he had, at times, a calming influence, it was obvious that he was not invested. He would say in meetings and in conversations that he was just a visitor.

The faculty was very supportive of me and knew that I was stretched. They also missed Kay and did what they could to help me. At Christmas time teachers organized a sing-a-long on the stage which was taped and sent to Kay. The teachers also surprised me with a gift card to take Lea out to dinner.

I visited Kay a couple of times during the year to catch up with her and keep her in the loop. She was always so appreciative, not only of my traveling to her home in Princeton but also of my commitment to being the best substitute I could be for her. I wanted to continue Kay's "brand" in the way she interacted with all stakeholders and the positive culture she had introduced.

Fortunately, Kay returned to work the following September.

After Kay's third year in Millburn, the superintendent decided to retire from New Jersey and oversee a school district in New York State. Kay looked at his departure as an opportunity to work with the fantastic people on the board of education at that time. So Kay was hired to be the superintendent, but within about six months was challenged by serious heart issues, compelling her to retire.

Once again, the door opened for me to move up, only now to decide whether it was my path to become the principal of my school. This was also serendipitous as I valued what I had learned during my time as assistant principal, but I no longer wished to continue in the "vice" role. Because I expected Kay to be principal for the long term, I had interviewed in a few other districts to see if I wanted to be a principal elsewhere. But Millburn Middle School was my home away from home where I was intimately aware of both the positives and the challenges. While I knew that I wanted the job, my decision would require conversations with my Higher Self and my better half. I had a 3-year-old and another baby on the way and wanted to be sure that my new responsibilities jived with my vision of family life at home.

For me, moving up the so-called ladder would elevate my vocation as a teacher. My school was my mission in life. I loved what I did and where I did it. I cared about my colleagues. Stepping into the principal's role would be like becoming head of the family.

It was already my goal to create a middle school that, like the stage of development itself, was not just a phase for kids and their parents to "get through."

According to the Roman statesman Seneca, "Luck is what happens when preparation meets opportunity." I think luck has another more behind-the-scenes component, specifically that the said preparation is nurtured by others, our helpers and guides. I was lucky enough to work in a place like Millburn and even luckier to have supporters and mentors and occasions to grow and assume greater challenges of leadership. Opportunity also had to do with timing; for me, it was how my life intersected with the timelines of other people's lives and careers and also about a shift in time that ushered in new challenges. It was "time for a change."

When the moment arrived for me to have to make an unanticipated decision about becoming the principal of my school, it felt like destiny came calling.

On a happy note, as I write this book seventeen years later, Kay and her husband, The Rev. Dr. John Mark Goerss, a retired Princeton church pastor and Princeton University chaplain, treated Lea and me to dinner to celebrate my retirement after sixteen years as Kay's successor.

I aimed to continue to use our successful and supportive organizational template while placing greater emphasis on the nature of middle level learners. I worked to "grow my school" to accommodate the influx of additional students. And I hoped to establish stability and continuity after a period of revolving door leadership. Between 1995 and 2002, the middle school had six principals (including two interims) and the district had four superintendents.

I was almost immediately approved by the board as the interim principal. Timing is everything, and when that superintendent's chair was empty once again, the vacuum was filled by others. The board, I had heard, wanted to make sure that I was the best possible candidate for the job, not simply the next-in-line default candidate. A couple of months later, after I had to interview for the very job I had been doing for some time, I was appointed principal. Since I already held a tenured position, it would only take two years to acquire tenure in my new post. I understood that I was on the clock and everyone was watching to see how I performed in order to determine if it was time for another one of those nationwide searches.

When it came to hiring another superintendent, it seemed that New Jersey and New York had a reciprocity agreement for recycling retired superintendents. A new superintendent freshly retired from New York State by the name of Dr. Richard Brodow was appointed to run the district. He would become one of the most beloved superintendents to the teachers, administrators, and parents in the district, and also one of the most beleaguered in terms of the shifting composition of the board and some alliances in the community. During my first meeting with him, after some pleasantries, he acknowledged that I was in my first year as principal and said, "I have the responsibility of determining if you are the right person for the job. I will not hesitate to decline tenure if I feel that you are not the best candidate." While I already knew that my future rested with his approval, I was also keenly aware of at least one board member who wanted to do a broader search, feeling perhaps that I was riding into office on Kay's coattails, precipitating an eerie sense of deja vu.

Was I smart enough? Determined enough? Working hard enough? Good enough?

During my second year, my tenure year, I was asked to compose written answers to some questions the board had for me. I referred to this as "Final Exam I." The four questions focused on middle school philosophy and programming as well as my vision and goals for the next five years.

Not long after I submitted my responses, I was served with "Final Exam II," with far more questions - eighteen - that left no stone unturned and required an additional Saturday in my office.

I responded, in detail, to all of the questions. It was not hard since I was the one facing the space crunch head-on as the person who had to schedule the building, and Kay had always included me in on all of the issues. That's what happens when you work on a team.

A team, in fact, that Kay referenced in a letter to the superintendent while she was principal proposing that I be appointed her co-principal.

I like to think that these extra steps were actually a way for me to display several things about myself: first, the depth of my responses reflected an unrivaled level of knowledge about middle schools in general and the specific challenges surrounding my middle school; second, that I had a vision for my school; third, that I possessed leadership and problem-solving capabilities; and fourth, that I possessed strong writing and communication skills. While I would never have wished it the way it happened, Kay's absence put me in the driver's seat as an apprentice principal, and that gave me real experience in the role with my mentor guiding and encouraging me from afar.

Something Kay once said that stuck with me was "it is always better for a new principal to follow a principal who was not loved." Well, I used to think, that does not bode well for me! In actuality, though, following in Kay's footsteps was a continuation of what we both started together under her collaborative leadership model.

# 12. Old Age and Growing Pains

AT TIMES I HAD WONDERED IF THERE WAS A GIANT NEON yellow sign painted on our school rooftop that read, "Register your child here" for all the incoming flights to Newark and New York. Our office staff did in fact receive telephone inquiries from inflight passengers. We experienced serial summers where our enrollment spiked by 50 to 75 new students, significant enough to raise class sizes and affect specialized programming such as English Language Learning and special education, where pupil enrollment is capped by law.

In 1999 fifth graders returned to their neighborhood elementary schools, only now there were five instead of four. Construction expansions had been completed at the elementary schools, and the former South Mountain School, leased to a day care program, was renovated and returned online.

With all of this drama at the elementary level going on, middle school administrators wondered how long it would be before anyone figured out that if the expanded elementary schools were maxed out with enrollment, then the middle school was already behind the eight ball with all those students heading here.

The lack of space was a primary challenge of my early leadership years.

In 1999 voters approved a bond referendum in the amount of $15.5 million, in part to construct eight classrooms at the middle school. This addition was already insufficient before construction commenced. We were told a smaller project was what the public would approve in a bond referendum. Ultimately, that meant the next superintendent would have to seek further public funding for construction.

Indeed, in 2005 Dr. Brodow launched a more comprehensive, and costly, bond referendum to add space at the middle school as well as at the high school. The pivotal questions seemed to be how much space and where. The former became a political hot potato, and the latter a logistical challenge.

In order to prepare for the referendum, the superintendent enlisted the services of an educational consortium to conduct enrollment projections; and because this was Millburn, a place where things tended to be done using an unconventional or dramatic approach often referred to by school personnel as "The Millburn Way," the board contracted with another company and then for good measure did their own projections. While there was some variability, they all told a story of growing enrollments for the foreseeable future. The years from 1996 to 2004 saw the overall middle school enrollment increase by more than 400 students. Later, an additional two hundred pupils pushed our total to just under 1,200 by 2010.

Millburn Middle School, a majestic building with columns, lanterns and globe light posts, was originally constructed in the 1920's as the community's high school. Our school was boxed in by Old Short Hills Road, NJ Transit train tracks, and a densely populated residential neighborhood. In essence, our school campus was landlocked, denying any possibility of expanding property lines for new construction. All new additions, roadways and parking lots would be constructed on campus at the expense of shrinking outdoor recreational space.

This classical building was my home away from home for 30 years. Photo by my son, Mike Cahill.

A Long Range Facilities Planning Committee, consisting of parents, community members, and school administrators, was convened to explore and study options to meet the demands of increasing enrollment. Our role as administrators included educating the group about how our school was configured and providing tours of the physical plant. We supplied information about our space needs based on the program we offered, including the number and types of rooms to accommodate the projected enrollments, as well as recommendations from department supervisors.

During this process, I was asked what the maximum number of students on a team should be. A utopian middle school would support 60-85 students per team. However, 100 students on a team was a more realistic view. My thinking concluded that 120 pupils was the upper limit of the range indicative of the need to hire an additional team for a grade level.

As part of the information-gathering process I had multiple conversations with supervisors and teachers. For example, the success of our instrumental program was also its greatest challenge. So many students wanted to be in the band that we already had to divide the band into two groups and schedule an every-other-day class rotation. We had to plan combined rehearsals on the auditorium stage prior to concerts. In the referendum, we asked for a much larger band room with more storage and also private practice rooms.

Our guidance counselors had offices slightly larger than a cubicle that could hardly accommodate one or two parents or teachers for meetings. Also, since teachers did not have telephones in their rooms, they often searched for an empty counselor office in order to have private conversations with parents. We included a conference room to mitigate both of these needs.

Students were already splitting the lunch period into two 20-minute segments in the cafeteria and the auditorium, so it made sense to request an auxiliary lunchroom.

Since we had only one art room, we had to schedule art-on-a-cart in academic classrooms for the overflow classes. Art teachers lacked adequate storage for student projects and art supplies.

Our school's special education population and faculty were also increasing, so we requested small group instruction rooms.

Our numbers justified another gym.

We were desperately in need of additional science labs and regular classrooms.

The committee assimilated all of this information into the referendum.

Overcrowding in our school was about more than the number of students in classrooms. Hallways became congested, especially during critical times at junctures between buildings. Gymnasiums lacked the space to allow *all* students to participate for the entire period, and kids were jammed into locker rooms. Cycle classes such as art, music and technology stretched the space, supplies, and electronic devices.

Our packed school stressed teachers in ways not so obvious to outsiders. For example, a teacher who was lucky enough to have the same assigned room for all of his or her classes still had to vacate when not teaching in order for another instructor to teach in that room. The home teacher therefore could not set up an activity or a lab experiment before the next class. The home teacher had to share space on a whiteboard and provide storage. Many of the home teachers waited for the cart teacher to arrive, understanding that the commute from other parts of the building could be daunting. The home teacher had to find another quiet place to work because, unlike our high school teachers, they did not have a desk in a nearby office. Sometimes home teachers did not want to vacate their classrooms while their colleagues were teaching, and I had to involve myself to alleviate pressure on the cart teachers by making it a rule and enforcing it, when necessary.

Teachers on carts had to travel down the same packed hallways, or maybe even take the ancient elevator, within the 4-minute passing time. The teacher on a cart would likely move around the building all day long, developing coping mechanisms for technology, materials, and communications.

The fire code maximum capacity for our lunch room was 278 persons, but most of our grade levels had already exceeded 300 students. When we had grade level sizes lower than code, we had comfortably accommodated all of the children in an entire grade level for the full lunch period, which prior to 2001 was a dedicated 25 minutes. At that time, though, grade levels did not have to share classrooms with other grades. We'd more than doubled our enrollment since then.

In order to comply with the fire code, and to make room for many more students coming our way, we had to add 15 minutes to the start of the school day to convert that 25-minute lunch to another regular 40-minute period. The second step was to split the 40-minute lunch periods into two 20-minute segments. While half the kids were eating in the cafeteria, the other half were sitting in the auditorium.

The middle school did everything in its power to flex during the years when we accommodated the fifth graders and also later when we experienced our own growth spurt. Until 2004 pre-kindergarten classes had been housed at the middle school, but it became necessary to reclaim those three classrooms. Small offices were transformed into special education classrooms. A former metal shop was divided into two classrooms. The library reference room was converted into a classroom. A wall was knocked down between a teacher media center and an audio-visual equipment closet to create a technology lab. A team locker room was converted into a P.E. weight room. The stage in the auditorium served as an instrumental music class, and the cafeteria was tapped as another P.E. space. Without creating a split session where students would attend either morning or afternoon classes, and addressing all of the concomitant challenges that come with staffing and parent work schedules, there was nothing left to do but build.

To say that the township was divided on this $40.2 million referendum for both schools is to understate the civil war that raged on. A community group known as We Love Millburn aggressively opposed this bond issue, and when your PTO presidents, usually the most ardent supporters of school initiatives, are against something, then you know you are in trouble.

This bond referendum was ultimately defeated by voters in December 2005, and work immediately commenced on another referendum that was far less ambitious and scuttled everything at the middle school except instructional spaces, a girls' locker room, and a multi-purpose room.

Voters did approve this scaled-back bond in the amount of $21.3 million in September 2006.

The multi-purpose room was a consolation prize for losing the gym and cafeteria. While parents and even board members expected the multi-purpose room to serve as an auxiliary cafeteria, its function as an instructional space trumped its use for dining. With some physical education classes approaching over 220 students, it was essential as a fifth PE space. PE classes were already utilizing two gymnasiums, a weight room, and the cafeteria when it was not being used, prepped or cleaned, even with its brick columns menacing the active play of our students. Parent concerns, however, about the 20-minute timeframe in which to purchase and eat lunch never abated, even if it was their very own lack of support, ironically, for the original referendum that caused it to be shot down.

Another ramification of the rejection of the original 2005 referendum was the delay of construction in time for the 2008 arrival of what was going to be the second of three consecutive years of hiring more teachers in each grade level. Our enrollments for both sixth and seventh grades that year exceeded 380 pupils. Without the additional space we could not staff this rising seventh grade class to have four teams like it did in sixth grade, and this sparked another significant public feud.

A group of parents lobbied to have portable classrooms (a euphemism for trailers) plopped down in our teacher parking lot so that the seventh grade could have its fourth team. Despite their good intentions, this was a terrible idea for reasons of our students' physical safety, security of the premises, inclement weather, traffic and noise from trucks and machinery, and the fact that middle level students in general are just unaware of their surroundings. I cynically wondered if these same supporters would have allowed me to place *their* kids on the "trailer team" or whatever other undignified nickname it might acquire.

But this was a vociferous bunch that had support from some members of the board of education. One board member interrogated me publicly about my recommendation to maintain three teams, even if it meant higher class enrollments. In this *Twilight Zone* moment for me, I was on the firing line defending my stance that the safety of our students was our #1 priority. "What little support (Superintendent) Brodow received Monday night came primarily from middle school Principal Michael Cahill. Cahill said issues of safety, supervision and practicality outweighed the need for a fourth team. 'We will keep the kids in the building, we will use our current seventh-grade teachers and we will give them a good program,' Cahill said. He told the parents 'there is flexibility at the middle school' to keep educational opportunities open for all students." (Harry Trumbore, "Parents Trash Trailer Choice," The *Item of Millburn-Short Hills*, 5/8/2008).

Of course, there were multiple contexts embedded in this public discourse. Parents were emotional about their children being deprived of what they deserved to have. School board members were embroiled in internal tussles with the superintendent. And I came from a place of knowledge and experience about kids at this age, the limitations of our facility and campus, and how our school delivered its comprehensive educational program. I had also lived through other construction projects. I took my decision-making role very seriously, and my thinking also derived from my own parenting instincts.

Parents naively thought that if enough trailers could be leased for an entire team, students would not have to travel back and forth into the building. Of course, the reality is that students had other classes in addition to their academics, and they would have to return to the building for lockers, physical education, lunch, and arts, music and tech cycle classes. The swarm of participants in chorus, band and orchestra would have to attend small group lessons as well as ensemble classes and rehearsals.

Trailers are not equipped with restrooms.

What about students who received support or special education services? What about guidance appointments or kids needing to see the nurse? How would we communicate announcements, drills, and especially emergencies? An evacuation, drill or not, would pose heightened risks.

A member of the audience at this inquisition came to the podium and put me to the test. "Then why do we have to build more classrooms if you feel that higher class sizes would benefit from the same quality of instruction?" A board member's question also elicited an honest response from me that higher class sizes would impact the delivery of the curriculum.

In my role as principal I had to choose the lesser of two evils.

It became incumbent upon me to figure out a proposal to implement support systems for seventh grade teams. The community voiced its concern about the vulnerability of the language arts program, specifically the frequency of writing and the ability of teachers to provide constructive feedback given a caseload of 130 students. I hatched a plan to hire an additional language arts teacher who siphoned 25-30 students from each team for instruction. I simultaneously created a writing lab cycle course in which language arts teachers could coach their own students with their various writing assignments. In effect, I used a two-prong approach to reduce the number of students for language arts teachers while increasing teacher contact time through the writing lab. The district hired a paraprofessional for each team to help with grading, prep, and clerical tasks and also purchased additional laptop carts expressly for seventh grade. This was a temporary situation stemming from an ongoing crisis of space. Time was not on our side.

Yes, class sizes and team enrollments were higher than what teachers and students were accustomed to, but I had made the decision that this was a far safer alternative than sending middle level learners outside the building in any kind of weather and worrying if they were going to reach their destination safely in what would effectively be an active construction site.

Writing about this reminded me of another time I met with resistance when I advocated for the safety of our students. Just outside the entrance to our parking lot, traffic from three roads converged to form long lines of cars and buses approaching the middle school every morning. This quaint and quiet area of Short Hills, situated on narrow winding lanes with cobblestone trenches on both sides, was not designed for the volume of traffic or the size of the vehicles that traverse these roads today. In addition to the rising number of parent cars, 18 school buses dropped students off at the bus loop, and 80 staff automobiles vied to get into the teacher parking lot, all at the same time. On top of all that, middle school kids from the Knollwood section walked to school on these same roads, dwarfed by humongous SUV's.

Many parents and I shared worries over the years that kids walking to school or being dropped off in the middle of traffic (yes, you read that right) were in danger of being struck by a vehicle. Since there were only so many police officers and crossing guards available to handle traffic around all the district's schools, I wrote a letter to the mayor about my fear of a child being hurt, or worse, hopefully providing grist to increase allocations for traffic and safety personnel. Shortly after I sent my letter, the only response came from the superintendent of schools informing me that future concerns would be communicated to the township via central office only. It was a slap on the wrist for breaking the chain of command, despite the fact that the district and the township were both aware of the situation. But a letter from the principal was now a part of the record in this matter, and I could sleep at night.

Eventually neighborhood routes were established to separate school buses from cars in order to expedite the unloading of buses, but the strategy only worked as long as a police officer showed up to enforce the plan. Traffic continued to bottleneck where the roads united, however, prompting an assistant principal, security guard and teachers on bus duty into the street to manage the flow of traffic and student safety.

The November 2006-approved addition had to be erected on the only sliver of land available on our campus, sandwiched between the main building and the annex. We voiced our concerns to the architects about the high volume of pupil traffic in an area where essentially four buildings would merge. As a result, additional stairwells included in the construction supplied alternate routes to different buildings and floors, alleviating the congestion that occurred during the change of classes and especially after lunch dismissals.

The construction of the newest addition furnished enough space for us to accommodate the highest number of teams we had ever had, twelve. Of course, the days of teachers having their own classrooms became a distant memory as administrators tried to schedule what I called the "a la cart" teachers into some of the same rooms during each day, or at least in rooms used by their department in order to share materials and resources.

Today the footprint of the facility is reminiscent of an airport in how terminals jut out of the main hub. Over the years at least four extensions have been added with another one already approved by voters as I was making my exit.

Overseeing the expansion and updating of our building continued to be one of the primary goals of my administration. I learned a lot about blueprints, construction, code, and systems. Once a referendum was approved by voters, it was just the beginning of a long process of planning, communicating, and constructing while keeping youngsters out of harm's way and continuing to learn, despite the noise, odors, dust, and interruptions.

One unexpected event inside our building, which I will never forget, forever impressed upon me the importance of cautionary measures and quick action to safeguard the well-being of students and staff. It took place on the second day back from Christmas vacation in January 2000 when I was the assistant principal and the only administrator in the building. About a quarter of the ceiling in the upper gym collapsed. It was as though the sky itself came down.

I was called to the upper gym by physical education teachers not long before because they heard rumbling sounds from above in that part of the room. They kept their students away from the noise, but they wanted me to know they were concerned. Foolishly, I walked into that quadrant of the room and looked up, trying to listen and see what was happening. The teachers quickly escorted me away, fearing something might fall on me. That's how scared they were. We could hear a loud shifting noise, but there was nothing anyone could actually see beyond the tiles of the dropped ceiling. Not long after, when the room was empty, ceiling tiles, metal frames, plaster, and concrete would come crashing down in the very place I had been standing, enveloping the gymnasium in a white dust cloud.

Apparently the dropped ceiling was hanging from another above it. Its weight and the force of gravity over time gradually pulled down both dropped ceilings as well as chunks of the original ceiling, culminating in the BOOMS and shifting sounds I had heard for myself.

Thankfully, no one was harmed, but I still see in my mind's eye the students and teachers using the upper gym as well as the perfectly straight line of elementary-age students who came to the middle school for aftercare as they were marching toward the upper gymnasium around four o'clock that afternoon. One more left turn and then a right turn into the space where they could shake, rock, and roll before settling down for a snack and homework. The SAM program children and their chaperones had not yet learned that the upper gym was sealed off. The memories of that day served as a perennial reminder of the top priority of leadership to provide a safe environment for everyone at all times of the day and night.

Building codes changed over time, and the new eighth grade wing had much larger classrooms, more suitable for the largest students. Hence, its name. The rest of the building was also arranged to match the size of the children with the proportions of the rooms, and also to create neighborhoods of classrooms by grade level. Sixth graders were upstairs in the main building because the oldest building had the smallest classrooms. The seventh graders were scheduled into the upper and lower annex rooms which were larger than the sixth grade classrooms but not as large as the eighth grade ones. Just like the students.

For a couple of years, we did in fact have one trailer housing two classrooms because we were short a couple of rooms. These instructional spaces, occupied by two classes of sixth graders, were conveniently located on the front lawn just yards from the side entrance to the building.

There were those who suggested that we add a lawn chair, some flamingos and a clothesline to endow the trailer with a measure of Short Hills neighborhood panache.

# 13. Angels and Makeovers

THE PLACE IS A DUMP.

The referendum cast a spotlight on the middle school as residents toured the facility to better understand the wish list in the bond referendum, and this resulted in a negative perception of the middle school's appearance, probably more so by the parents of younger elementary age students who would be coming down the pike.

Little had been done to improve the interior or exterior of the building during the years preceding my role as principal. When you work in a big and busy place like this every day and your focus is on all of the educational and people-related concerns that are a constant, in addition to the rising enrollment and building expansion, and all of the unexpected events that occur daily, maybe it is natural not to really notice the deterioration. Maybe you just learn to live with it. School building administrators also know that a tidy sum of money is needed to renovate older buildings, funding that rarely seems accessible or even appropriated in longer-term capital improvement plans. Building maintenance projects rank low on the list of spending priorities when tight budget allocations could be used in other ways, such as for technology, or are needed for unforeseen rainy day projects around the district.

It doesn't help that old buildings do not look anything like newer schools. Ours was an older school laid out in the traditional egg-carton design. The rooms were small and in need of painting, the lighting was dim, the lockers were aging, and the tile floors were worn. It would be impolite to describe the bathrooms.

In a letter-to-the-editor of the local paper, one resident referred to the middle school as a "dump."

Parents who relocated to the township would have a visceral reaction when they toured our building. Many of them shared with me how their children were coming from more modern schools. I knew what they were talking about as I had visited several middle school campuses in New Jersey. Contemporary buildings are designed to be more compatible with the latest thinking about instructional practices and technology with airy and spacious gathering places fitted with flexible furniture for innovative and collaborative activities.

Clearly, our facilities, they discovered, were not up to par with the stellar reputation of our school district. In my welcome remarks during the new family orientation held in August, I actually began to emphasize what I believed was true, that our programs, teachers, and student opportunities, not our physical plant, were the reasons for our reputation.

A member of the long-term facilities committee had suggested that we raze the middle school building and construct a new one either in its place or somewhere else. Few options existed for the "somewhere else," possibly a tract of land near a highway or another property owned by the board that was too small and faced environmental and neighborhood challenges. Even if we could bulldoze this building, we would need another school online first, and at a time when we were growing too fast to catch up. I remember feeling shocked about the suggestion, even though this forum's charge was to evaluate any and all options. Another proposal by the board that caught me off guard was to tear down the new eighth grade wing so the district could replace it with a two-story building.

I could not imagine destroying our auditorium, the artistry of which is not usually replicated in modern performance venues. Our library also had a huge wood fireplace flanked by candelabras. Columns, elegant lighting fixtures, high ceilings, tile arches and woodwork accented hallways and entrance ways. Even though this old building would never be comparable to a new building, it was my hope that steps would be taken to preserve and blend the aesthetic classical elements with more up-to-date functionality. At least the two new wings of our building offered spacious, modern classrooms.

After the construction of the new addition, all ceilings and lights in the hallways of the older structures were replaced, as were all of the lockers. Some simple yet still expensive updates made the inside brighter and endowed the building with more of a shine. Windows and eventually the many aging external all-glass doors were replaced as well. Geothermal wells were installed in our back field to provide cooling and heating in most of the classrooms in the older buildings. I will always remember the day the company decided to conduct a test, after months of work on this project. So much water spouted out of the holes in the pipes, it was as though they had installed a sprinkler system! It was a good thing the test took place after school.

Two major concerns, the painting of classrooms and hallways and the lack of any curb appeal in front of our school, were addressed by a surprising benefactor. You might say that it was the hand of God.

A local church needed a temporary place to worship while it was renovating a recently purchased building, so the South Mountain Community Church rented out our auditorium. In the movie *High School Musical*, the drama teacher refers to her school's auditorium as a "temple of the arts." Now, our auditorium was a real temple, too, at least on Sundays. The church knew firsthand what our needs were and adopted Millburn Middle School for its "mission." I penned a thank you to the church that appeared in The *Item of Millburn-Short Hills*, on September 27, 2006. The following excerpt from "Volunteer painters teach life lesson" tells the story:

*Bob Griner, the pastor of the local South Mountain Community Church that rents our school facility for worship services, offered the middle school administration the opportunity to have the entire school painted for free.*

*It was not because he saw what we saw.*

*It was not because he wished to help our community during a time when caps on budgets and a defeated referendum meant that funding for a paint job the size of the middle school would not be a priority.*

*He simply wanted to give back to the community and at the same time offer opportunity for service to others. The opportunity came through the Paint the Town program.*

*Even I asked him if other communities needed the help more than ours did. In Griner's eyes, a school is a school, and every community needs help. It is true that many other communities who took part in the summer Paint the Town project were of a lower socioeconomic status. This did not matter to Griner; Millburn Middle School had a need, and help was on the way.*

*All the way, that is, from Texas, Kentucky, Mississippi, and Florida. In addition to local church members, six teams of volunteers, most of whom were active participants in faith groups, made it their "mission" to volunteer to paint schools during the summer.*

*Volunteers ran the gamut from toddlers to senior citizens. High school students, young parents and their children, grandparents, and every-one in between paid for their own travel and lodging from the South in order to volunteer at Millburn Middle School. Many of these people experienced heat waves, blackouts, airport delays, long hours of driv-ing, and substandard housing.*

*To hear them tell of it, it was just another part of this interesting sum-mer story about a trip up North to perform community service.*

*When in my official capacity I tried to thank them for their service, I was thanked in return for providing such an opportunity.*

*The group's objective was to help repaint the inside of Millburn Middle School in just 52 days. Aside from the school library and some stairwells, the entire school was painted.*

*Bob Zeglarski, the district business administrator, estimated the volunteer effort saved the district time and money to the tune of $70,000. The result is a cleaner, brighter learning environment and an interior building of which we can again be proud. It is hard to put a dollar amount on that.*

*The people who traveled from near or far to paint Millburn Middle School provided a "real life" example of how persons of any age can help a community.*

*We want our young adolescents to learn that they too have opportunities to help others without the expectation of something in return. Paint the Town, and South Mountain Community Church, offer a meaningful model of both spirit and generosity in caring about the community.*

The project involved 175 gallons of paint for 39 rooms, six hallways and the cafeteria. The number of volunteers participating between June 28 and August 18, 2006, was 135.

It felt like a Habitat for Humanity Project, except for schools. In this case, a school in one of the wealthiest school districts in the nation.

A year later Bob Griner and his volunteers, many of whom had painted our school the year before, returned to landscape the front lawn, again at no cost to the district. The volunteers labored to remove older shrubs and trees and replaced them with plantings that were symmetrically arranged and spaced. The new plantings included flowering shrubs, evergreens, and cherry blossom trees. The South Mountain Community Church raised donations tallying $14,000 and provided free labor to undertake this community project. The new landscaping transformed the face of our building and graced it with the sense of pride it deserved.

The era in which additions were constructed can be seen in the style and color of materials used. For many years the exterior of the 1950's annex was covered by sherbet orange metallic panels. During my time as principal they were replaced by silver panels, but the boxy metallic building still looked to me like a large trailer in contrast to the stately older brick building sitting right next to it.

Another hue of orange was the color of the circulation desk in our library, an area of our school that begged for an update. In 2007 the middle school P.T.O. donated $52,000 to remodel the entire library. An area with bookshelves was converted into an instructional media space with a SmartBoard. Shelves were reconfigured to create an open space with more tables and chairs - all brand new. A new circulation desk was more centrally located, and comfortable seating areas made the library more inviting.

It became increasingly evident that even our auditorium warranted a makeover. The auditorium was constructed as part of the original 1920's building, and its gold lattice ceilings, floral plaster medallions, Corinthian columns, and gilded chandeliers, often found in Broadway theaters, fashioned a spectacular showpiece for the performing arts in our school and community. We estimated that the seats, a shade akin to pumpkin, were at least thirty-five years old and had deteriorated to the point of springs sticking out of the cushions and seats falling off the backs of chairs. The aging process was accelerated by frisky students jumping and kneeling on them every day during the non-eating part of the lunch period.

The house lights behaved erratically and would suddenly turn off, or on, in the middle of a presentation or production without anyone even seated at the control board. As the lights blinked or turned dim and then bright, whichever administrator was speaking would just calmly say, "It's okay. It's just the middle school ghost." The kids became used to it, though at first they would sit up straight with their eyes wide open, murmuring, "Whoa, what's that?"

The refurbishment of our auditorium made it a better illuminated, technologically updated, and more comfortable theater. New and sturdier cushioned blue seats matched the stage and window curtains. The old fluorescent light "cans," literal cans projecting out of the ceiling containing white fluorescent lamps that took forever to warm up, were replaced with dignified, and brighter, recessed lights. The orange stain on the trim and woodwork was transformed into "humble gold," a warm and subtle contrast to offset the cream-colored walls. A highly anticipated sound system was installed. The installation of air-conditioning delivered welcome relief during the spring musical and concerts, and especially for the June move-up ceremonies.

I admired the workers who labored over the summer and into the school year because they genuinely cared about the task of preserving the artistic elements of the room while simultaneously transforming the space into a more usable, comfortable, and modern venue. The renovation that began at the close of the school year in June 2012 breathed new life into our own "temple of the arts."

The icing on the cake, for me, was the restoration of the 1906 Steinway Grand Piano that was thought to be donated to our building by a local professional organist during the 1940s. Steinway records revealed the piano was originally sold to a customer in Paterson, New Jersey. In the spring of 2013 the Millburn Middle School P.T.O. donated $20,000 to restore the piano rather than purchase a new one because, once restored, it would look and sound better than a piano that could be purchased at a comparable price. It felt, too, like they wanted to preserve another piece of history, one that had called our auditorium home for decades.

As I look back upon this time of renaissance for Millburn Middle School, I will always have a feeling of awe when I consider the generous and giant acts of kindness from so many angels, from town and far away, who made personal sacrifices and/or donated their time, energy and money to upgrade and enhance where we lived and worked every day.

# 14. Stuck in the Middle

"YOU WORK IN A MIDDLE SCHOOL? UMM..WOW...REALLY? Why? Was that, like, your dream?"

Strangers, likely recalling an awkward stage of their lives they would rather forget, offered condolences or exlaimed, "That's gotta be rough!"

A Benedictine monk I met in a doctor's office, upon learning that I was a middle school principal, whispered wide-eyed, "we both carried that same cross" and promised to pray for me.

The look of unease in some eyes betrayed what they were really thinking: "Are you insane?"

A fair question, if you don't get who middle schoolers are.

Indeed, the key to understanding my most important role as the instructional leader is linked to discovering who middle schoolers are and their metamorphosis, accompanied by all sorts of possibilities, challenges, and discoveries over the three years they spent in our school. It was the reason for my existence and my joy in coming to work every day. Every decision - whether it was about content, instruction, hiring, activities, safety, character education, or discipline - was made with their unique developmental traits in mind.

During my undergraduate studies, I do not recall classmates dreaming of teaching middle schoolers. When I graduated from college I also saw myself more as the high school English professor, but that was before I ever taught in a middle school. Over the years I have had opportunities to teach at the high school level, but it was a conscious decision on my part to stay at the middle school. I was stuck in the middle.

Reconfiguring middle schools from junior high schools was actually a movement intended to put ninth graders where they belonged, in a high school, and removing the words "high school" because the point was that a middle school was not a high school or even a "junior" high school. Middle schools comprise more compatible students who are all in a phase where they are no longer children and not yet adolescents. This cauldron of hormonal chaos is officially known as "transessence" and generally consists of students in grades 6, 7, and 8. The Carnegie Corporation's *Turning Points* research, an often referenced bible of sorts for me, offers a middle level framework that matches specific developmental and learning constructs with the characteristics of children in this evolutionary phase.

Middle school marks what is a bittersweet time for parents as their child journeys closer to young adulthood. The three years of middle school are a time of intense physical, cognitive, social, and emotional growth. The extraordinary changes students undergo make this stage of development remarkable and unique.

I reflect on how the world, and in turn growing up, has changed in so many ways since the time when I entered sixth grade (let's just say it was in the early 1970's), not just in the superficial ways of style (bell bottoms and platform shoes) and pop culture but also in the more profound "rethinking" about family, marriage, and sexuality. Families have been redefined and children more often come from single parent households, shared custody arrangements, interracial marriages, and blended families. A growing number of students have two moms or two dads. Kids, beginning in middle school, are identifying as transgender in a world, at least in more progressive thinking camps, that eschews labels and embraces "sexual fluidity."

The words and wisdom of parents as their children's first teachers compete with the powerful pull of the media, especially social media, and hundreds of cable channels and open access to the internet. Cell phones have replaced more personal communications and social connections. Video games challenge our students to compete in hunting and killing "people."

If, as a kid, you want to stand out as a competitive athlete, to make the high school team or hope for a college athletic scholarship, you had better "major" in one sport and devote all your time, year round, to training camps, travel teams, and off-season practice from a young age, at the expense of enjoying a broader participation in a variety of athletics or other activities. All with no guaranteed outcomes.

It was never easy entering adolescence, a life-cycle transfiguration of grand proportions from which emerges a young adult. This stage of development commences with the onset of puberty, which can begin as early as ten years of age. A powerful challenge for preadolescents is the task of defining who they are while also carving out a group identity. It is an age of curiosity and taking risks. The strive for independence from parents combined with peer pressure, a veritable Molotov cocktail, can compromise their safety and well-being.

The preadolescent stage is a time when students often begin to experiment with smoking or vaping, alcohol, drugs, gambling, and sex. In their quest for acceptance, their decision-making can be impaired. No middle school is immune to these coming-of-age trials, and our school has dealt with kids trying out all of these more adult pastimes over the years. Entrepreneurial students sold commodities such as sneakers or established betting websites. Some students became sexually active by seventh grade, and in this modern day of sharing everything one does on social media, they Snapchatted or texted compromising pictures, porn, and sexting messages. If school personnel even suspected that a student was under the influence of alcohol or drugs, and they have, including at school-sponsored social events, they were legally bound to "code" the individual to require a physician screening.

In fact, drinking was one of the reasons I discontinued our eighth grade dance - not so much because our students were imbibing at the dance, but because eighth graders pregamed at someone's house, arriving at school already tipsy before the dance even started. Of course, this betrayal of child welfare and the law was enabled by either the negligence or support of older siblings or adults.

The Millburn Municipal Alliance Committee (M-MAC) was a proactive community organization dedicated to the prevention of alcohol and drug abuse by children. Although M-MAC included in its membership parents who had children in the public schools, ironically, it was sometimes other parents who were their greatest adversary, not just those who failed to lock up the liquor cabinet and/or who left their kids home alone, but also parents who espoused a divergent point of view. For example, one parent told me that she allowed her middle school kids and their friends to drink in her basement because she was supervising them and, after all, they were not going to be driving themselves home. Another parent explained that it was inevitable that kids were going to drink, so it would be better for them to experience drinking now while under her tutelage. Their "suspend reality" thinking abandoned important concepts about not promoting alcohol to 13 and 14-year-old developing brains and bodies, violating the law, risking addiction, impairing student judgement, and escalating unwanted behaviors.

The continuum of preteen development, though, is such that other students still play with dolls or Legos, which of course have to be hidden from view. The few remaining kids who still think Santa Claus is real are disabused of their belief by seventh grade.

Negotiating the social stratosphere can be a challenge for individuals of all ages.

Those of us who work with middle level students understand their foibles but also recognize how wonderful these emerging adults truly are. These kids are curious, earnest, caring, daring, and social. Add energetic, positive, friendly, and hopeful. Middle schoolers are just beginning to develop awareness and social skills as they advance from thinking almost exclusively about themselves to developing empathy. I have devoted an entire chapter to the multitude of ways our pupils have been engaged in peer leader activities that promoted and supported service initiatives literally around the world.

Middle school educators witness not only their students' external growth but also how their hearts and spirits open up to care about others as they channel their energies to embrace worthy causes that benefit people, animals, education or the environment. This is the time of their lives when they will be most influenced by their teachers and many other adults in their extended families and schools, athletic programs, religious institutions, and neighborhoods. They are searching for mentors and role models as they take their place as leaders in the world and architects of their own futures.

I realized that our school lacked a mascot, and I wanted a figure that reflected our students. I chose the mustang, not just because of the alliteration, but also because of their shared characteristics with our pupil population. Mustangs are spirited and wild and band together in a herd. Sound like middle schoolers? They have an energy that is difficult to harness, but are also an image of beauty to watch, just like our kids. Mustangs are a symbol of the pioneers who expanded westward, and middle schoolers are trailblazers in their own right as they mature and evolve.

I introduced our new mascot at the beginning of the 2007 school year, and peer leaders assembled a bulletin board in the main hallway that celebrated the formal induction of our new mascot with photographs and information about Mustangs. From then on, the mustang logo appeared on banners around the school and on all documents and publications, not to mention all the swag.

From an instructional standpoint, there is nothing easy about teaching middle schoolers, especially as the content rigor and expectations increase in preparation for high school. And while that is one important component of what middle school teachers do, middle school is not simply a "feeder school." The middle school mission is much more comprehensive.

One of my favorite assignments, when I was an eighth grade language arts teacher, was to have students interview their parents about when they were middle school age. This was a great project because kids in the 11-14 range begin to see the world and their parents in a different light. A context emerges for their own lives as they seek to better understand and connect to their family history, culture, religion, traditions, or even the era in which their parents grew up. Parents talking - and laughing - about their own experiences and how times have changed helps students understand their stage of development in the life cycle and also how much DNA rubbed off (what Garrison Keillor refers to as "the dread of heredity"). The sweetest reward is that they actually talk to their parents, something that becomes less assured as students mature into preadolescents.

Each year of middle school is different in terms of growth, expectations, and behavior. Sixth graders are ready for change. It is nerve-wracking for them in the period of time leading up to the start of middle school. They are changing the place in which they learn, and that new setting is significantly larger. What is most on their minds? Questions like these: Will I be able to open my locker? Who will I sit with during lunch? Will I get lost? Of course, they ponder other questions as well, such as, Will I get a lot of homework? Will I like my teachers? Will I make new friends? Will I be able to do the work?

Some rising sixth grade students already possess transitional or survival skills while others are just initiating or developing them. Day-to-day logistics require more self-reliance for opening a locker, finding classrooms, and rehearsing procedures for lunch, PE, locker room, cycle classes, buses, etc.

Incoming sixth grade parents have often expressed to me that their children were ready for greater academic challenge. Teachers at the middle school level are required to be certified in their subject while elementary school teachers have broad certification to teach all subjects. So our specialists jumped right into their content areas using their knowledge, preparation, and understanding of preadolescents to provide greater depth of learning and applications. Over the years parents have shared with me how social studies and science teachers, especially, have inspired dinner table conversations generated by their children about classroom topics that excited them.

When it comes to social cues and awareness, sixth graders in particular are raw material. Boys lag behind girls. At times, a lack of awareness about how their words and actions might affect others creates what might look like a bullying situation, but in reality often represents their lack of maturity, filters and social skills. These kinds of interactions come with the territory. Our comprehensive peer leadership program has also doubled as a character education program, including a sixth grade cycle class with a curriculum to teach students how to speak to each other, respect the personal space of others, and practice conflict mediation skills.

At times our youngest students - we referred to sixth graders as our "babies" - needed an adult connection for even a token measure of reassurance. Some students would find a reason to wander into the nurse's office while others struck up a friendship with the office staff. We had a sixth grade girl who would occasionally open the door to the main office and ask the office staff, "Do I look like I'm going to throw up?" The secretaries never missed a beat, "No, hon, you're good." And the reassured student scampered off to her next destination.

By the end of sixth grade most students are sprouting wings. They strut confidently in the hallways, know more peers, and convey a feeling of owning the place.

Seventh grade is the black hole. There's no other way to put it. As our guidance counselors reminded us, it is literally the middle of the middle. Their preadolescent bodies have been hijacked by hormones, causing growth spurts and all the distractions fueled by puberty. Pupils develop secondary sex characteristics, and questions about sexual attraction and gender identity often manifest.

Today more students are identifying as transgender, and the last several years have catapulted principals and schools into an emerging field within education that has required greater understanding of transgender individuals and how to support them in school. To this end, we formed a committee whose participants all read and discussed a book written from the perspective of a transgender student. We researched policy and legal opinions regarding such questions as whether school personnel were required to inform the parents of children who declared, publicly or privately in school, that they were transgender. I found myself on the line between thinking parents had a right to know what concerned their child (and perhaps what their child's peers and other parents already knew) and being concerned about placing pupils in danger of parents who could possibly reject or abuse their son or daughter. Administrators also had to be cautious about unwittingly "outing" transgender students in any documentation, for example, about a bullying incident in which a transgender individual was a target. Such reports could be read by the child's parents or Board of Education members, who are often parents.

As a committee we talked about how to accommodate bathroom and locker room facilities, and our concerns about the discomfort that this might cause other students, as well as the adults who supervise locker rooms, when kids were undressing. Transgender students also requested that we change their names and pronouns. We found ourselves in uncharted waters with many questions and concerns. Thanks to funding from the P.T.O., our group met with an expert in the field who was also invited to speak on this topic to parents during an evening presentation. All of these activities helped us to grow in our understanding about transgender students, even if this became a political issue that was subject to evolving guidance from the federal government.

Students become more social in seventh grade, and coming of age rituals like bar and bat mitzvahs and confirmation reinforce the idea that they are no longer children. While they are surely growing cognitively, they face greater short-term challenges when it comes to self-discipline, time management, and focus with regard to their academic work. In my school this was a critical period of time related to placement, because how a student fared in seventh grade determined his/her level of math in eighth grade, which also had implications for high school coursework. It was the perfect storm.

Seventh grade ushers in changes in student affect, especially moodiness. Students often will push away from their parents and more toward their friends, sharing less and less at home. Dr. Goerss used to tell parents to leave their unrecognizable kids with us and pick them up in eighth grade when the children they knew and loved would return. I have suggested to parents over the years that their temperamental middle schoolers would be more responsive or inclined to open up if conversations happened more naturally during a hike, car ride, game of ping-pong, or pilgrimage to their favorite restaurant.

Almost like a ritual, seventh grade teachers would come to my office every year to vent. "They don't listen. They don't follow directions. They don't do homework." At first I thought it was a specific group of children who were being less than cooperative, but then I figured out what it really was, and I would remind the teachers that they teach seventh grade. There's a special place in heaven for seventh grade teachers.

Over the years some boys of the seventh grade variety have been known to carry pocket knives to school. They claimed not to remember that they had left them at the bottom of their backpack, while others "forgot" to take them out of their pocket after an alleged recent scout activity or weekend camping trip. Once, a knife fell out of the bottom of a boy's pants, but this particular piece of cutlery was a paring knife. I asked him why he carried a paring knife, not a pocket knife. Either way this was a breach of our code of conduct, but my question reflected a combination of concern and curiosity. The unretractable sharp edge of a paring knife could have cut him and also accounted for the hole in his pocket and the reason it fell down his pant leg and out for others to see. He explained to me, with all seriousness, as if I were the one having trouble understanding, that it was indeed a pocket knife because it was a knife and he kept it in his pocket.

Eighth graders returned to school having gained maturity and focus. Many or even most understood that how they performed in eighth grade was linked to where they wanted to land in their freshman year, so they began to plan ahead. Our Peer Leadership program provided opportunities for them to lead, serve and shine. At their move-up ceremony, they presented like the young adults they had become, the middle school metamorphosis miraculously accomplished.

This did not mean, along the way, that they were unable to fire up their pubescent brain for a notable cause, like The American Cancer Society's campaign to support breast cancer. To help raise awareness, our students took it upon themselves to don shirts, buttons, and other paraphernalia bearing slogans like "Save the Tatas." "Tatas" are all the rage on the hormone highway of middle school. The superintendent's edict was to ban any reference to tatas, but I suggested that the board attorney be consulted first. The superintendent was resolute. The mother of one tata supporter, an attorney, called me and then the superintendent while waiting on a platform for her train home from Washington, D.C., declaring that it was against the law to prohibit student self-expression. She was apparently correct because the very next morning we welcomed back student enthusiasm for tatas along with all the fan accessories.

Middle school is a fantastic time of life, and middle level learners deserve to have teachers who understand what students are going through, as they not only teach them knowledge and skills but also inspire them to think, create, and explore. Mark Oppel, an eighth grade language arts teacher, was also the extraordinarily talented director and choreographer of the annual spring musical. As part of a cultural arts program funded by the P.T.O., Mark also taught a playwriting workshop to all of the eighth graders.

Toward the end of the year he selected scripts to be staged during an evening in the spring. These plays were read by faculty members with some improvisation and basic blocking. While many of the scripts were quite imaginative and a good deal of fun, one could not help but notice that others portrayed the kinds of issues that our middle schoolers faced in real life, such as dealing with the loss of a loved one, coming out to parents, or navigating family and peer dynamics. I still remember an innocent and humorous skit simply about the interaction of family members on a long car ride. Of course, the teachers in the skit knew how to make it even funnier with their delivery. This workshop was a unique opportunity for our students to integrate writing skills and the arts to convey something authentic about life or about themselves.

The primary way for me as principal to leave an enduring imprint on my school was by recruiting the right teachers. I was keenly aware that teacher candidates had to understand and be able to relate to middle schoolers. A new supervisor, who did not have much middle school experience, and I watched a demonstration lesson at the end of which the supervisor apologized for moving the applicant along in the process. The supervisor found the candidate's high-octane teaching style to be a bit much. I cut my administrative colleague off by saying, "This is the perfect middle school teacher!" I was not above sneaking into a classroom through the back door of another school to check out a teacher who applied for a job in Millburn. Another time I was escorted into an impromptu interview in my assistant principal's office because she and the science supervisor were so enamored with an experienced teacher who had ducked out of her own school during lunch. It was love at first sight.

My interview questions always included inquiries about the characteristics of middle level learners and what instructional practices were most compatible with their stage of development. The best possible learning environment is characterized by a symbiotic relationship between teachers and students, and teachers and teachers. Inspired teaching and learning exists when teachers and students connect, and this is only possible if teachers understand the unparalleled cognitive, physiological, and social-emotional changes taking place within the middle level universe. Life, and learning, can be messy in the middle.

I personally see a threat to the legacy of middle level research and practice. Outside forces such as standardized test designers and publishers and state department officials and sometimes even central office administrators think they need to "raise standards" and force middle students to learn more, learn faster, and think more abstractly than they are developmentally capable of. Offering high school level content, such as algebra, geometry, and advanced levels of world languages, adds more rigorous academic coursework and stress, for the students who made it into these classes and for the others, and their parents, who felt as though they should have. It is incumbent upon middle school principals, curriculum personnel, and teachers to be mindful and to honor this unique stage of development with a compatible, high-quality program of learning.

It has been suggested by some through the years that the mindset of the middle school staff, including its administrators, mirrors the traits of its students, almost like we are stuck in middle school mode throughout our lives. I take that as a compliment! I believe there is a thirteen-year-old inside all of us. Being around middle level students keeps one young and in touch with new generations of kids, ideas, and changing culture.

While we have had our share of middle school hooliganism over the years, my colleagues and I shared a laugh almost every day. Kids at this age are funny, and if you do not have a sense of humor you simply will not appreciate this fascinating transformation of children "in the middle."

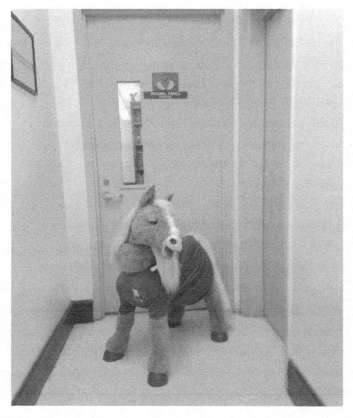

MMS Mascot, wearing a Mustang shirt, guards the principal's office.

# 15. Pressure Cooker

A PROFILE OF THE MILLBURN HIGH SCHOOL CLASS OF 2017 published on the district website revealed that Millburn's mean SAT score for reading/writing was 638 compared to the New Jersey mean of 545 and the national mean of 560. The mean Millburn math score was 631 compared to the New Jersey mean of 549 and the national mean of 555. Advanced Placement scores were detailed by subject, but overall 1,222 tests were administered of which 96% of students scored 3 or above, 86% scored 4 or above, and 57% scored a 5. Millburn had 17 Semifinalists and 34 Commended Students in the National Merit Scholars Program. 96.4% of this class planned to attend a four-year college while 1.8% intended to enroll in a two-year school.

The community eagerly anticipates the annual list of college acceptances published by the high school guidance department, a manifest that is subsequently dissected to tally how many students gained admission to Ivy League universities and top-ranked schools. Not surprisingly, realtors herald the good news. In June 2017, one real estate website wrote about where Millburn High School students were attending college under the caption "Millburn High School Class of 2017 Once Again Proves Millburn's Pedigree."

The choice of the word "pedigree" resonates within this community. On the surface, it is a word that refers to an elite class, in this case one of the wealthiest communities in the nation. The term also has to do with passing on a heritage, a legacy of achievement, opportunity, and financial success by parents who can afford to live here, and who themselves are college and Ivy League graduates. Probably, the caption intended to refer more specifically to the historical reputation of the school system itself.

It's why people come here. What drives property sales is also what, I believe, fuels the expectations and the anxiety that have manifested even more so in recent years. The reputation of the district - its brand - has created its own challenges.

Yes, this is the chapter about stress in Millburn, the "place" in placement.

Expectations are epitomized by this class profile and the community's fixation with college admissions. The pressures to succeed begin fairly early, but have substantial impact already at the middle school where enrollment into high school accelerated classes is predicated on academic achievement in the eighth grade.

As someone who spent three decades in the township schools, I had observed a new dynamic within the community that intensified the competition to be a prime student. Fewer families were continuing to reside in the township after their children graduated, so new families kept moving in. It appeared that families were drawn to Millburn for the schools, though not necessarily for the community. They coveted a Millburn diploma and a ticket to a top tier school. They wanted a timeshare in that Millburn pedigree, too.

Families relocating to Millburn expected to take advantage of all of the opportunities for their children to stand out. A new generation of parents and more "transient" families used the schools to get their kids on the right track, transforming the school system into a mill of sorts for students to gain admission to competitive colleges.

What was the impact of this new community dynamic on the middle school? It meant that the middle school did not just more than double its enrollment, it doubled the number of parents and students craving to be in accelerated levels. Even new families transferring their children after the start of a new school year automatically expected their children to enroll in accelerated classes.

While parents are the primary drivers of stress, this crisis is conflated by a number of other factors and realities.

First, some children require more time, sometimes extending into high school, for them to blossom academically. Others are not capable despite intense micromanaging by their parents. One of the indispensable tenets of middle level education is that each child is on his or her own journey. Pushing students into a level of challenge for which they are not yet ready obviously causes stress, and it also poses the risk of embarrassment in front of peers and a failure to live up to parental expectations.

But some parents are impatient with any notion of academic performance aligned with cognitive development, a lack of acceptance or understanding that a child is not yet mature enough to handle advanced coursework. An illustration of this view is found in an excerpt written by a parent: "There are a lot of kids in Millburn getting A's, and getting pulled into honors classes. So many, in fact, that they (the school) don't seem interested in making more. The B students aren't supported or particularly helped to become A students."

A school is not an assembly line, or a laboratory. When did a B become a bad grade?

Second, accelerated level students today are not like the traditional "honors" students of old whose thinking enriched class conversations and challenged peers and teachers to see things from new or multiple perspectives. Those scholars possessed or endeavored an interest in the content and the context, reading beyond a textbook or anthology. They forged connections to movements, historical figures or ideas with ease. True accelerated learners kept teachers on their toes. All of this despite their participation in the spring musical, music ensembles, sports teams, bar or bat mitzvahs, or family events. And they did not complain about the amount of work or the teachers, recite excuses, or require the level of tutoring that goes on today.

Students, even those in accelerated sections, now require constant reassurance that they are doing the right thing, in the correct way, and are on their way to an A. Even with all the resources literally at their fingertips, ironically, many students lack the magical spark for learning. The emphasis is on the grade and the placement. And they become somehow frozen in fear of failure, redefined as anything less than an A.

Third, kids in general are different from even ten years ago, and middle school age children have grown up in a world markedly unlike that of their peers before them. In general, they do not seem to be resourceful or resilient and are more reliant instead. This could be the result of helicopter parenting morphing into its new iteration of bulldozer parenting, which eradicates all obstacles and challenges, the very things that promote learning, growth and resilience.

Fourth, preteens have unfettered access to devices, including in their bedrooms. It is quite possible, and probable, that therein lie two major reasons explaining why, if students are properly placed, homework takes so long, grades are dropping, and students are not getting enough sleep: distraction and time eaten up by social media posts, online activities, and games.

Fifth, educators see a generation defined by shorter attention spans. I believe that cell phones specifically have affected our children's ability to sustain their effort to learn, or even to listen, as these devices drive their need for immediate gratification with every text, email, and post. We have to be honest that adults are equally affected. I am not the only one who sees that kids are no longer reading books and articles, the very activities that increase their knowledge, spark interests and conversational ideas, and broaden their vocabulary.

No doubt volumes could be written about how technology impacts every aspect of our lives. Kids are still kids. Supervision, structure, and boundaries are critical parenting tools to enable already distractible and social preadolescents to focus, do their work, and sleep. A lack of parental oversight can undermine a key family connection during a time of competing interests for the attention of their middle level children.

Sixth, stress is the most significant problem facing teens today. Students are so anxious they have panic attacks, stomach pains, fainting spells or emotional outbursts, often at school. School refusal is on the rise. Children with mental health issues cry out for attention through cutting and other forms of self-mutilation. Kids are medicating themselves through drinking, drugs, and now vaping.

All of this was a part of my Millburn experience, too. Our teachers, counselors and nurse observed increased symptoms of stress in our students. Indeed, signs of stress have been simmering for years in Millburn and also in other communities that have resorted to bringing in guest speakers with expertise in this area and establishing district wellness committees.

The numbers of risk assessments, occurrences of suicide ideation, and actual suicides are on the rise. Adam Clark's article, "Gone at 15," published in The *Sunday Star-Ledger* (10/20/2019) cited a 2019 Pew social trends survey that found that "about 70% of teens ages 13 to 17 said anxiety and depression are a 'major problem' among peers…." Clark also quoted a 2019 Pew research study: "Across New Jersey, and nationwide, adolescents and teens are reporting alarming rates of depression, anxiety and suicidal thoughts."

One also has to consider other reasons behind this growing phenomenon of stress, including living in a post 9/11 world with monthly lockdown drills in an era of ongoing and unimaginable school shootings around the nation.

What else is stressing kids (and parents) in today's schools? National standardized tests that assess new and tougher national curriculum standards, especially content requiring greater cognitive thinking at a younger age.

Stress in districts like Millburn is exacerbated by the growing enrollment and demographics of the student population. Pupils themselves strive for perfection and in the process create a negative synergy in school with their peers. The size of the student body intensifies the competition to be one of the highest achieving students in a larger pool of high-achieving individuals.

Over the last ten years of my administration we tried to be responsive to the stress affecting our students by implementing several measures to alleviate academic pressure:

- Eliminated the A+ grade because everyone was expected to earn an A+.

- No longer published an honor roll because conversations centered on whose names were *not* on the High Honor Roll or any honor roll.

- Discontinued final exams, although an eighth grade "final exam experience" was later instituted because former students complained they were not prepared for cumulative assessments at the high school.

- Created school policies to facilitate team coordination of assessments, projects, and volume of homework in order to manage overall student workload.

- Required teachers to post homework assignments on the internet for parents to check.

- Prohibited group projects off school grounds (this was prior to the advent of GoogleDocs) because it was impossible to gather students together.

- Declared "no homework nights" on the official school calendar so that parents and students could attend concerts and other evening school activities.

- Banned homework during religious observances, long weekends, and vacations.

- Divided the school year into trimesters to afford students and teachers more time for curriculum instruction and assessment and provide parents more time for interventions.

- Established time frames for the return of graded assessments, essays, and projects so that students could learn from these experiences.

- Mailed report cards instead of distributing them in school in order to avoid comparisons and meltdowns.

- Dispensed with publicly awarded medals, trophies or academic honors. What started as an awards ceremony morphed into a move-up exercise.

- Instituted a student safety committee to generate interventions for students who needed support, mentoring, or positive peer connections.

I spent the early weeks of summer, with help from other administrators and guidance counselors, reviewing a packet of information about each child moving to the seventh and eighth grades in order to finalize placement decisions. In the seventh grade we offered two accelerated opportunities in the subjects that required more developed skill sets, mathematics and language arts. All eighth grade content areas had an accelerated level. The packet contained a final report card, the aforementioned teacher checklists, comments noting observable change in student performance - for better or worse, standardized test scores, and a holistic writing sample.

In our school the term "accelerated" literally meant the highest of the high-achieving. Parents thought I was splitting hairs between a grade of A and A minus. Since we had eliminated the A+ grade, the grade of A reflected a wide band of final averages ranging from 94 to 100. I have had grade level populations where one third of the students in a subject earned a final average of A, another third earned an A minus, and most of the remainder finished in the B range. An A-minus student could be in the bottom half of the class. Some parents have called that grade inflation, but it actually reflected the skewed performance level of our students. I discovered early in my tenure that nearly sixty percent of our students attained the 90th national percentile score or higher on what was then the Terra Nova, a standardized achievement test. It was poignant that a pupil with a national percentile score of 85, indicating that he/she performed better than 84 percent of the students in the entire country, could find him or herself in the bottom third of our school test group, or "local" percentile.

While a grade of A was the key that automatically unlocked the accelerated door, it was possible, depending on the checklist, standardized test scores, and teacher feedback, that students who earned an A minus were also ready. These students, numbering usually between 250 and 300, were the focus of my summer review.

If a child did not earn an A, receive at least 7 out of 10 checks on the checklist, or have a top standardized test score, then after reviewing multiple measures of student performance, it was not for any one reason a child was not considered ready. For those on the borderline, I would distill how students performed on quizzes and tests - content mastery - apart from the other components factored into the overall grade. At times I would call a teacher over the summer to better gauge a student's probability for success in accelerated coursework. On occasion I contacted parents and said, "I don't know what to do with him/her!" Sometimes I would even pull elementary files and review prior years' test scores and report card grades and comments, piecing together a broader profile of a student's potential.

I wanted students to be in the correct placement for their sake.

Parents tried to pick apart the characteristics checklist. Some requested to see the scientific research that validated the attributes on the document. Other parents saw this screening tool to assess readiness as a conspiracy against their kid. Several claimed it was discriminatory.

Early on as principal I allowed myself to be bullied by the dual lawyer parents of a pupil who subsequently spent an entire year in algebra never earning a grade greater than a C, experiencing tremendous pressure, requiring a tutor, having to repeat the course, forgoing the opportunity to reach calculus by senior year, and ultimately feeling like this child disappointed everyone. The pupil was just not ready, and I vowed that I would not permit that to happen to another student if I could help it. While standing up to parents who are angry or emotional is hardly ever easy, sticking to a decision based on student data and teacher feedback rescues a pupil from all of the heightened anxiety and stress that accompanies an incommensurate level of instruction.

Instruction in math actually added another layer of stress to the placement process, especially in eighth grade. No subject better illustrated the intersection of critical thinking, abstract reasoning, and problem solving with pupil readiness to learn than algebra. Algebra has traditionally been studied at the high school level, but our eighth grade teachers taught the high school algebra course to those students who demonstrated readiness on teacher-constructed and standardized assessments.

In recent years, though, there has been a greater push for kids to take algebra earlier, or at least by eighth grade, even though this was to their detriment in terms of not having solidified their arithmetic and pre-algebra skills. Why was this happening? One of the factors we knew for sure was that high school guidance counselors began telling everyone that students had to have studied calculus by senior year in order to gain admission to a highly selective university. Of course, this meant that students had to have taken algebra in eighth grade. Unfortunately, this resulted in extraordinary pressure being placed on middle school children to be in a course for which many were cognitively immature.

Even the State of New Jersey embarked on a quest to fast-track more students into algebra by publishing the middle school algebra enrollment percentage as a component of each district's annual report card. But there was also a catch: if a course was named algebra, regardless of its scope or expectations, students would also be required to take and pass the state algebra exam. Our students had always done well on those tests because the content of the test matched the level of instruction for students who were ready to learn it.

With pressure mounting from parents, high school guidance counselors, the district, and the state, the safety net may disappear, propelling more students into algebra even though the pupils near our own cut-off scores were already struggling.

Millburn and other high-achieving school districts are in crisis. Millburn has always had competitive students, demanding coursework, and parents who tried to manipulate the placement process, but today's bulldozer parents seek to pave the way for their children to be in accelerated levels by discrediting the criteria and the process and also by attempting to eliminate qualifying assessments. Then they complain about the pressure the school puts on kids. The problem in recent years is that pupils and their parents want the moniker of accelerated or advanced placement, but they do not want what comes along with it, namely, additional work, intense rigor, and more time carved out of a life now encumbered by tutoring and private classes in addition to clubs, sports, music, and religious studies.

During my final year in Millburn, parents created an online petition with over 300 signatures in which they complained about homework, forwarding said petition to me, the superintendent, and the board of education. What was ironic to me was that there were names on the homework petition who had called me to push their kids into *more* accelerated classes - yet here they were, objecting to the amount of work. When flash mobs gather on petition sites or email servers, there is no level playing field for conversation, correction, or clarification, and individuals who would destroy the integrity of a course rather than acknowledge that their child is not ready for it hide in the virtual crowd.

Something has changed indeed. It seems that kids in general are more anxious and dependent upon their parents who want them to have all of the opportunities that cause more stress, but without the stress. One of my colleagues summed it up this way: Welcome to Millburn, Harvard-bound with no homework or stress.

Millburn is not alone. Just a couple of years ago another high-achieving New Jersey school district dealt with a parent divide with one side advocating for the "right" of gifted students to a rigorous education while the other side wanted to decrease the pressure they claimed was coming from the schools.

Technology today affords a faster turnaround time for students, and their parents, to receive notification of grades. School databases such as PowerSchool now "publish" each and every graded assignment or assessment so that students and their parents have full ongoing access. This is, of course, good and bad.

Millburn High School was the first district school to use this application, and I vowed to hold off as long as possible. My hand was forced when the elementary schools agreed to open the parent portal feature. Parents began seeing the grades before the students did, and they started texting their children at school or ambushing them when they walked in the door.

With each published grade came a recalculation of how high the next grade had to be in order to maintain or achieve a specific average. Parents, and some students, literally became obsessed with checking grades, and we knew this because PowerSchool counted how many times the gradebook had been accessed. While having up-to-date information is always helpful, the portal became a purveyor of stress, especially for those parents and pupils who could not regulate their compulsion to check for updates and whose placement into an accelerated class might have already been precarious.

Ever since I arrived in Millburn, there existed a culture of parents having bragging rights about their kids' placements. Often, parents themselves were gifted learners, charting their children's academic path guided by their hubris. I recall a humorous interaction I had with a mom who waved her hand above her head to indicate how smart she was, and then moved her hand higher to show how much smarter her husband was. Proclaiming themselves "educated people," she ticked off the mostly Ivy League undergraduate and graduate schools they had attended. She then held her hand somewhere between her level of smart and her husband's to demonstrate how bright her older child was, "who got the best of both of them," but she dropped her hand, and her smile, when it came to her younger child, beseeching me, "Mr. Cahill, I need you to put my baby in at least two accelerated classes next year."

I lost count as to how many parents have referred to their own curriculum vitae when challenging a borderline placement decision. "Did you know I went to MIT? Do you know what I do for a living? Do you know where my husband went to school? Are you aware that both of her parents are doctors? Where did *you* go to school, Mr. Cahill?"

Numerous parents submitted that I should just enroll their child in one accelerated class because it would be good for his/her self-esteem. But self-esteem cannot be bestowed, it has to be earned through hard work and persistence. And a gamble like that could have an opposite and devastating repercussion.

This was not a community that took "no" for an answer. Parents' efforts to push their kids into accelerated classes bordered on desperation. Over the years parents falsely accused me of barring their children from accelerated coursework by adhering to a quota system. Families had tutors write letters to recommend placement in the highest math group, including even a letter from a Princeton University professor.

Each summer parents would pursue the issue of placement with central office administrators. Parents' calls would continue into the new school year, sometimes until Christmas. I was once ordered to appear in front of an administrative law judge about our placement process, and was prepared to do so until the day before the court date when, to my surprise, the district assuaged the complaining parent by offering a solution for the following year at the high school.

I have had parents yell, cry, insult and threaten. Phone calls with exasperated moms would lead to subsequent calls from their husbands. A father inquired of me, "What can I do to make you understand that Alice Rose has to be in algebra?" I have been badgered and called a "self-made god" and a sexist.

This despite the fact that I was completely transparent about our process and provided specific information in my responses to inquiries about each child's placement as evidenced by the volume of detailed emails and the number of hours on the phone that I spent talking to parents.

In their conversations with me, some parents actually named classmates of their children who had earned accelerated placement and declared their progeny to be "much smarter" than so-and-so, challenging the process and my decision-making. Parents often saw only their own child; they did not see our student through the lens of the classroom teacher or in comparison to other pupils or benchmarks of performance. Sometimes I would redact another child's work, such as an essay, to share a model of what was considered to be "accelerated ready" so parents could compare the benchmark paper to their own child's writing skills.

I was not without empathy for parents and children who were disappointed, but I had to be fair and faithful to what was a comprehensive process, for the benefit of all, including myself. That's not to say that I was not receptive when parents shared with me personal information about family, medical or impactful events that might explain a temporary dip in performance that was otherwise exemplary. Making exceptions is different from acknowledging that there are exceptional circumstances. I learned early on that making an exception generated many more requests, or demands, for exceptions. A school is like a public fishbowl where everyone is watching.

I believed in our process because it was a thoughtful one that considered each individual child. Ironically, the whole point of it was to generate opportunities for more students to participate successfully in an accelerated level class.

Years after their children graduated from middle school, parents would approach to remind me that I had denied their child placement in an accelerated class. I dreaded attending parent social fundraisers because inevitably someone would revisit a placement issue. I eventually stopped going.

Early in sixth grade parents began to place pressure on teachers for re-grading, extra credit points, after school help, recommendations for tutors, and suggestions. Others criticized the test, or the point values, or the grading, or the weighting of the grade, or the teacher's "style." Parents have offered bribes for better grades, and not just in sixth grade.

One evening a mother actually interrupted dinner with my family in a restaurant to talk about her sixth grader's likely final grades and the child's prospects of making it into accelerated coursework the next year.

It was inevitable that parents compared teachers and teams. "You put my kid on the harder team, with the more difficult language arts teacher, the team that gave more homework. It's impossible to get an A with Mrs. McGillicuddy, the other math teacher is nicer, that teacher hated my kid." Sometimes, parents outrightly blamed teachers for grades lower than A because teachers should have known Melissa needed more motivation, or because teachers weren't challenging enough (as in "John was bored in his class"), or because they were just "crappy teachers."

During many of my conversations with parents they came to the realization that if they resided in a different district their child would be in the accelerated grouping, not possible in Millburn because of the population.

Even parents of students with Individualized Educational Plans (I.E.P.s) have attempted to coerce the Child Study Team to write "must go to accelerated" as an accommodation on this legal document for a child receiving special services.

Parents have written to me expressing hope that neither my family nor I would contract a disease for which their child could have been the future scientist to discover the cure if only I had placed the child in algebra in eighth grade. Another parent called her child's placement "inhumane" and said "your cut-throat decision takes away my child's future." Her sarcastic and condescending conclusion was that her offspring could pump gas for a living.

I understand how divisive it can be to have levels of learning, and in a competitive school environment students measure themselves against not only the criteria for readiness but also the performance levels of their twin, siblings, friends and peers. If the community insists on "tracking" students, then schools must identify and accommodate learners who merit a standard of scholarship conceived only for the highest-achieving students. Without a doubt, it is how parents themselves view and handle these realities that have the most powerful impact on their own children's self-image and stress levels as they move forward.

In the summer of my final round of placement ordeals, I received an email with the following subject caption: YOU ARE KILLING MY CHILD!!! I barely had time to read the email when my secretary informed me that a parent had arrived unannounced and insisted she would sit for however long it would take to meet with me. I invited this mother in shortly thereafter and while I listened to all that she had to say, I remained steadfast that her child did not meet the requirements despite her open sobbing. All of a sudden she stopped gasping for air and inquired if I might consider placing her child in a different accelerated class, if she and her child could not have "the one they wanted." I told her placement was not negotiable, to which she responded, "Mr. Cahill, everything is negotiable."

Another mother pointed her finger at me during a PTO meeting and said, "You are the cause of stress in this school!" When I asked her why, she replied, "Because you have to get an A to get into accelerated!" During that exchange, I suggested that our school should consider if it was really even necessary to have accelerated levels in seventh grade. The refrain from those around her sounded like a chorus of converts at a revival meeting; "Yes, yes, we believe! We have to have accelerated classes!"

This mom's public recommendation was that students with a final average of B should be allowed to be in accelerated levels. It would not be out of the ordinary in most schools to expect students to achieve at least an A range average to qualify for an accelerated class. If our school placed students who earned a B or better into accelerated classes, it would include almost everyone. The mandate to continue offering accelerated levels, paired with the pressure to lower the bar so that almost everybody could participate, framed the conundrum I faced, even if the overarching goal of accelerated placement for all was based on wishful but unrealistic thinking.

This parent made the elephant in the room visible, though, something I was unable to accomplish at those wellness committee meetings where parents and school personnel gathered to discuss our students' level of stress and what to do about it. No one (meaning the parents who predominantly made up the committee groups) appeared open to hear or willing to talk about the connection between the stress of being in an accelerated class, or the pressure to place in, for children who were not yet ready to handle an academically intense program.

In the wake of the March 2019 college admissions scandal where wealthy celebrities paid obscene amounts of money to get their kids into schools like Stanford, Alexandra Robbins, author of *The Overachievers*, wrote in an article entitled "Kids are the Victims in the Elite-College Obsession" (The *Atlantic*, 3/12/19): "Overachiever culture has done this to us. It has caused drastic changes in schools and homes, relentlessly prioritizing prestige, high-stakes testing, and accountability at the cost of families and schools. It's a myth that going to a certain type of school is a 'roadmap to success,' but parents desperately want to believe that by controlling the system, they can guarantee success for their children, even if it's a narrow, superficial, winner-take-all definition of that word."

Some folks just want to manage the symptoms of their child's stress by petitioning for longer lunches, less homework, outdoor recess, and stress management activities such as yoga. Schools bring in therapy dogs for stressed kids to hug, pet, and play with. Mindfulness has become a buzz-word in education as of late. Some stress-busting strategies are obviously more effective and have the potential of becoming life-long tools than others that are just a Band-Aid or a distraction, a fun way to forget life's challenges momentarily. But brainstorming ways to manage stress is easier than having an honest conversation about how to prevent it from happening at all. Even the parental push for a block schedule, a format they dubiously believe will reduce the amount of work, is not going to be the panacea for stress parents hope for because it does not address the source.

This public discourse caused me to have a flashback to when I was first hired as principal. In an interview published in the local paper I was quoted as saying that one of my goals was to continue working on what Dr. Goerss had already started with regard to accelerated coursework. In his article "Cahill New Principal at Middle School," in The *Item of Millburn-Short Hills* (12/20/2001) Harry Trumbore reported, "That same concern to ease unnecessary pressure on students who are at a difficult time in their lives leads Mr. Cahill to consider partial elimination of leveling, or tracking students in the seventh grade. Dr. Goerss previously eliminated leveling in sixth grade." As a result, a mob of moms literally stormed the main office, warning me, "If you remove any more accelerated courses, you will be history!"

I did indeed remove more accelerated levels the following year in the seventh grade, and I included a representative from this posse to be on my leadership team as we together studied the pros and cons and various proposals about what to do. Our school's and district's traditional approach of differentiating the learners instead of the content continued to lock instruction into a system that depended on the proper placement of students. It should come as no surprise that the proper placement of students was the thorniest and seemingly never-ending challenge of my principalship.

Parents and, to some extent, students were the drivers of this unhealthy and unsustainable culture. I wasn't "killing" anyone. I wasn't "the cause of stress in this school." The fact that I invested much time and energy into the appropriate placement of pupils was evidence of my intent to prevent or reduce stress *for kids*. School personnel are not responsible for, nor can they control or manage, the pressures parents put on their children to be in accelerated or advanced coursework, even if parents deflect their own accountability for the outcomes onto teachers and administrators, the school, or "the system."

Kevin Chan, a member of the Millburn High School Class of 2017, spoke truth to power about the "place in placement" in a guest column that appeared in The *Item of Millburn-Short Hills* (3/28/2017). In "Stressed Millburn students bring it on themselves," Kevin wrote:

"The Millburn community defines success as a report card of A's and a resume loaded with activities. I believe this Millburn portrayal of success is largely a result of family pressure and the social climate of the student body itself. As a school district with a high average household income, it's no surprise students are encouraged by family and peers to follow the same path many in the community have already taken. While the MHS administration is part of the Millburn community, it is not responsible for the community's attitude towards success nor its stress culture....The school administration and Millburn teachers have never told us to overburden ourselves just to get into that Ivy League school....Many of Millburn's classes, especially at the Accelerated and AP level, come with a heavy workload. It's part of what has made MHS so academically successful for years. With all the students who have taken classes in years past, the workload of most classes is well known. The workload should not come as a surprise, and if it is overwhelming, lower-level classes should be taken instead."

# 16. Guiding Lights

"WHICH ONE OF THESE TEACHERS USED TO WORK IN A morgue?"

Always comfortable on the stage, Guidance Coordinator John Rogers embraced the role of Master of Ceremonies as he disclosed the past careers of three teachers whose lives were now open books in front of four hundred eighth graders in our school's version of a game show called "What's My Line?" Guidance counselors had wrangled staff members to participate in this Career Day Assembly panel, and the task for the audience was to match job titles with panelists. Over the years teachers, staff members, administrators, and even a superintendent came clean about the different kinds of work they performed prior to a career in education.

Mr. Rogers held up the poster with "Mortuary Assistant" written in big red letters as he walked behind each of the seated staff members. He gauged which panelist garnered the loudest hootin' and hollerin' and awarded the poster to the teacher selected by the audience. For the big reveal, once all the posters had been allotted, the MC called upon the teacher who performed the duties of a mortuary assistant to stand. Of course, the panel teased the spectators by having more than one staff member stand up and sit down several times until one finally remained standing, but it was not the one the students had predicted.

The purpose was to show students that individuals usually perform various types of work in their lives. The "game" also demonstrated that student guessing relied on what little they knew about a staff member, including his or her subject area, as well as preconceived ideas about looks, gender, and physical attributes. When I participated on a panel, I revealed my own stints as a summer custodian and also as an after-school cooking teacher for high school students, mostly boys, much to everyone's surprise.

Career Day was a really big deal in our school. I believe there was no other career day like it anywhere, and it involved a considerable amount of time and preparation on the part of the guidance team.

In the weeks leading up to Career Day, traditionally held in January, the eighth grade counselor administered a career interest survey to the entire grade, analyzed the results with students, and linked career categories with job descriptions in these fields. (Counselors more than once heard from parents who called to declare that their child was not going to be a stewardess!) A day for students to conduct research on their selected careers in the school library soon followed.

After the game show, the keynote speaker was introduced. Our keynoters have spanned a variety of career fields, including a joint presentation once by a local rabbi and minister, with several alumni returning to share their career journeys and insights. One of my favorites was Elliott Kalan, a former student in my eighth grade language arts class, who at the time was a writer for "The Daily Show with Jon Stewart." Kalan, who won several Emmy Awards, told our students that the things he liked to do as a kid - drawing comics, telling jokes, watching TV - probably helped him, but he warned that one also has to work hard and be persistent in pursuit of the job he or she wants.

After the assembly, students returned to classrooms where they listened to a rotation of speakers - movie critics, surgeons, detectives, construction managers, brokers, attorneys - representing the colors of the career rainbow. The vast majority of presenters were parents who were also recruited by guidance counselors beginning on Back-to-School Night in September. The culminating Career Day activity had students compose a letter of introduction to their high school guidance counselor, incorporating some things they had discovered about careers and themselves in this exploration.

The afternoon was spent viewing a movie that continued the themes of career preparation and growing up. A favorite film was *October Sky* based on *Rocket Boys,* a memoir by Homer H. Hickam, Jr., which told the tale of a transformational time for a young man inspired by Sputnik and encouraged by a teacher to launch rockets. Homer Hickam's team won the National Science Fair, and he went on to college, his ticket out of the coal mines of West Virginia. Mr. Hickam became a NASA engineer.

The guidance team embarked on several major innovative school projects every year, including Career Day, all of which added dimensions of learning that supplemented our academic program. The goal of Dialogue Night was to jump-start communications between parents and preadolescents at home. The program typically began with a brief orientation followed by break-out sessions facilitated by peer leaders where students and adults responded to questions. Parents and their kids, intentionally separated for this exercise, were to continue the conversation at home after the ice was broken on sensitive topics by their peers. I have often heard parents say as they were leaving that we should sponsor more activities like these, or that they did not know or realize something about kids growing up today.

Our school had a goal of achieving 100% student participation in service learning. Because so many students were already participating in peer leadership, only a minority of students could not or would not commit to ongoing weekly meetings and projects. Guidance offered opportunities for these outliers to participate in one activity during the course of the year, such as serving food at the Morristown Community Soup Kitchen, working at St. Hubert's Animal Welfare Center in Madison, or cheering students on at the Special Olympics. As someone who has accompanied our fan group to the Special Olympics, I witnessed how our enthusiastic cheering spurred the athletes on to be their best. The smiles, excitement and motivation of the Special Olympians were the pay-off for our pupils who came out to support their efforts.

I doubt that principals in other schools thought that maybe they should ask their guidance counselors to do less, but that was becoming my position as I worried that this talented, multi-tasking team was spending too much time planning and stressing about these bigger school events.

My guidance team was an important part of my narrative as well as the story of our school. John Rogers, Jill Canastra, Dominick Pisa, and Denise

Worthington spent many years together as a team of counselors during much of my time as principal. Their knowledge and collective wisdom about middle level learners, the middle school model, and our school community made them integral participants in discussions about program proposals, school climate, scheduling issues, and building initiatives. I was fortunate indeed to have worked alongside guidance professionals who shared my vision for our school and who could be relied upon to offer perspectives, opinions, and ideas on how to accomplish our mission together.

While we had appointed meeting times on the calendar for our official "administrative-guidance meetings," in reality we talked all the time, individually and spontaneously. And this deepened the bond and respect we had for each other in the work we did together for the benefit of our students and our school.

Guidance counselors are the connective tissue in schools, highly skilled in diplomacy, communications, and painting the bigger picture for students, parents and teachers. Everybody, including the principal, went to guidance seemingly for everything. This was so true that I added a second column every year in the September P.T.O. Newsletter advising parents where else they could turn for specific types of assistance. Parents sometimes needed guidance counselors more than their children did, especially since middle school is an age where communication between "tweens" and parents ebbs. And because middle school does not invite the access to which parents had become accustomed in their elementary school settings, parents expressed their frustration by saying things like, "My kid doesn't tell me anything" or "How am I supposed to know?" or "He forgets everything!"

A task that loomed large for guidance counselors was counseling parents about their child's placement levels. Parents turned to counselors to better understand the process and individual data points, but more often to plead with them to intercede on their child's behalf. Counselors found themselves in a predicament because advocacy had to be about what was best for the student, even if it was not what either the student or the parent wanted to hear.

After having gained the experience of working at each grade level, guidance counselors understood the progression of expectations and the teaching styles of instructors. Counselors assimilated intel about their students to create a learner profile about their personalities, academic progress, and social interactions and tapped into clairvoyant powers as they pivoted toward the next school year in terms of a "best fit" team selection and anticipated level placements.

But while the American School Counselor Association promotes a ratio of 1 counselor to 250 students, Millburn Middle School counselor caseloads ranged from 350 to over 400 students. Even though spikes in student enrollment were well documented during my time as principal, we nonetheless even lost a position after a guidance counselor retired. That position was held by the aforementioned John Rogers, to whom I referred as "our very own Mr. Rogers," not only because of the surname he shared with popular children's show host Fred Rogers, but also because he, too, was a gentle, child-centered, and thoughtful man who sometimes wore the signature vest or sweater and who likewise embraced the teaching power of role playing. John Rogers' dedicated service of forty years made his name synonymous with Millburn Middle School.

John Rogers came to Millburn Middle School as a substitute language arts teacher who also apparently became "stuck in the middle." Subsequent to his years as a classroom teacher, Mr. Rogers reinvented himself as a guidance counselor and later was named Guidance Coordinator, at which time he assumed all of the administrative, communication, scheduling, testing, orientation, special projects and meeting responsibilities that typically accompany a leadership role, and then some.

"Dean" Rogers sponsored groups for kids and hosted fireside chats for parents called "Wanna Talk About It?" by the fireplace in our library. He composed a reflective monthly column in the PTO newsletter called "GUIDELINES" where John burned the midnight oil drawing from his experiences, research, and extensive reading about parenting preadolescents. Mr. Rogers was the first person our new students and their families met when they registered, providing a warm welcome, a tour, a heap of reassurance and a key personal connection.

John Rogers was an aspiring actor while he was a substitute teacher, but even after he was bitten by the teaching bug, acting remained his avocation. On one occasion, unbeknownst to me, John was dressed up as Dracula performing for fifth graders in the hallway outside the library on Halloween. Flying by at my usual pace, I was admittedly startled, and bemused, to turn a corner and come face-to-face with Dracula himself. At other times I ran into the auditorium during the lunch periods to see what the ruckus was all about. I could hear someone shouting from inside the main office. It was John Rogers loudly hamming it up with his shovel and scarf, advertising for student volunteers for his neighborhood buddies program that aided local seniors with snow removal and other chores. Apparently, Mr. Rogers did not think there was already enough drama in middle school.

John Rogers' passion for acting played out on our stage every year as he joined the cast of all of the spring musicals since 1975.

"Director" Rogers also used acting as a catalyst to facilitate discussion about values and doing the right thing by training his Mental Health Players to perform skits about typical adolescent challenges. The well is deep when it comes to the predicaments of growing up, such as making or losing friends, being the new student, cyberbullying, peer pressure or family situations. After the players performed the skit, student actors remained in character while Mr. Rogers moderated a conversation between the audience and the performers about their words, deeds, and choices. These interactive presentations became a component of the sixth grade leadership classes.

For example, a student, Diana, becomes jealous of newcomer Danielle's relationship with her best friend, Charlotte. Diana attacks Danielle on social media by calling her "pathetic" and "a loser who will never fit in here." When questioned, Diana becomes defensive and blames Danielle for creating the situation.

Mr. Rogers would mine a deeper understanding of the characters, their actions and feelings. "What motivated Diana? What were some other ways that Diana could have handled this situation? What is our responsibility when we use a powerful tool like social media? What do you think it's like for a new student who doesn't know anybody? Is it possible for Diana and Danielle to be friends? How can Charlotte embrace a potential leadership role here?"

In one of his PTO newsletter GUIDELINES, Mr. Rogers quoted a sixth grade student, an audience member, asking the characters in one skit, "Why can't you just treat each other with respect and talk this problem over?"

His most famous Millburn Middle School Mental Health Player alumna, Oscar-winning actress Anne Hathaway, was a guest on *Good Morning America* in 2011 when she said, "Mr. Rogers was an amazing guidance counselor."

During that same interview "Annie," a former student of mine as well, referred to me as "one of her favorite teachers of all time." Anne was a student in my morning accelerated language arts class, one of only nine students whose desks were arranged in a circle with mine. This class had a workshop feel to it because of its size and also because it happened to be a period when kids could munch on a morning snack. We chewed on granola bars, apples, and Brutus's motives in *Julius Caesar*. Anne was a participant in our school's spring musicals, and since I was in charge of stage techs and the school newspaper, my job was to snap pictures of the cast which I still have.

I was fortunate to have seen the interview with Anne live on television. However, I did not expect Anne's reaction to my name or her kind words about me, so I was surprised and touched. It goes without saying that I am a huge Anne Hathaway fan and am immensely proud of who she has become, as well as how accomplished she is at her craft. Millburn parents on vacation in places far warmer than New Jersey in February sent me emails telling me that they had watched, too.

Eventually, as our enrollment climbed and the other counselors were bearing the brunt of that growth, John Rogers was once again assigned students. I had included requests in my budget for additional guidance counselors, but I knew hiring more personnel was not likely. When John retired, he was not replaced, leaving us with just three counselors, one per grade level.

But there are consequences to every decision, fall-out that cannot be valued in dollars and cents but in lost opportunities to connect and changes in the delivery of services that stem from defaulting to a mode of coping.

Consider that lopsided ratio of students to counselors and how pre-adolescents on their journey to adulthood undergo unprecedented growth since the time when they were infants over the course of three years in middle school. The road to adulthood is fraught with obstacles and challenges, academic, emotional and social, turning the guidance office into an "ER" where counselors now had to perform triage and concentrate on the students who were in crisis, and there are many more in crisis.

As our former Guidance Coordinator used to say, "This ain't your parents' guidance!" With the enrollment and caseloads soaring, the time had come to connect with kids in non-traditional ways. Years ago I came up with the idea of creating a compendium of resources aimed at helping students become better learners. The guidance department and teachers contributed to what became the *Millburn Middle School Companion Guide*. This school publication grew to more than 90 pages, featuring information about active study, note-taking, mind mapping, test-taking strategies, writing rubrics, evaluating internet websites, and research protocols. Every student received a copy on the first day of school. Guidance counselors used the *Companion Guide* as a tool to teach lessons conceived by them as part of a developmental guidance curriculum, including topics such as learning styles, teacher-pleasing behaviors, learner self-assessments, study skills, self-advocacy, and time management. Topics counselors would address individually with counselees were now delivered en masse as they took their guidance show on the road to classrooms.

Counselors also scheduled meetings with students in networking and social skills groups, lunch bunches, changing families, newcomers, and other small group discussions. But they were unable to schedule even one meeting with every child during the school year.

In fact, when combined with the hours they spent on the phone or in person with parents, attendance at team meetings, and demands on their week by the child study team and 504/Intervention and Referral Service Committee (I&RS), most of the remaining time was devoted to students who needed ongoing monitoring and counseling. This was an overwhelming ratio of students per counselor.

A 504 Plan refers to Section 504 of the Rehabilitation Act of 1973, a law passed to provide accommodations in schools or the workplace for individuals who have physical or mental impairments. Typically, pupils were referred by teachers who funneled their concerns to their guidance counselor. Parents also often requested 504 accommodations for their children. It was hard not to notice the multiple requests for extended time on tests, including standardized tests, that came from parents of eighth graders on their way to the high school and the SAT's.

I recall a time when I discussed the need for additional counselors with Board of Education members, and I compared how our high school literally had twice as many counselors with only about 350 additional students. One board member told me that the high school counselors had the important job of getting students into college. This was a poignant statement about priorities, reflecting a lack of appreciation for the turbulent transitions of preadolescents as well as their correlating impact on academic performance.

In one of my final meetings with the Middle School PTO Executive Board, just prior to my retirement, some parents noted that their child never met with his/her guidance counselor. How does any principal justify that? More to the point, how does a principal in a well-to-do district rationalize this omission? Counselors used to see every pupil at the very least once a year for a birthday visit, but now even that was no longer possible. When I first arrived in Millburn, every student received guidance passes four times a year, once per marking period.

All kids should know, and have the opportunity to be known by, their guidance counselors. In today's world of atrocities such as mass shootings in schools, even more so.

Guidance counselors kept me abreast of what was going on with individual students and group dynamics. It was important for me to know about and sometimes weigh in on matters. Their amazing recall of the details of student experiences and insights made our counselors critical participants in special education and regular education accommodations meetings. Our counselors offered their repertoire of strategies not just for their own counselees, but for all of the children in the school.

Counselors have a unique position in schools where they can be a mommy or daddy figure and address behaviors or issues without being the parent. Students knew that, unless they divulged any thought or intent of harming themselves or others, counselors could be trusted to keep the information confidential. Students, and their parents, have gratefully acknowledged through the years how the counselors made such a difference in their child's development.

Likewise, counselors huddled with teachers to achieve greater understanding of a learner, and also met with students to broker agreements about teacher expectations or behavior. Through their intuition, sensitivity, and quick response they prevented problems from escalating.

For a long time the overarching theme in guidance, for students and their parents, was resilience, beginning with the fifth grade parent orientation where counselors used learning to ride a bicycle as an analogy for their children becoming middle schoolers. At some point parents have to let go! The counselor would talk about letting kids skin their knees, get back on the bike, and figure it out by learning from their mistakes. While resilience continued to be a priority, the theme of persistence had been gaining momentum as a timely and relevant message for today's preadolescents.

At our fifth grade parent orientations, Mr. Rogers spoke from the heart as he painted the home as a demilitarized zone where parents should try to de-stress with kids, listen to what's in their hearts and avoid what I called "the rat race of measuring up" to other students or what was important to other parents. He pointed out that what kids remember most are the simple things. Mr. Rogers gave voice to the need for "unconditional love" from parents and "the courage to be imperfect" for children whose brains during the middle level years were not fully developed, even if they had an off-the-chart I.Q.

Without a doubt, our middle school guidance counselors' individual counseling, developmental lessons, and thematic messaging provided an antidote for students and their parents in this culture of stress predicated on academic achievement.

Whether guidance counselors were tracking down students with organizational challenges, participating in a host of meetings, conjuring innovative programs or quietly laboring behind the scenes to cushion a fall, create an opportunity for growth, or follow up on a disciplinary matter, their job was critical to fostering a middle school culture of advocacy, communication and support.

Our guidance team consisted of the warmest and most dedicated, creative and energetic individuals who genuinely cared about our students and our school. Jill Canastra came from another district with middle school guidance experience. Dominick - Nick - Pisa had been a social studies and leadership teacher in our school where he also co-founded the Peer Leadership program. Denise Worthington started out as a special education teacher in our school and later became a learning disabilities teacher consultant (LDTC) at the high school. Their varied backgrounds and singular interest in creating successful pathways for students, individually and collectively, made our school a proactive and stronger student-centered middle school.

# 17. Not So Black and White

I HAD NOT GIVEN MUCH THOUGHT TO WHAT IT WAS LIKE TO
be one of the few African American students in a predominantly white school
like mine. But when you participate in extended school trips like the aforementioned expeditions to Costa Rica and Europe, you experience opportunities to know students in ways that you might not be able to otherwise because
you spend more time together during traveling, activities, and socializing.

Costume Party in Spain: Students donned ponchos and sombreros and
pointed pistolas at their favorite language arts teacher in a more innocent era.

A pupil of mine on one of these trips who was African American was just
outstanding in every way. The student was smart, athletic, witty, and friendly,
and I took for granted that this individual fit right in. In one exchange we had
on our travels, though, I will never forget how the student summed up the

experience of attending school in Millburn: "Mr. Cahill, do you know how hard it is, every day, when you do not look like everyone else?"

When Niche.com selected Millburn Middle School as the #1 middle school in the nation, it was despite the fact that their website assigned us a lower grade in the category of diversity. Frankly, that grade of C+ for diversity was better than I would have expected, and what diversity existed reflected the growing assimilation of Asian cultures (*PublicSchoolReview.com*, 2016), primarily Japanese, Chinese, and Korean, as well as families of Indian nationality. Our African American population was consistently the smallest demographic (1.5%), while the size of the only somewhat larger Hispanic population (6%) had also remained static. The term "diverse" is usually a reference to African American and Hispanic enrollments.

During my years as principal I hosted many visitors, including teams from local district schools and school leaders from as far away as India and Norway. In my conversation with an administrator of an exclusive private school in India, he explained how families had to be able to afford the tuition to send their children to his school as compared to here in America where parents can register their children in excellent public schools like mine for free. I stopped our tour and explained, "People have to be able to afford to live in this community in order to send their children to school here." I continued, "A couple of miles down the road is a school in Irvington that had no books in its library, so Spanish teacher Senora Nilda Gaud's LEER (Spanish verb "to read") Peer Leaders collected donations of books and delivered them to the school so the children could have reading materials."

Irvington, a town wrestling with issues of poverty and crime, composed of a greater population of African Americans (85%), was such a juxtaposition to white affluent Millburn.

In fact, according to a *New York Times* (5/17/2018) article, "New Jersey Law Codifies School Segregation, Suit Says," written by Sharon Otterman, a recent lawsuit in New Jersey contends that the state supports *de facto* segregation precisely because students have to attend schools in the municipality in which they reside. The article cites a UCLA study that found New Jersey to be the sixth most segregated state for black students, and seventh most segregated state for Latino students. It means there are school systems that are largely composed of minority students and others that are primarily white, some in close proximity to each other, like Irvington and Millburn. Students are growing up in parallel universes just miles from one another.

As an undergraduate I was assigned to read a book that opened my eyes to see how disparate communities like Irvington and Millburn had dissimilar educational purposes. *Slums and Suburbs* (McGraw-Hill, 1961) was written by Dr. James Bryant Conant, a former Harvard University president. In his introduction he wasted no time outlining how public schools serve different populations: "In the suburban high school from which 80% or more of the graduates enter some sort of college, the most important problem from the parents' point of view is to ensure the admission of their children to prestige colleges....In the city slum, where as many as half of the children drop out of school in grades 9, 10, and 11, the problems are almost the reverse of those facing the principal and guidance officer of the rich suburban school. The task with which the school people in the slum must struggle is, on the one hand, to prepare a student for getting and keeping a job as soon as he leaves school and, on the other hand, to encourage those who have academic talent to aim at a profession through higher education." In a greater sense, the contrast is that the urban student will be stressed in the pursuit to survive while the suburban student will be pressured to maintain the standards of achievement and quality of life set by his or her parents.

I could not have anticipated during my undergraduate years that the entirety of my professional career would be spent in affluent suburbs. I was the student in Conant's "city slum" and later the teacher and principal in the "rich suburban school." I acquired a comparative understanding and a unique personal perspective about divergent educational goals and lack of equality in education based on where one lives.

In my public high school education in Hoboken, I was never challenged to perform at the same high standards that I learned to provide for my own students. While I was taught by many caring and devoted professionals, the program of study overall, including in the "academic" or college prep track, was rudimentary when compared to schools in communities like Millburn.

I was never assigned to read even one book throughout high school. Instruction in writing was almost non-existent, with the most prominent assignments consisting of basic essays. I was never assigned a research paper in any English or history class, though I was required to write one for Advanced Chemistry. My entire junior year of English was wasted when the instructor ordered the class to copy the text of Greek plays handwritten on the board by a student or dictated by the teacher. When my senior year Honors English instructor realized that no one understood his allusions to *Julius Caesar*, an eighth grade unit of study in Millburn, he asked if anyone had read it. Mr. Musto could not abide this lapse in literary learning, and though it was not part of his course of study, he scraped together enough books for our class. In general, the curriculum lacked rigor, often missing the classic literature that was a core part of the American high school experience.

Because many, even most, of my teachers had themselves attended the Hoboken schools, they never experienced the difference in expectations and content learning between this urban comprehensive high school and suburban college preparatory schools. And working in the Hoboken school system was often based on whom you knew, not what you knew. When it came to curriculum oversight and the evaluation of teacher performance, I don't ever remember - not even once - seeing an administrator observe a class in my four years of attending public schools. But students like me conducted our own observations about which teachers were hard-working and genuinely invested apart from those who were ineffective or frequently absent. It is not a stretch to be able to see how students from my high school arrived at college already in arrears in terms of knowledge and skill sets.

Hoboken was a far more diverse community. The demographics of my class consisted of 40% Hispanics, 10% African Americans, a smattering of Asian, Indian and Middle Eastern cultures, and less than 50% whites. Depending on one's abilities and aspirations, students completed coursework in one of three tracks: academic, commercial or general. Peers in my graduating class who did not go on to college - the majority - opted for vocational or secretarial training, studied for civil service exams to become police officers, firefighters or postal workers, or entered the workforce. Or they married and started a family.

Was the overall program intended for a population of learners, as Conant suggested, that focused more on working than continuing their education? Did the diversity and socio-economic make-up of my high school peers, as well as their general attitudes toward education, shape, even curtail, at least some teachers' expectations? To be sure, there were students who could not wait to be free of school (and a good number of them dropped out as soon as they could) and others who felt that teachers and their subjects lacked relevance. Perhaps this was because they could not imagine themselves as college material or doubted that they could afford to pay for any postsecondary education. They were often children of immigrants from Cuba, Italy, India, and South America or working class parents who had no college education and who struggled to make ends meet, often requiring welfare, food stamps, subsidized housing, or the support of a network of extended family members. Indeed, the only option for many was to get a job.

Conant's writing resonated with me as I watched students transfer to Millburn Middle School from other school systems, especially more urban districts like Hoboken. These pupils were generally not on grade level and usually disadvantaged in terms of content, skills, and overall expectations. In a word, there were gaps. New students with the greatest gaps were unable to keep up with their Millburn counterparts. To accommodate these pupils, based on what we learned about them from their records or after observing their progress in classes, we enrolled them in our supplemental support classes, such as reading, replacement math, and study skills. It was our goal, however, that they would eventually return to the regular education setting.

It could be unclear if students required more than a supplemental education boost, so if students failed to make progress in a support class, or if they evidenced signs of learning challenges, we were required by law to test them for eligibility for special services.

Some African American parents accused me of trying to "lock up" their kids in special education classrooms. Our teachers and guidance counselors continually monitored the progress of all students. At Intervention and Referral Committee meetings, members brainstormed strategies and accommodations to try out in the regular classroom first before moving a child into a remedial setting. But sometimes perceptions have an element of credence, and after one of our guidance counselors surveyed how many of our African American students were enrolled in support classes, he came to me wide-eyed about the tally, informing me that a high percentage of our smallest demographic was enrolled in support classes. However, many of our African American students on the rosters of remediation courses were also transfer students.

The mother of one black transfer student about whom we had so many concerns would not consent to enroll her child in supplemental skills instruction. It was challenging to communicate with home, but when we were able to connect, the parent refused to move forward with our recommendations. Weekly wringing of hands signaled the frustration of teachers and guidance because the pupil was unable to complete any work, lacked structure and supervision after school, and refused or "forgot" to attend after-school help sessions. Everyone worked together for the two years the child had been in our school, and then the family moved again.

Another African American transfer student's parent's voicemail response to a letter inviting parents to come in to discuss supports at school illuminated parental opposition: "I will be there and I will be coming possibly with a social worker of my choice and possibly an attorney. I am very upset and I am going to tell you why when we sit down and we discuss it. I am not agreeing to this and I do not want it addressed to me again. Do you understand? I do want to sit down and meet with you. I'm gonna tell you up front: 'Hell no!' I'm not saying 'no,' I'm saying 'hell no.'"

This outcome repeated itself with other students passing through, including families of Asian and Hispanic cultures, who sometimes stayed just long enough for us to figure out what we should do or led us to believe we were finally closing in on our goal of providing assistance. Then the student was off to another place where more time was lost and the gap would widen. Other families initially resisted our offer of help just as hard, though eventually they came around to see what we saw, an unhappy child struggling to read and trying to compensate in a class where he or she could not understand or contribute, oftentimes starting to tune out or act out.

The mandate of education is to provide each child with what he or she needs.

Parental opposition and their lack of context at times hindered our ability to serve the range of students within our larger demographic of high-achieving pupils. Like my former student, we have had high-achieving African American students whose parents, quite possibly, were even more demanding that their children receive a rigorous accelerated education, suggesting that offering services had nothing to do with race but instead about where students spent their primary learning years.

The difficulties of attending school where most other kids are of a different race can be exacerbated by sensitivities and mistrust. Sometimes what a few of our African American preadolescents perceived as racism was not what they thought it was. For example, Lincoln Center Institute for the Arts provided cultural programming for schools. Our PTO funded a production about Africa with black actors wearing costumes and masks dancing to exotic music reminiscent of *The Lion King*. An African American student seated in the front row walked out in the middle of the performance because the pupil thought the actors were making fun of Africans.

To be sure, we have investigated, confirmed, reported, and addressed incidents of racism and Anti-Semitism in our school. But sometimes I was not sure that even the use of the N-word was necessarily intended as racism. Now, that does not mean that it did not require our attention. It would become complicated because sometimes kids would hurl racial slurs and invoke other ethnic stereotypes in a mutual swap of friendly fire with their peers, often those whom they considered to be their pals. Was it racism? Was it bullying if friends were equally slinging racial epithets at each other? They were indeed acting their age, and it was obvious they had a lot to learn. Greater confusion resulted when African American students said they could use the N-word, but nobody else could.

Students in a class were making up a story about a bear attack when one of them added "black bear," to which another said, "If it was a black bear, then it would have robbed you, too." When the child's parent was contacted, the parent's reply was that the kids were being impulsive and it was "just a stereotype." Wasn't that the point? Stereotypes are negative and hurtful and, recalling the conversation with my former student, I wondered if the parent ever considered how an African-American child in the class would have felt. One of the goals of the new HIB laws, it seemed to me, was to protect targeted populations maligned by such stereotypes.

The middle school used different approaches to spotlight African American contributions to the history of our country and in many fields of study, and advisors would help peer leaders write and deliver public service announcements, sometimes using a contest format, during Black History Month or to honor Dr. Martin Luther King, Jr.

I considered Neville Clarke, our African American head custodian for many years, a hero and a role model. Most of the baskets from our annual Thanksgiving food drive went to nearby inner-city residents thanks to his untiring concern for others. Neville retired in 1999, but that did not stop him from continuing to pack a truck, until 2015, and driving it to the Little Friendship Baptist Church in Newark, New Jersey, where he distributed cans, bags, and boxes of food. For years I introduced Neville for a wave, and sometimes some words, because I wanted our students to see what I saw, an exemplar of generosity, kindness and service to the community.

Neville Clarke having some fun. Neville gently reminded this principal that God, not I, was really in charge.

Our school nurse, Pam Palmieri, coordinated our annual Kris Kringle project and, with details about age, gender and size supplied by Neville, homerooms fundraised and purchased gifts for specific children so that they could have a warm garment and a toy for the holidays. This campaign was what fueled our team's auctions and pig-outs in order to purchase as many gifts as possible.

The enactment of the updated Harassment, Intimidation, and Bullying (HIB) law by the New Jersey legislature required, among many other provisions, that schools conduct a Week of Respect to formally provide anti-bullying messages and activities. I opened my first Week of Respect with a reference to Jackie Robinson: "In the first half of the twentieth century, a young man by the name of Jackie Robinson made history by becoming the first African American to play major league baseball. He was a pioneer of the game, who faced many racist fans, but he was quoted as saying, 'I'm not concerned with your liking or disliking me...All I ask is that you respect me as a human being.' Sixty years after Jackie Robinson's baseball career ended, there continue to be concerns about racism as well as other forms of discrimination against people for the way they look, where they are from, what they believe, their sexual orientation, their interests, their friends, what they wear, and the list of labeling and dividing goes on. It is because of this that the State of New Jersey has enacted what is being called the toughest anti-bullying law in the entire country."

One of the best presenters lined up with our Week of Respect activities was a performer and psychologist by the name of Dr. Michael Fowlin, aka Mykee. Mykee would portray several characters, using monologues and a variety of voices, to expose unique internal challenges that rendered his characters afraid to be themselves because of the intolerance, judgment and exclusion of others. Mykee had a way of making students empathize with his characters, leading them to recognize or question something about themselves or their beliefs, including the pressures of living in an affluent community. While he was funny and engaging, his presentation touched our evolving youngsters in a personal way as he portrayed an array of individuals struggling with identity, sexual orientation, expectations, and stereotypes. The impact on students was profound, some of them in tears or needing to talk to their guidance counselor. It was amazing how he could reach inside kids' hearts in a 45-minute assembly. It was important for all of our students, black and white, to experience such a gifted teacher who was also a person of color.

When Senator Barack Obama was elected President of the United States, I immediately knew that our student body needed to watch his historic inauguration as our nation's first African American President. It was the first time we had ever planned for students to see a Presidential inauguration on a large screen in the auditorium in real time.

Niche.com was right, the world is a lot more diverse than our school or community. In a way, it is another one of those "suspend reality" moments recognizing that our kids grow up in a bubble where their interaction with different people, especially people of color, is limited. Over the years it became a goal of ours to showcase the contributions and service of African Americans on our stage as well as on the world stage.

# 18. An Era of Curriculum Upheaval and Neglect

ONCE UPON A TIME, THE MILLBURN PUBLIC SCHOOLS funded a full cohort of academic supervisors. The district's existential purpose to provide an up-to-date, approved, and meaningful program of instruction rested on the expertise and guidance of those who served in these indispensable leadership roles. These content specialists led the process of establishing detailed curriculum frameworks from kindergarten through twelfth grade. If the instructional program was our district's central nervous system, the supervisors were the spinal cord.

Supervisors had been a fixture in Millburn since before I arrived in 1987. These professionals worked collaboratively with building administrators to recruit faculty, evaluate staff, and resolve personnel matters. The timing of their classroom visits yielded feedback on how well the curriculum was being delivered in addition to whether instruction was progressing on the expected timeline.

Unfortunately, in 2010 the board of education voted to eliminate the five academic supervisors for language arts, mathematics, science, social studies and world languages. They severed the spinal cord.

It could not have happened at a more consequential time.

In that very same year, the New Jersey State Board of Education's adoption of the Common Core State Standards (CCSS) set off a cavalcade of revisions in learning standards that mandated the modification of curriculum to align with a new standardized test known as the PARCC (Partnership for Assessment of Readiness for College and Careers). These major reforms demanded content expertise and department leadership that were no longer available, at least not in my school.

In 2011, New Jersey adopted a new anti-bullying law that mandated specific personnel roles and added deadlined processes that monopolized the time of building administrators now saddled with the challenge of distinguishing spats and dirty looks from legitimate instances of bullying, leaving less time for building administrators to even tinker with curriculum and content standards.

In 2013, New Jersey passed AchieveNJ legislation to overhaul the evaluation of school personnel, hitching the evaluation of language arts and mathematics teachers - and principals - to student performance on the aforementioned PARCC. Even though teachers' evaluations, and possibly livelihoods, now relied on how their students performed on a new standardized test, there was still no content specialist to guarantee quality assurance that pupils would be properly prepared for an assessment that measured newfangled "21st Century learning."

All of this was happening while technology integration had become a reformation unto itself.

Even lesson plans had to conform to a new format.

Seemingly, everything about the leadership tasks of principals, and more so about any aspect of instruction, content, and assessment for teachers, was simultaneously changing at the speed of light.

Without the proper supports in place to do it well.

The decision to cut the supervisors was a money-saving measure for the district but, as you can see, the tasks of supervisors not only lived on but also assumed greater significance. The district made provisions for this everywhere else except at the middle school. The elementary schools maintained their "instructional supervisors." At the high school, the board budgeted for a new hybrid position with the title of "department chair." The middle school once again became the proverbial neglected middle child.

What I saw happen in my school as a result of no direct curriculum and instruction oversight was how the same department teachers on a grade level strayed from the curriculum and each other. As the curriculum aged, teachers added new activities or media to expand thinking and connections for pupils, which in turn extended the time spent on a particular unit, shrinking or even eliminating other units. Liberties were exercised that resulted in adjustments to course requirements, such as varying expectations for the amount of formal writing, the number of reading tasks, the types and frequency of classroom assessments, and the assignment of homework and projects. The result was a curriculum that had not been approved and a student learning experience that depended on which teacher he or she had.

Without a doubt, the challenge and drama of this era of curriculum upheaval was intensified by the absence of middle school department overseers providing directed, specific, and thoughtful curriculum reform and formulating well-developed and consistent goals and expectations for instruction. In what world or, for that matter, in what other district, including a less affluent community, would it have been okay for a board of education and central office administration to disregard proper curriculum oversight, quality of content instruction, and teacher accountability in one of its schools?

Supervisors were the conduits that threaded the curriculum through the elementary, middle, and high schools. In fact, they encouraged middle school teachers to observe classes at the elementary and high school levels to understand where our students were coming from and where they were heading. After their demise, our schools struggled even to communicate for the purpose of creating a cohesive instructional program. And how could a systemic program have even been possible if the three middle school grades were voted off the island?

This orb we live on keeps spinning, and in time much of what generations before us have learned has evolved. Historical events have drawn new maps and shifted political alliances in parts of the world. Science and the use of technology have forged new understandings, and advancements, regarding climate change, genetics, medicine, energy, and artificial intelligence, to name just a few topics from our curriculum. For our courses to teach accurate, appropriate, and contemporary content would require the leadership and coordination of experts immersed in current developments within their fields.

What I call the "connectedness of supervision" had also disappeared with the supervisors who linked together professional development, department expectations, and curriculum presentation as the context for the evaluation of a teacher's overall performance. Supervisors were like clinicians who could diagnose, remediate, train, support, coach, and encourage their teachers; they often focused on instructional techniques that were compatible with the level of challenge of a course and the developmental stage of learners. But they were also responsible for holding teachers accountable. *Departmental supervisors understood the content, the delivery, the timeline, and the teachers in a way that no building or district administrator ever could.*

Supervisors were professional developers who utilized various approaches to improve the art and science of instruction. My favorite was the math department's use of Lesson Study because it focused on the intersection of instructional strategies and curriculum content. A teacher volunteered to teach a lesson. A group of colleagues helped design and prepare the lesson. The lesson was taught to children in front of colleagues and invited guests, including college professors, school administrators, and visitors from other districts. A frank debriefing session followed. Imagine teachers of all stripes gathered together to talk about teaching and learning! This kind of ongoing professional engagement - scrutiny, really - required collegiality, openness, trust and more than a dash of courage. The experience of watching all of these professionals be critical in a "What's the best pedagogy to teach this concept?" approach made me proud of our profession and our teachers.

Without a dedicated supervisor to lead the way, valuable teacher improvement endeavors such as Lesson Study fell by the wayside. And that's not all.

The importance of the role of a department supervisor as a mentor for new staff, and especially for teachers new to the profession, cannot be overstated. During my own novice years of teaching in Summit, I was fortunate to have had a school-based English supervisor. Jean Canning observed me formally and informally nine times during my first year. Many were unannounced visits. During our frequent one-to-one meetings, Jean offered suggestions and support as she helped me to discover the nature of learners at this age and apply compatible instructional practices. All teachers at that time were expected to incorporate the components of Madeline Hunter's Instructional Theory into Practice (ITIP) as the framework for conceiving lesson plans. Jean had file cabinets full of sample lesson plans, ideas, and materials to augment my thinking and improve my teaching.

Needless to say, I learned so much and felt supported, especially in a schedule that assigned me to teach two grades each with two performance levels for a total of four different preps in my first year of teaching. Jean's evaluations of me assessed my growth as a teacher and how, or if, I was implementing her recommendations and utilizing the department archives. When the time came to summarize my annual performance and progress, she used an evidence-based approach by collecting my lesson plan book, my grade book, and two portfolios of student work from each of my five classes.

In Millburn, supervisors played a supporting role for teachers, parents and administrators in our school. These content leaders provided ongoing guidance and resources to teachers for curriculum and instruction, at times researching and assembling activities and lessons which they modeled or co-taught with their department staff. Supervisors even provided direct instruction to children who required greater differentiation than was available in the classroom. These experts addressed questions about the curriculum and the placement process, especially in mathematics, in order to help parents reconcile their goals for their children with the reality of course content and performance levels with a longer-term understanding of where it all led. As principal, supervisors became my eyes and ears and helped me to steer our school in new directions.

It is difficult to explain the importance of supervision without sounding like I am, as the new superintendent put it, "whining." As the building principal, an observer not certified in every content area, I soon came to realize that watching a lesson could not inform just any evaluator about the accuracy of the lesson information, or if the lesson's content was within the scope of the approved course of study, or that the teacher had reached the expected milepost. Evaluation of this variety was cursory, focusing primarily on delivery. Administrators could concentrate on teacher actions, organization, and student engagement, but it would be difficult to offer substantive recommendations for improvement or, for that matter, document qualitative reasons for not renewing a teacher's contract or declining to grant tenure.

Ongoing improvement and accountability were supposed to be the drivers of the teacher observation and evaluation process.

Eventually, the effort to evaluate a teacher's performance became even more surreal, as every New Jersey district was forced to adopt a state-approved teacher evaluation model under AchieveNJ. Ours required each teacher to undergo ten 10-minute observations, most unannounced, every year. Administrators were also expected to vary the timing of observations, i.e., ten minutes in the beginning, middle or end of the 40-minute period. Now I do think you can tell some things about a lesson in ten minutes, though if you were not present in the beginning it would require the evaluator to discover the antecedents of the lesson to determine if the instruction, content and activities were congruent with the lesson objectives.

The observer was allocated 1,000 characters (including spaces and punctuation) in a box on a screen to capture the lesson and the post conference as well as include feedback and recommendations. This streamlined process forced an efficiency of words that achieved business-like goals of documentation while checking off another item on the principal's expanding to-do list.

Though I could not possibly carry out all of the roles of the supervisor position, it was nonetheless my responsibility as principal to provide curriculum oversight, understand how our teachers had to modify content and expectations to comply with the new common core standards, and support the work of teachers. In addition to the question about tending to matters of curriculum and staff development was the added challenge about how the three middle school administrators could possibly conduct all of these new observations while running a school. In spite of my whining, the superintendent did see the need for the middle school to add an administrator.

So a new "Program Chair" position was established to assist with observations and evaluations and to provide oversight of supplemental support classes. However, after the State of New Jersey passed one of the most comprehensive anti-bullying laws in the country, our Program Chair became the *Anti-Bullying Specialist*, requiring her to investigate all allegations of bullying. She also chaired the referral committee for children who were possibly manifesting learning challenges under the state *child find* mandate.

We hardly saw her. In a school full of preadolescents, there was a ton of conflict. In a developmental stage where kids now grappled with nine teachers per day instead of one, an epidemic of organizational and learning challenges surfaced. Our Program Chair was submerged in investigations, research, communications and paperwork.

Now there was plenty more work to be done that required a fourth building administrator, but the goal of comprehensive supervision and support of content areas became even more elusive.

I assigned my administrative team members to various subjects for the purpose of conducting teacher evaluations and attending to department concerns. An assistant principal handled tasks such as supplies and book orders. We conducted a drop-in at monthly department meetings, reflecting the truly token attention paid to completing requirements as opposed to thoughtful dialogues on what, why and how learning should happen in the middle level classroom of the 21st Century.

As a full-time building administrator it was just not possible to be all things to all people. How could three building administrators have the content wherewithal and time to update learning standards in five subjects in preparation for a new test on the horizon?

Despite my responsibilities and time constraints, though, I assumed ownership of everything that happened in my school. I involved myself in shaping or influencing curriculum in various ways after the departure of our supervisors. One example is how the School Leadership Team and I introduced a new sixth grade novel. A special education parent representative told me about a recently published book entitled *Wonder*, written by R.J. Palacio (Knopf, 2012). I read the book and wholeheartedly agreed that this work of fiction, a story about a homeschooled boy with a facial deformity returning to a mainstream school setting, was a perfect match for teaching important lessons about respect, tolerance, friendship and growing up. The sixth grade teachers embraced the novel and created "Wonder-ful" lessons. I loved the freshness of a new story, especially one so relevant to our sixth graders.

It was important to me that departments collaborated using an inter-disciplinary approach, and one way to accomplish that was to involve myself in designing research activities. For example, in sixth grade, together with teachers and the library-media specialist, Amy Ipp, we created a project called the "Great Greeks", combining the social studies and language arts departments. Sixth graders would learn how to conduct research in the library, using links for sources specifically selected for them by Amy. Pupils would learn note-taking and proper formatting and documentation, and their research would culminate in group slideshow presentations while draped in togas and crowned with plastic wreaths of laurel.

Later, when schools pivoted toward an emphasis on innovation, the research project dropped the "r" and was renamed the "Great Geeks", blending science and language arts. The focus shifted from the Greek divinities and ancient writers, philosophers, and statesmen to more contemporary "Famous Geeks" such as Einstein, Pasteur, Hawking, Franklin, and Darwin.

I had also wanted to ensure that we were continuing to meet the district's protocol for students to learn how to write a research paper. Sadly, the wind was knocked out of our sails when language arts teachers learned that their annual evaluation would be based, in part, on how children in their classes performed on the PARCC. So, instead, I teamed up with sixth grade language arts teachers to purchase a "common core ready" reading anthology to update the curriculum in the only way possible without a curriculum content leader onboard.

The new teacher evaluation rubric kindled a backlash from teachers everywhere, not just in Millburn. It was significant for Millburn, however, in how it changed our modus operandi. Teachers in Millburn historically did not prepare students for standardized assessments by teaching the test. To be sure, information about the test and a sample essay assignment to familiarize students with assessment rubrics would have been an expected exercise in advance of the test administration. However, other school districts, especially in urban areas, forced children to complete endless drills in and outside of school in preparation for the test. Millburn teachers believed that the best preparation was to teach content and skills; thus, preparation for the spring administration of the standardized test began on the first day of school.

Now it was our turn to teach the test, too. One language arts teacher spoke up on behalf of her department. "You can't expect us to continue with the research project. We don't have the time to do that anymore now that we have a different standardized test, and one that is much harder. And my evaluation will be based on how my students perform on a test I don't know anything about!"

The state's data-driven emphasis on teacher accountability was perceived by teachers as a threat, not just to their livelihoods, but also to their professional expertise in terms of the wisdom and understanding about teaching and learning that accrues with experience. It rerouted teachers away from teaching children knowledge and skills within a context of content to drilling the standards and test format. After years of messaging that encouraged teachers to differentiate instruction and to employ more authentic methods of assessment, teachers were now forced to prepare all pupils for a more challenging standardized test that did not distinguish expectations for the gamut of learners and learning styles assembled in their classrooms.

One of our early deductions about the Common Core Content Standards and the PARCC was that students were expected to have greater skill proficiencies at a younger age. It seemed as though we had entered into a new era of education, one that simultaneously accelerated learning and anxiety for kids, parents and teachers. It was unfortunate, but the teacher in me understood that there was no longer any time to spend on more fun and collaborative, albeit time-consuming skill-building projects.

I used to warn our math teachers that I did not speak math, and our Connected Math curriculum, different from what has been referred to as either traditional math or "new" math," came with a language and Kool-Aid all its own. I jested that subscribers of the Connected Math program were part of a cult, so devout was their fidelity to this constructivist and integrative approach, a curriculum consisting of a series of investigations, such as the "Locker Problem." Grade level math teachers worked very closely together and were generally, and literally, "on the same page," so it was no surprise to me that our math teachers knew just what to do to realign the Connected Math curriculum themselves to conform with the Common Core standards. But it was eye-opening when the Common Core/PARCC implementation shifted math curricula to the grade below, resulting in sixth graders now struggling with seventh grade math. Sixth grade teachers shared their frustration with me about the increased challenge and stress for their students to learn higher level concepts.

Other content areas beyond the two that "counted" on the PARCC also required the ongoing attention of building administrators. I was fortunate to have assistant principals who could apply their content expertise to guide curriculum updates. Theresa Gonnella was once the district's K-12 science supervisor, and Dan Brundage had led the Health and Physical Education department. John Leahey, our K-12 music supervisor, directed his department's compliance with new requirements. The curriculum of some subjects, such as social studies, leadership, and art, received little attention while world languages was an ongoing saga.

The State of New Jersey mandated that children be instructed in a world language every year, although it did not specify how long or how much. Millburn's original goal was to teach half of a yearlong high school course in each of the sixth, seventh, and eighth grades, gradually building language skills and fluency reinforced by plenty of time for practice. However, this sensible, slow, and steady approach resulted in scheduling/programming repercussions at the high school.

The solution seemed obvious to me because world language had displaced a reading course in sixth and seventh grades. Our students had had the benefit of a double dose of literacy by having both language arts and reading during two pivotal years of expanding cognition. By replacing our sixth grade reading course with a world language, we were in effect terminating the formal teaching of reading skills in fifth grade. I noticed two things in the aftermath of dropping reading: first, our Terra Nova reading scores declined and stagnated; second, parents began complaining that we were not teaching study skills. Reading skills are study skills.

For me, the correct course of action would have been to reinstitute reading in the sixth grade, borrowing some of that class time to introduce French and Spanish in order to meet code and so that students could select the language they wished to study starting in seventh grade. Under my plan, our students would have completed one high school year of language study over two years in grades 7 and 8.

Another brainstormed idea was to teach a sixth grade course on Latin roots, prefixes, and suffixes. In effect, more literacy skills while simultaneously satisfying the language requirement.

Because this was Millburn, the prevailing thinking - certainly not mine - was that our middle school children should be able to cover high school levels 1 and 2 during their three years with us, completing all of level 2 world language in eighth grade. Told "our kids could handle it," I was overruled.

Though it looked to everyone on the outside that Millburn students were finishing two high school years of language before they left middle school, the truth was that it could not be done. Learning does not happen by decree. It is not possible to teach middle schoolers in the same way one would instruct high school students. A year, or two, of maturation makes a tremendous difference. Ironically, high school language instructors still had to deal with the reality that our students still did not complete all of the units of the second level.

I whined about this, too, but even the new regime at central office did not want to hear the middle school principal yammer about building a better reading foundation and reducing stress for students who now had to learn a new language at a pace and sophistication more typical for older students. This curriculum change also pushed more advanced language coursework later on at the high school where students were required to take a minimum of two years of language, but where highly competitive colleges wanted to see three or four years on high school transcripts.

Here was a prime example of how Millburn was throwing more fuel on the fire to be a formidable competitor in a race whose finish line probably did not make much difference for most students, but added to the stress of almost all students.

The addition of STEM (innovative classroom activities involving science, technology, engineering, and mathematics) in our cycle classes led me on quests to neighboring districts and private schools to see their facilities and gain inspiration from their curriculum. I was accompanied by STEM teachers and the district technology teacher trainer, Elizabeth Bagish, to meet with instructors and supervisors as well as observe lessons.

These visits led us to develop a blueprint for new courses. We talked about what students should learn and at which grade level, creating a sequence of coursework. I was fortunate to have staff members who were teacher leaders and who could coalesce the possibilities into the specifics of what our students would learn and in what order. My role was to share in the search, support their efforts, and follow up. We knew from the beginning that coding, design, 3D printing, and robotics were dynamic and evolving fields of study, and in a short time would have to be updated again, building on what kids would already know when future classes of students arrived at the middle school.

While I had suggested some curriculum additions, deletions and modifications, or new courses, in different departments over the years, the bulk of my effort had been to support the teacher experts.

In the years since the supervisor role was eliminated in Millburn, New Jersey passed so many reforms that I was compelled to express my opinion not only about the volume of significant changes impacting our schools, but also about how these political mandates attempted to standardize education throughout the state without deference to the nature and needs of individual districts. My "Viewpoint" editorial was published in The *Item of Millburn-Short Hills* on September 19, 2013:

> *A massive reform movement in education is underway in New Jersey. Educators around the state are watching our political leaders and*

*education officials hand down a one-size-fits-all "remedy" to overhaul public education. New teacher evaluation models, additional testing and data collection, new federal Common Core curriculum requirements, new standardized testing, and local reporting of "readiness for college and workplace" are all components of the template they have assembled to standardize the "what" and the "how" of New Jersey's public schools.*

*This model of reform does not distinguish between the successes of high-achieving, community-involved districts like Millburn and other districts where radical changes are a moral imperative for children who deserve better.*

*I wonder if any of our legislators and leaders have thought through what impact these changes, and the array of costs associated with them, will have upon our students and schools. I doubt that parents understand how all of these changes and requirements are going to affect the culture of our classrooms and schools.*

I went on to explain that teachers had to establish two Student Growth Objectives, each of which would require two assessments, a pretest and a post-test, in every academic class as well as physical education, health, art, technology, etc. These assessments were referred to as "benchmarks."

As if it were my idea, several parents complained to me: "Really, Mr. Cahill, even in gym (physical education class), the one place where our kids can blow off steam, they now have to take written tests?"

I introduced the new teacher evaluation model. During year one of implementation, I conducted 140 teacher observations, and my three administrative teammates completed even more.

In my concluding paragraphs, I described what I saw as the impact of these reforms on education and specifically on Millburn:

*School districts like Millburn are being forced to spend time and capped budget funds to implement broad reforms that are not aimed at us. Politicians are changing the culture of education, intentionally or perhaps unwittingly, by making too many changes at the same time and forcing all districts to standardize the work of teachers instead of promoting district-based models of improvement based on high standards.*

*Our teachers are feeling the pressure to teach the same content in the same way and in the same amount of time. This poses a threat to the flexibility of teachers to assess and adjust instruction in order to achieve student comprehension of content and to extend, enrich, and nourish student thinking and connections. For these reasons, I believe that districts like Millburn stand to lose the most in this movement toward standardization. A national Common Core curriculum, testing, and the collection of data now narrowly define the work of teachers in a society, it seems, allowing education to become a business where students from different districts are viewed as the same assembly line product.*

On top of all of these things, teachers were also asked to integrate technology. If it were not for Liz Bagish, departmental teachers would not have had any training, support, and resources. But the cart was already before the horse! Integrating technology would have been more effective if departmental teachers had had a content supervisor who could have spearheaded conversations to determine the purpose and use of technology beforehand and incorporated actual lesson plans into an expanding repertoire of strategies and outcomes. By not doing this as a group, teachers became independent operators who retained different levels of comfort and expertise, and as a result, students again experienced inconsistent outcomes.

It is safe to say that prior to 2010, education changed at a snail's pace, which made it all the more ironic that there were no K-12 supervisors in place when systemic content leadership was needed most. In a very real way, the board and administration were no longer investing in the district's greatest asset, its teachers. As president of my professional association of supervisors and administrators, on multiple occasions I advocated for the return of supervisors.

As I was exiting the district, there was a plan in place to hire a couple of supervisors who would play overlapping curriculum and teacher evaluation roles in the middle school, high school, and central office, but at the cost of losing the middle school program chair position. But, just like building administrators, supervisors lacking content knowledge can only focus on more generic facets of classroom instruction and whatever trends *du jour* define 21st Century teaching.

Education had undergone a tsunami of change in the seven years before my retirement, and just looking at these shifts in practice one could easily see the need for expertise and leadership directly connected to the subject matter and to the teachers who delivered it. I believe that not having K-12 content area supervisors had diminished Millburn's stature as a leader in the field of education. Millburn now looked to other districts to see what they were doing.

My administrative team and I did our best to carry the weight of reform, simplify the process, streamline goals and tasks, and research the answers to questions. We were all learning as we went along, including how to collect and analyze more data, and my approach was one of reducing requirements to simplest terms and keeping our eyes on the real prize, the actual learning that took place every day.

# 19. The Baby and the Bathwater in 21st Century Schools

INSTRUCTION IS CHANGING IN WAYS THAT CAN BE EXPECTED to coincide with the times. It was inevitable that technology would become a platform for teaching and learning, one now ironically more widely used as a way to homeschool children, even before COVID-19 forced schools to shutter. Districts where high school students are depended upon to earn wages and/or who are unable to attend school during traditional school hours for a variety of reasons are already picking up the tab for their students to learn online. It's no longer a stretch to see in the crystal ball, especially after a trial run during a pandemic, how technology can facilitate the ultimate change in education: learning without a teacher or a multi-disciplinary, multi-sensory interactive environment.

Instructional practice even in schools is becoming increasingly dominated by "project-based learning" and technology collaborations. The state trainer for the PARCC assessment encouraged teachers to shift the amount of "teacher talk" in a lesson to predominantly "student talk." These popular buzzwords as of late, representing what is trending - pretending? - as instructional and curricular innovation, are taking their toll on teacher morale. Teachers want to engage with learners on a human level. Abandoning storytelling, anecdotes, and examples as a way for teachers to relate, illustrate, inspire, and foster empathy is becoming an existential threat to the original network of "wireless connections" forged in the classroom.

Content must be taught with clarity and accuracy. Frustration sets in when teachers have to watch and listen as they hear students acquiring, interpreting or passing on misinformation. A science teacher, encouraged to have students teach other students, posed the question, "Michael, what am I supposed to do? I am on the sidelines listening to students making statements that are inaccurate."

When a school system does not fund content-based supervisors, it means that generic supervisors who lack expertise in a subject will not understand what foundational knowledge, concepts, or ideas are being sacrificed to the gods of watered-down instruction as schools seek to create student or technology-driven classrooms instead of learning-centered ones. A crappy lesson on a Chromebook could win accolades from a supervisor who does not have a grasp of the content just because the teacher used technology.

The unequivocal success of the Millburn schools has led teachers and parents at times to pose the question, "If it ain't broke, why fix it?" One could not fully subscribe to the premise of this question as it is an imperative for all of us to continue learning and especially to prepare our students for *their* futures. But there remained more than a kernel of truth inherent in the argument to preserve the content and best practices that have elevated learning and achievement to such heights.

Content, in recent times, seems to have taken on a negative connotation, hence the question, "Why do they have to learn it when they can look it up?" Students need to learn a fair amount of content to be educated, functional, deep-thinking human beings whose fund of knowledge forms a point of reference and informs a point of view. How much content and exactly what should be taught requires devising common expectations through conversations that must include educators of every level, including those institutions of higher learning to which our students aspire to attend, as the work of schools and teachers continues to evolve.

More than anything, schools - and I suspect not just Millburn - need to return to the idea of a vision. The vision to which I refer is more than the philosophical statements displayed on district websites or printed materials. The vision in a school district is a function of leadership that enables changes in practice and substance that are based on rationale, research, and thoughtful reflection, while remaining true to the district's core values. In a word, changes - and the desired outcomes - are *intentional*.

When districts or schools are not guided by vision and research, they tend to jump on the bandwagon of what other schools are doing, and the implementation of new practices and ideas, including the use of technology, is haphazard, resulting in unanswered questions, frustration, and sometimes embarrassment. I have experienced situations where parents did more due diligence than district personnel by undertaking research, composing thoughtful questions, and expressing concerns.

Of course, the best way to approach change is to include a wide swath of stakeholders, from the ambitious to the resistant, so that the outcome is an inclusive proposal that will bring about change via a careful, deliberate process. This undertaking necessitates an investment of time, a huge challenge in and of itself, and in people, too. Even for those who do not agree with the direction, a rationale guides and supports new expectations and lends credence as to how and why these reforms benefit learners. It anticipates potential potholes, unites everyone on the same page, and endows the end result with the integrity it needs for implementation because it is what is best for kids.

A role that I found myself playing as principal, especially as a middle school principal, was that of "the guardian." We knew what effective teaching looked like. As we continue on in this 21st century of innovation, we should carefully explore how we can retain those heuristic features - the human experience, engagement, creativity, culture, learning how to learn - as we become a more technology-dependent enterprise. To this end, my hope also is that classrooms of the future do not abandon important research such as Dr. Howard Gardner's Theory of Multiple Intelligences which identifies "multiple types of human intelligence, each representing different ways of processing information." Facilitating learning that incorporates as many modalities as possible, not just screen time, activates the brains of all learners. For me, Dr. Gardner's work is also a declaration that not everybody can, or wants to, be a coder, mathematician or engineer. Our unique "intelligence" leads us on a path to realize our potential in a career where we find satisfaction and fulfillment. My own journey is proof of this fundamental, life-guiding principle.

What exactly is meant by incorporating technology? I have seen entire lessons based on teachers' PowerPoint slides. These were boring presentations from which students took copious notes and teachers added little from their own well of knowledge. This was merely a substitution for using an old-fashioned overhead projector and transparencies. Slides could have been distributed, or shared on GoogleClassroom, as notes that served as gateways to in-depth learning and inspired further inquiry.

Technology utilized for the sake of using technology, or as a substitution for Xerox copies, is not a transformational advancement of teaching and learning. For example, how is it different for students to be assigned independent reading of a passage and answering follow-up questions posted on Google Classroom by their teacher instead of using a print source and lined paper? While there are efficiencies and cost savings, there is no innovation.

For technology to be an effective tool it should add value to learning. It should allow students - and teachers - to go where they have not been able to go before, to experience and explore, to integrate and to appreciate, to arrive at new and deeper understandings or to change perspective, and to inspire ways to connect, apply, and build upon their discoveries.

The district eventually introduced Dr. Ruben Puentedura's SAMR Model of technology integration to help teachers understand this concept. This taxonomy of levels - Substitution, Augmentation, Modification and Redefinition - delineated the continuum of technology applications in the classroom. While it was easy enough to implement technology practices in the first two levels, the transformative integration occurred in the third and fourth tiers. This framework was revealing to our teachers, and it made apparent that the higher levels required first their own brain's imagination and innovation.

I have seen transformative technology used in the classroom, and the most impressive added value resulted from the ways a teacher incorporated media, the arts, maps, and culture in order to present a holistic understanding of a particular unit instead of a one-dimensional view. All at once an iconic painting of the American Revolution was in front of an American History class telling its own version of a budding nation, or a video of Dr. Martin Luther King, Jr.'s "I Have a Dream Speech" at the Lincoln Memorial engrossed students in a watershed moment of the Civil Rights Movement. I have seen language arts teachers connect the study of a novel to a YouTube video about an individual who overcame the same challenges as its protagonist, or to a brief segment of a film that was reminiscent of the characters and symbolism in a literary work, or to a TED Talk related to the central theme of a piece of literature. GoogleEarth transported social studies classes to historic sites to understand how location, natural resources, and trade routes impacted culture, religious beliefs, and ways of life. With powerful telescopes, microscopes, and scanners, science teachers displayed what no one could surmise with the human eye.

At the highest level of the SAMR model, learning is "redefined" by the plethora of technology tools and online resources available for students to create (documents, blogs, web pages), communicate (posts, publications, virtual bulletin boards), collaborate (Zoom meetings or chats with peers/professionals/institutions in a field of study/schools in other countries) and teach (quiz games, documentaries, demonstrations). Without a doubt, technology has the potential of helping learners achieve a previously unimagined level of understanding as well as formulating possibilities for them to apply what they have learned in new and creative ways, including solutions to "real world" problems. It is in this space, beyond the engaging, entertaining, and enlightening powered by technology, that the promise of the deepest thinking lurks in that computer lodged between the ears of our students.

Should students be using technology exclusively all day at school, especially since we know that they spend so much time on their own devices when not in school? Will that result in a generation of passive learners who do not read or speak to others? And do not know how to interact with others? If we are not careful, the overuse of technology can culminate in sufficient passive teaching and learning where one might wonder if it is even necessary for students to come to school to do what they could do at home, or elsewhere, on their own time table.

By the way, as we purchased more and more laptop carts and provided technology in-service learning opportunities for staff, a group of teachers shared a timely and ironic news article with me about how the computer whiz executives of Silicon Valley were sending their kids to private schools that did not utilize technology in the classroom until middle or high school and limiting their own kids' use of tech at home as well.

I have already seen middle schools in our area swipe the books from their library shelves to convert these sizable rooms into makerspaces for S.T.E.M. classes. Friends and colleagues have admonished me to "get over it" as an inevitable outcome. It seems to me that schools in general have jumped on the bandwagon to support what is called "21st century learning" at the risk of begetting a less literate generation of learners. It should be every school's goal to promote reading, and that also requires a librarian who knows how to connect kids with books. It is heartening to me that some schools are fighting back to keep their libraries.

One reason our middle school already had more laptops than we would have had is that several years ago we implemented a 1:1 tech study wherein the district purchased enough laptops for our entire seventh grade, half of them Macs and the other half Chromebooks. In the middle of the year, the teams switched their devices so that all of the students and teachers could experience using both. Aside from comparing functionality and cost, we learned that we had a lot to learn. Teachers had varying degrees of comfort and facility when it came to technology, and we had to answer basic questions such as: Were teachers expected to use technology every day? Were departmental teachers supposed to be using the same activities, videos, websites, etc.? It was the early stage of technology integration and, to the consternation of many, a "building the plane while flying it" approach because there were no supervisors presiding over the marriage of content and technology.

For administrators, we were taught important lessons by our students about the things they can do on technology that they should not be doing in school, or anywhere else, including social media, games, pornography, selling things and gambling.

An abundance of literature supports the belief of educators that "hand teaches brain" in a way that cannot be replicated on a keyboard. Note-taking trains the brain to record and recall information. In addition to writing and taking notes or outlining, we cannot lose the importance of practicing the skills of listening, speaking and memorizing. All of these are life skills that will serve learners well in the practice of their future careers and the exercise of their lives. The question that requires consideration, for teachers and supervisory personnel, is how can we as educators offer a *balanced* repertoire of strategies and activities that incorporate technology instead of being replaced by it?

School leaders have to be visionary as they assimilate new thinking, technologies, and innovative ideas as their venerable institutions try to keep up with changing practices and curriculum standards, as well as expectations from communities, colleges, and corporations. But maintaining relevance and being futuristic have to be parallel objectives to administering to the needs of the developing children in front of them right now, and providing them with opportunities to grow cognitively, emotionally, socially, and morally in a safe and nurturing environment.

Principals must be courageous enough to stand by their convictions about what is best for the students and the school, even if they are not popular, for being the guardian and the gatekeeper sometimes comes with a target on their back.

My thoughts and feelings about all of this curriculum reform are summarized in my "Principal's Message" in the *MMS PTO Newsletter* of February 2015. They had to do with my vision, the focus of which was primarily on what was best for our students, and the struggle to continue to evolve while preserving the elements that made our developing students, and our school, so special:

*I have been contemplating lately about how all the changes in education fomenting around us are influenced by entities on "the outside" of school buildings like ours, and they include government and business, testing and publishing companies, colleges, and societal shifts in* thinking. We continually hear terms like "skill levels" and "proficiencies" and "college readiness." Additional tests and time spent on testing are a new reality in schools. A big part of the new landscape of teaching and learning means using more tools of technology.

I know change can be a good thing. I realize making change is difficult. It seems to be that more than at any time in history, schools are undergoing dramatic changes and all at the same time. It can be overwhelming.

What we have to continue to focus on, however, is our vision for who and what our students can aspire to become. And while that includes proficiencies and skill levels, it means much more.

As I observe classes, I see wonderful dialogues taking place. These classroom conversations engage students in meaningful discussion and debate. They, too, involve those higher level critical thinking skills as students form opinions and are enlightened by what they hear in an exchange of ideas in a classroom or cooperative group. They do some other things as well, including developing public speaking, collaboration and social skills. Not every moment is a Google moment, not every search requires a search engine, and with all the demands on testing and time I am afraid that we risk losing important interactive components of the learning process.

Here is an important tenet for us to protect: middle schoolers are in formation. This unique age group needs and deserves to have a developmentally appropriate curriculum and program. We teach students about metacognition - learning how to learn - as well as about their own learning styles and how to develop coping mechanisms, organize themselves and manage their time. Learning about the values of community participation, leading and service are important to a developing citizenry. And they take time as well.

*Important, too, is promoting well-rounded, informed individuals where learning is messy and incorporates investigations, deliberations, and creations. Students are coming into their own, and there is a distinct difference in the presentation and pacing of instruction for students in this age group.*

*The value of what transpires every day in our classrooms cannot always be measured on a test or captured in a teacher's evaluation. We cannot let the test and the technology become the curriculum. And even if the conversation that is taking place outside of school does not take into consideration who our students are and how to help them become young adults, it is incumbent upon us to make sure that we don't throw the tween out with the bath water.*

# 20. Get the Nurse

I FEEL LIKE I WORK IN A HOSPITAL.

It is one way to describe the increasing health, especially mental health, demands of administering a school today. This size-up is not exclusive to Millburn and it is much more than about seasonal maladies, chronic conditions, and attentional challenges. Anxiety and stress are more prevalent in schools and society in general, and places like Millburn generate their own unique and arresting level of stress. In addition, public school districts are mandated to incorporate students whose disabilities would once have dispatched so-called "handicapped" learners to an alternative educational setting. All of it adds drama to a day-in-the-life of a school, its principals and, most of all, the school nurse.

A friend informs the guidance counselor that Jasmine is cutting herself again. Burt, a student diagnosed with oppositional defiant disorder, refuses to leave when the teacher tries to remove him from the room. Raymond, known as a "runner," absconds from class, heading for an exit with his aide in tow, unable to keep up. Shannon is so anxious that she has to call her mom every period today. Bobby has a meltdown because his social studies teacher told him to put away the sci-fi thriller he was reading so he could pay attention and participate in class. The school psychologist huddles with Ethan in a stairwell trying to help him understand that his behaviors affect how his peers see him.

Not fiction, and only a slice of life in schools today. This chapter speaks to the changing composition of our students and how their evolving needs impact the roles of administrators, child study teams, and nurses.

Meet Pam Palmieri, the school nurse who has been an integral part of the inner circle since we started this journey together. In fact, it was in the spring before I began as principal that Pam was scheduled to interview for the position, but because my daughter Caroline had made her late but grand debut into the world, I missed the interview. I knew I was in good hands with Dr. Goerss and the panel of teachers interviewing candidates.

Caroline was born ten days beyond her official due date, and after the first couple of days of waiting and anticipation I posted a sign on my office door that said simply, "not yet" for all the inquirers. On the Sunday morning Caroline decided she was ready, she hardly gave her father enough time to drive to the hospital. The doctor and the doula both missed her birth. A nurse on the other side of the room into which we were just ushered was absent-mindedly telling Lea to breathe when yours truly was the first to lay eyes on his second child.

The biggest change, and greatest challenge, for school personnel in the last decade had more to do with the state of our children's mental health. The fact that schools have put into place a risk assessment training and protocol is evidence of its need.

Risk assessments are conducted by a member of the child study team - a social worker or school psychologist - for a student who has threatened to harm himself or herself or someone else. It is usually the former, reported by a peer or sometimes a teacher or counselor in whom the student confided. Depression afflicts more middle schoolers with feelings of inferiority, difference, isolation and/or hopelessness than one might imagine. More than 30 students underwent a risk assessment at the middle school during the first four months of one school year.

In "Teen Suicide Soaring: Do Spotty Mental Health and Addiction Treatments Share Blame?" Jayne O'Donnell and Anne Saker, *USA Today* (3/19/18) cited a study by the Centers for Disease Control and Prevention that concluded, "The suicide rate for white children and teens between 10 and 17 was up 70% between 2006 and 2016." It further explained that while black children do not commit suicide as frequently as white children, a greater increase of incidents occurred during that same time period.

The National Institute of Mental Health website, also using statistics from the Centers for Disease Control and Prevention (2019), summarized findings that ranked suicide as the second leading cause of death for children and young adults between the ages 10 and 24.

In "Gone at 15," Adam Clark (The *Sunday Star-Ledger*, 10/20/2019) published an intimate, compelling, and detailed story about teen suicide and the woefully inadequate resources for children suffering from depression, including overstretched school nurses and a shortage of counselors and therapists. Clark embeds statistics that portray a mental health crisis in New Jersey and throughout the country: "In 2017, there were 100 documented suicides among New Jersey's 15 to 24-year-olds, the highest number and rate since the 1990's, according to federal data." Clark also cited findings from the National Alliance on Mental Illness that "about 1 in 5 teens aged 13-18 is living with a severe mental disorder."

When statistics become students we knew, we suffer the personal realization of how tragic it is when young people see no other way out. Between 2014 and 2017, sadly, three former Millburn Middle School students committed suicide, two while in high school and another as a college freshman. And there have been other credible attempts, including at the middle school.

School avoidance has become a phenomenon of its own with students refusing to come to school despite the interventions of administrators and counselors, police visits to the home, consultations with mental health professionals, evaluations by the child study team, and even assistance from the NJDCP&P (New Jersey Department of Child Protection and Permanency). Pam was the first to call home to inquire about absences, not just on behalf of the health of the child but out of concern for possible contagious disease. Sometimes years hence we would discover the root cause of school avoidance to stem from issues of bullying, sexual orientation, cultural differences, family dynamics, transitional challenges, academic stress, or serious mental illness. It was likely that chronic absenteeism resulted from a comorbidity of conditions and factors.

Another indicator of drastic change over the years has been the increase in the number of classified students enrolled in public schools. The mandate to provide the "least restrictive environment" often became a litmus test as to whether the regular school environment, with all of the support services, special classes, and extra personnel, was an appropriate one.

Years ago, when I was a teacher in this building, our staff included three special education teachers, one per grade. That total number grew to 18. When I retired, our special education program offered replacement classes, in-class support, study skills, and an executive functioning course instead of a once daily "resource room" period.

One huge difference is that public schools now have more pupils who are classified as emotionally disturbed (ED) or with behavioral illnesses. Students have paranoid schizophrenia, bipolar disorder, obsessive-compulsive disorder, or overwhelming anxiety while others suffer from oppositional defiant disorder or severe attention-deficit/hyperactivity disorder. Afflicted students often have outbursts and require more monitoring during the school day. Others have behavior plans that require constant management and oversight, necessitating even period-by-period feedback reports, keeping case managers, a behaviorist, paraprofessionals, the nurse, and administrators literally on their feet.

During my time in Millburn each child study team member (CST) was assigned to case manage all of the classified children in a grade level. However, middle school CST members sometimes had 60 or more students for whom they were responsible, an overwhelming number, especially considering that some of those cases were quite involved or litigious.

Our Life Skills program, a contained class that accommodated pupils with developmental disabilities and autism, had students at times who became physically aggressive. A 911 call to the main office precipitated a speedy response from the nurse, assistant principal, security guard, and child study team member. Most of the students had one-to-one aides who often made a tremendous difference by effectively anticipating and avoiding the triggers that could have resulted in self-injury or trauma to others. And when that did not happen, I witnessed the untamed physical and verbal rants of children who were unreachable, requiring them sometimes to be confined in a calming space until they stabilized or, depending on the situation, to be restrained. Along the way these temporarily irrational individuals have struck or injured aides, peers, their teacher, and administrators.

Schools today enroll many more students who have autism or autism spectrum characteristics, even if they are not formally diagnosed or classified as such. This is not surprising as the website AutismNJ.org cites Centers for Disease Control and Prevention statistics that demonstrate a prevalence of autism in 1 in 32 eight-year-olds in New Jersey and 1 in 54 nationally. New Jersey has the highest rate of autism in the nation.

Our child study team coached teachers to better understand, communicate and interact with these usually high-functioning and at times "quirky" individuals. But students with communication disorders are further challenged in the social arena and sometimes misunderstand or misinterpret the words or actions of other students, resulting in conflict or accusations of bullying, even if they consider these other individuals their friends. In an extreme illustration, a boy misread a situation as he and his friends were walking together in the hallway. He thought his friend purposely pushed him hard, so he walloped him. It was a fourth party who pushed the boy on the other end who in turn set off a chain reaction, resembling a physics demonstration in a lecture hall, as each boy plowed into the next.

Have I mentioned that surveillance cameras are the greatest gift to school administrators?

Sometimes children in crisis were escorted to the main office, requiring assistant principals and office personnel, including secretaries and the security guard, to try to help students to calm themselves and stabilize until a counselor or child study team member could assist, or until a parent could come. I have watched our staff console students, provide something to color, draw or fidget with, supply earphones so they could either listen to music or block out all auditory stimuli, or offer a stuffed animal to hug. I have also witnessed children become aggressive and try to elbow their way out of an office with an administrator blocking the door and a security guard in position. We have had students we knew were "runners" who have dashed out of the building, a scary proposition with that busy road just outside.

The most hyperactive students were the ones that stood out from the pack of already impulsive, distracted, and inattentive preteens. This behavior manifested not only in the classroom, but also especially in those less structured or supervised places where lack of self-control and high energy sometimes resulted in physical interactions, especially in locker rooms, gymnasiums, the cafeteria, and hallways. It did not take long for these students to be on the radar for administrators and the I&RS Committee, a core member of which was the nurse. Many of our students with ADHD did not perform academically as well as their peers because they were unable to focus or sustain their effort, sometimes resulting in lower grades or lower level classes and finding themselves in the company of a "shadow," a paraprofessional, to help them stay on task or even out of trouble.

I have called or met with parents at times to convey how I experienced their children as they walked (not really) the halls, engaged peers during lunch or behaved in classrooms. Parents sometimes replied, "I am not going to drug my child and turn her into a zombie."

Anybody who knew me would know that recommending prescription drugs would never be my first step; having said that, though, I think the right medicine could have made a difference if parents were unwilling to investigate other therapies. But doing nothing would continue to deny their children access to their educational program. Some parents just did not comprehend the seriousness of the problem and its repercussions. Other parents did not want to medicate because they feared it might alter their child's athletic prowess, especially if it could jeopardize a future college scholarship. But the challenge for a classroom teacher was that the child with ADHD, who was not accessing the program of instruction, was also making it difficult for other students to learn.

Ben's impulsivity and immaturity caused him to be an aggressor at times, as well as the victim of his poor decisions at other times, in his involvement with other students. Kids with ADHD have a bad rap because others might only know them through how they experience or observe them in a crowd, but I can tell you that many of our toughest ADHD students, like Ben, were sweet, honest and respectful kids who would apologize or say they did not know why they did something or admit that they just lost control.

The nurse is the pivotal connection to the well-being of all students. Pam had relationships with students as well as historical context and knowledge about their conditions and pharmaceuticals. She was key to our being able to help students who were being physically abused or at risk in some way. Students confided in her and opened up about what was stressing them.

In fact, The *New York Times* (10/16/2007) published an article about Pam Palmieri, written by Jan Hoffman, with the caption, "In a Competitive Middle School, Triage for Aches and Anxieties." The story highlighted the evolving nature of the school nurse job description, referring to our nurse as "a front-line medical manager, first responder, diagnostician, confessor, shrink." Later in the article, Pam shared her truth about our students being stressed out with "phantom illnesses, endless headaches and stomach aches" emanating from our competitive school environment. Our nurse also divulged a growing problem with school avoidance. In the article, Pam revealed how she even had to prop up those kids who were upset to the point of feeling sick because they were not invited to bar mitzvahs.

The article did not fare well with some parents and board members. Calling it a breach of confidentiality, some board members engaged in conversations about creating a policy that would have effectively prohibited most school employees from speaking to the press.

The bizarre thing for me as principal was that I do not recall anyone wanting to meet or speak with me or Pam about the substance of this article. It felt like another one of those "suspend reality" moments.

Some folks were upset about what they considered to be negative publicity when in fact even in affluent areas, or maybe especially in wealthy districts, stresses that are taking a toll on children could be relayed best by the caregiver in the school who observes them firsthand. The article captured a reality of school life for those of us who lived it every day in a pressure cooker environment. In retrospect, this was a missed opportunity, as the anxieties and risks that preadolescents experienced had escalated as Millburn morphed into a monochromatic population of must-be accelerated students.

What else could one see at school that supports the comparison to a hospital? The number of inhalers for children with respiratory illnesses like asthma. The students with diabetes who came several times a day to check their glucose levels or make sure their pumps were working properly. The lengthy list of pupils on each team with specific allergies, including foods, as well as those with allergies to pollen and bee stings that made life more complicated when it was warm enough to open windows or go outside for physical education or during lunch. The increase in FM systems or amplification equipment for students with auditory challenges. And the line at the nurse's door, especially during lunch time, of preadolescents who took prescription medications for ADHD, anxiety, and other conditions.

Allergies to nuts have been around for some time, but allergies to wheat, dairy, eggs and other ingredients had become more common, driving administrators to ban fiestas and other culinary celebrations of culture. A team of administrators and teachers were trained in the use of EpiPens in the event a student unwittingly consumed an ingredient that could lead to anaphylactic shock. Our school developed cleaning protocols for avoiding contamination in classrooms from celebrations or lunchtime group meetings.

A team of staff members was also trained in the use of Automatic External Defibrillators (AED) in case an individual experienced sudden cardiac arrest. We positioned several AEDs in key areas around the building, and training was part of the opening of the school year for all teachers.

The school nurse plays the lead role in response to all of these health crises.

The word "outbreak" strikes fear in the heart of the principal, especially because a school is an incubator that provides temperature and conditions conducive for germs to thrive, especially in winter. Pam would relay information from the county health department about an outbreak and how to prevent or curtail its reach. In 2007, our school had a confirmed case of MRSA, an antibiotic resistant staph bacteria, which sparked concerns about special cleaning and reminders to students about washing hands and not sharing cups, bottles or cans. Two years later came a national and global pandemic of

Swine Flu, which never materialized in Millburn, though we braced ourselves and reminded students again about proper hygiene.

Pam would keep me abreast of developments concerning illnesses as well as spikes in absenteeism. Influenza and stomach flu can spread very easily given the contagious nature of these illnesses. As a school we would have to monitor any infectious illness for the benefit of other students and the staff, and especially for teachers who were pregnant. Pam would also maintain communication with the other nurses, central office, and the county health department regarding any precautionary measures.

It was not uncommon to see kids walking around on crutches, pupils who were injured either in physical education class or sports practices or games. After winter break we prepared ourselves for the slew of students who would return from their February ski trips with sprains or broken limbs. Injured students did not participate in P.E. class and instead were assigned to the library tagged as "the walking wounded." Over the course of one year the library staff accommodated more than 130 pupils with injuries. Pam would meet with parents, develop support systems, and hand over an elevator key that was hardly ever returned.

Concussions also became commonplace and were now accommodated with learning plans, requiring professional training for our administrators, nurse, CST, and guidance counselors to better understand and manage expectations. We have had our fair share of repeat fainters, too, at times difficult for doctors to diagnose except for possible stress. Of course, we were as concerned about the causes of fainting as we were about possible injuries sustained from falling or sliding out of a desk. Pam also dealt with a number of students with epilepsy who experienced seizures during school hours.

We have had students with life-threatening medical conditions who required my ongoing communication with parents and doctors as well as more involved accommodations at school, situations too personal and specific to go into details about in this book.

In recent years our school has seen several students battle cancer, requiring them to be on home instruction or modified school attendance. When they returned to school, they often required rest or even a nap in the nurse's room. Tragically, a student succumbed to cancer during my time as principal.

Did I say that our school of nearly 1,200 students and approximately 125 adults had only one school nurse? Despite my budget personnel requests for more help in our health office, the formula for how many nurses should be on staff was based on the aggregate number of students in the district, not the number of students in a school. And our school student population far surpassed what was once the recommended ratio of one nurse for no more than 750 students by the American Academy of Pediatrics. Our school nurse had to do it all.

Nurses just don't sit and wait for something to happen. In addition to all the drop-ins who have real or imagined "boo-boos," or wanderlust students using the excuse of needing a lozenge, Pam dealt with periodic outbreaks of lice, chicken pox, and flu, dispensed medications all day, complied with individual student medical plans, addressed injuries and sudden illness, and accompanied children to the emergency room.

Pam also saw every child for updates on height and weight, vision and scoliosis screenings. She monitored compliance with vaccinations and completed paperwork for, and followed directives from, the county health office. She made sure every student had a timely physical. Pam directly and indirectly screened for signs of physical abuse, anorexia, cutting, or possible use of illegal substances. Her input on the I&RS Committee was an important component in developing a plan of action. It was she who had to recruit teachers for students on home instruction and troubleshoot to find solutions to accommodate students with unique medical circumstances.

Pam, as our school nurse, was an integral member of our school leadership team. I would know immediately if Pam had information, evidence or speculation about a student or something health-related brewing. We could talk about how to approach a possible problem with either one of us conferring with district doctors, government entities, or other nurses and administrators in the district. Our communication and collaboration was an important element of meeting our, as well as parental, expectations for a safe and healthy school environment.

Pam also reflected my vision of important middle school connections for kids. Students transitioning to adulthood present concerns about body image, hormonal changes, questions about sex and sexual orientation, and more recently about being transgender. All of these topics have to do with the physical and emotional, an intersection that seems like the natural purview of the school nurse, who in a very real way, and a point of The *New York Times* article, is also a counselor and advocate.

In a way, Pam reminded me of "Dear Abby" because she dispensed common sense and patience, calming children and adults alike. This was not only because in her professional training and background she had seen it all before, and much worse, but also because her instincts and intuition were important components of her assessment and response. In any kind of emergency, our nurse remained calm, focused and observant, the very characteristics that offer the best possible outcomes, in a hospital or a school.

# 21. Reinventing Leadership and Our Middle School

"PLOPs, PEEPs, AND PIPs SHOULD REPORT TO THE auditorium at this time."

It took me a while to get used to hearing announcements like this one over the public address system. Our peer leader group acronyms were fun and efficient, but also somewhat indelicate, perhaps betraying a resemblance between middle schoolers and their middle school teachers. Believe me when I say that I have heard even edgier suggestions from the more fertile thinkers among us. I did love their creativity and the way they identified each group's purpose, even if I was not entirely comfortable with all of the names.

A most amazing aspect of middle level learners is the shift from being self-centered to developing an emerging awareness of others and their needs. It is a social awakening where students begin to internalize the concept of justice and develop empathy. Middle level kids are alive with energy and inspiration. They embrace helping others, and it was our goal to channel their enthusiasm to lead and serve through our curricular and extra-curricular initiatives.

The word "curriculum" derives from the Latin root meaning "running." Curriculum is a current, like that of water or electricity, that powers the school's mission to educate the whole child. A strong vibe about academics already exists in districts like Millburn, but I have always held that academics alone are not enough.

Peer leadership had been a component of our school program long before I relocated from the classroom to the main office (a short trip, as my classroom for years was almost right next door). Becoming a peer leader back in the day was a knighting of students who stood out because of their excellent grades, exemplary comportment, and universal regard by teachers as born leaders.

Two of our teachers, Zsuzsanna Michael and Dominick Pisa, reframed the purpose of peer leadership to ask: "Why don't we expect *all* of our students to become leaders, and how do we help them to do that?" It was one of those times when the phrase "paradigm shift" actually turned an educational construct not upside down, but right side up. This new approach charted our character education program for more than the next two decades, connecting students not only to school and community outreach, but also to organizations that serve humanity around the globe.

While virtually all eighth graders who applied and interviewed were accepted into the program, membership was contingent upon remaining in good standing, both in school and in the peer leader program itself.

The hour after school every Wednesday was considered sacrosanct time for peer leaders to meet, first all together for general news, training, directions and messages, and then in groups to work on their goals. The various groups reflected a wide array of possible service opportunities. As you can see on the appendix at the conclusion of this chapter, where I highlighted peer leader projects during my last year as principal, each group had a specialization and one of those unique acronyms. It is not an exhaustive list of what peer leaders do or did, but readers can glimpse the diverse advocacy and beneficiaries that I believe made our school distinctive when it came to character education, leader empowerment, and service learning.

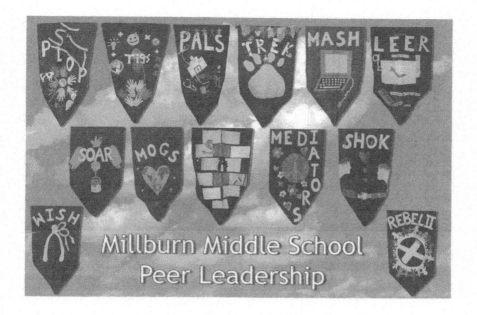

During the month of October, known in middle school circles as "The Month of the Young Adolescent," the middle school hosted a formal induction ceremony that included much pageantry as peer leaders paraded into the auditorium behind a banner that symbolized their special purpose, all wearing their peer leader T-shirts. Each group was introduced by its acronym and job description followed by the reading of the members' names. The spotlight shone on the peer leader inductees who also did all of the planning and preparation and most of the speaking. Invited guests included the DARE police officer and high school students who were former middle school peer leaders also on hand to administer the Peer Leader Pledge.

In 2007 Millburn Middle School was featured on the ABC nightly network newscast, *Nightline,* in a segment called "Echoes of Autism," about the transformative work of Millburn district psychologist Dr. Jed Baker. Through his training of our peer leaders he created a peer social support system in our school for students with Asperger's Syndrome, a form of autism. Dr. Baker had students practice doing something we took for granted, even before the advent of texting and other forms of digital communications: he had them practice talking. The art of conversation is a skill that is already tough enough to execute for a shy or awkward preadolescent, but it can be downright limiting for students coping with additional communication hurdles. These conversations generated important and enduring peer connections.

One realizes in moments like these that it was not just the students with a disability who were benefiting and learning. More "mainstream" students better understood the nature of spectrum disorders while embracing the opportunity to meet and come to know some pretty special individuals who happened to have a disability. Everyone involved moved forward, even if just a little, with a measure of acceptance, confidence, and perhaps commonality that we hoped would be turnkeyed to create a wider circle of tolerance and respect for students with disabilities in our school culture. For me, the cha-ching moment was when I would observe or hear about peer leaders and their new friends together at lunch or events sans the orchestration of an adult.

Peer leader groups changed from time to time, as other service opportunities opened and new advisors came into the fold. For example, several years ago Rebecca Nelson, a French/Spanish teacher, formed the group ECOLE (French for "school") to raise money for the promotion of literacy and education in French-speaking countries around the world. ECOLE raised over $2,000 to fund books and reading materials for the Little Rock Early Childhood Development Center, located in Africa's largest slum. The donation was instrumental in creating a space for reading at Little Rock dedicated as "The Millburn Library." Imagine what a great feeling it was for our students to know that they had made a difference in the lives of little children thousands of miles away on another continent.

I do not know of other middle schools who host a formal Thanksgiving program. For me, it always felt like a uniquely non-denominational yet spiritual gathering. It was a rare opportunity to celebrate American history, patriotism and culture together through speeches, presentations, videos and music. It came together thanks to our peer leaders.

The stage was transformed into a visual feast of colorfully decorated baskets and boxes of food waiting to be delivered to homes in time for the holiday. Homeroom students cut out turkeys, pilgrim hats, and cornucopias, making each container its own Thanksgiving greeting card. Prior to the assemblies, students packed the halls lugging hefty cartons of clinking cans and dry goods into the auditorium with their chatter adding to the animation of peer leaders rehearsing their roles for the imminent assembly.

Often there were educational programs planned that included readings, skits and short films made by our students. One memorable presentation was based on the book *If the World Were a Village* by David J. Smith, in which the whole world is viewed through the composition of a village of 100 people and the proportionality of nationalities, languages, ages, religions, etc. as well as factors indicative of quality of life.

The Thanksgiving Assembly included patriotic band selections and a choral performance of "Rain Dance" where the audience could hear the sudden gush of rainfall as the pebbles slid down inside the Native American rain stick. Representatives from Heifer International and the New Jersey Food Bank spoke about local and global poverty and hunger. It was a time for me to promote what I called "an attitude of gratitude" as I thanked our teachers and students as well as the peer leaders and their advisors. I have quoted Theodore Roosevelt, "Let us remember that, as much has been given us, much will be expected from us, and that true homage comes from the heart as well as from the lips, and shows itself in deed." I ended by telling students, "You have used your heart today."

At our 2017 Thanksgiving Assembly, representatives from Heifer International presented us with a plaque acknowledging the three Arks that our school, thanks to fundraising by peer leaders, had donated between 2006 - 2015. Each Ark represented a $5,000 donation to the organization for the purchase of livestock such as water buffalos, cows, pigs, sheep and goats, along with beehives, chicks, rabbits and more, in addition to funding training and support to develop sustainable farming, marketing and community development in villages around the world.

*Empty Bowls* was another way for our school to advance awareness of food insecurity in local communities and also to raise funds by hosting a community supper. Preparation started long before the event as various peer leader groups shaped, fired, and glazed the colorful bowls under the guidance of art teacher Claudia Sohr. These unique handmade bowls were included in the cost of admission and filled with piping-hot soup for dinner. My favorite bowl, of the several I purchased over the years, had watercolor strokes of denim and teal on a white background with flecks of yellow and reddish-orange.

Whole Foods generously donated tasty soups along with crusty French bread, and the P.T.O. purchased desserts. Guests were seated at long tables covered with white paper and crayons for doodling while waiting. Peer leaders were attentive in serving drinks, soups and desserts. Some were assigned dishwashing duty while others helped clean up after the event. Moms who attended this event watched with a sense of wonder and humor as their kids performed chores they avoided at home.

At our *Empty Bowls* fundraising dinner in March 2017, Community Food Bank of New Jersey honored Millburn Middle School with a plaque for our food donations and ongoing support.

As you can see from the appendix, much of the work that was accomplished by our students touched the heart, and it was our goal that in addition to learning about how to see a project through to its conclusion, students were also learning about the human condition and growing in empathy for people who did not have the blessings of health, wealth, or opportunity.

The peer leadership program complemented our mission to provide a values-based character education program. While the initial launch of the peer leader program was an extra-curricular enterprise, it eventually made sense for us to create coursework about leadership. Long before New Jersey established tougher laws about bullying, "Leadership for a Peaceful School" was teaching concepts regarding communication ("I statements"), bullying, tolerance, conflict, and mediation. The course established nomenclature and a standard of behavior in our school to which teachers, guidance counselors, child study team, and administrators could refer and build upon as they addressed conflicts and behaviors. It made a powerful statement to sixth graders about expectations at the middle school. It also acknowledged that students in this stage of development did not come equipped with social skills, so it was our job to provide them with some tools to learn how to interact with others.

I remember when Zsuzsanna Michael, a founder, coordinator, and the executive director of peer leaders, and I had a conversation in which she conveyed her observation about a lack of understanding in our students regarding their own capacity for leadership. My response was, "Let's teach them!" A seventh grade cycle leadership course was born. This innovative course had students using technology to research, write, and film scripts that were responses to the questions: What do you stand for? How tolerant are you? What would Gandhi do? What makes a great leader? And the declarative statement, "I am a leader." The content of this course studied historical and current world leaders and conflicts with an emphasis on nonviolent solutions to create peaceful and just change.

With the expansion of our leadership courses, I faced a unique challenge in advertising for a "leadership teacher." I was probably the only principal in the state conducting a search for a candidate who had experience teaching middle level language arts or social studies, familiarity with character education, facility with technology, and a grasp of the causes important to middle schoolers. The naysayers said I would never find such a person, but not only did I find the person I was looking for, I recruited someone who understood what we were trying to accomplish and could also help steer the ship. Over the years Steve Chernoski has held the mantle high as an innovative and enthusiastic teacher, curriculum developer, peer leader advisor/coordinator, mentor and role model.

The gamut of his instruction ran from basics to pushing boundaries. Steve could be seen escorting his sixth grade cycle leadership classes through the school while talking to students about what I call "the rules of the road." "What side of the hallways and stairwells should you be walking on? What do you do if someone's books fall? What should you do if you see someone being bullied? What should we be aware of whenever we open a door? We say 'please' and 'thank you' to others." Steve endorsed student-generated ideas and topics, even if somewhat uncomfortable, such as transgender students, to write about for the PEN, the peer leader online student newspaper. He exhorted his students to find out answers, even if it meant they should meet with the principal, or somebody smarter. He promoted experiments with kids to find out what daily life was like without a cellphone and always being "connected." His students' videos about conservation, recycling and resources conveyed timely and cogent messages.

Though it had been over twenty years since the establishment of this peer leader platform, both visionary co-founders, Dominick Pisa and Zsuzsanna Michael, continued to play coordinator or leadership roles. These founders advanced the planning, training, scheduling, and communication tasks - and the massaging inherent in any organization - that made everything happen. They also continued to be "idea people" and problem-solvers themselves. The organization never rested, and neither did the coordinators or the group advisors. It would just not be possible to have accomplished all of these inspiring achievements without the dedication, time, and leadership of all of the staff who made the program what it became.

This more inclusive paradigm of declaring all pupils who applied to the program a "peer leader" was not without its issues. Kids were still kids, and from time to time they made mistakes or behaved in a less than perfect manner. There have been pupils who were not thought of as "leaders" by their teachers and also sometimes by parents of their peers who considered their membership adversarial to the other participants and the program. These adults did not truly understand what we were trying to do. In fact, we considered all of our students "leaders in training."

Sometimes the greatest transformation occurred with the students whose acceptance into the program in the first place seemed dubious. One student who had more of a "mean girl" reputation prior to eighth grade dramatically transformed herself to winning a leadership award at the end-of-year ceremony. Another student who just had so many things going against him in his personal life, baggage from home that interfered with his academics and social life at school, found purpose, meaning and connection as a peer leader and improved his overall behavior, personal affect, and work ethic.

Whenever inducted peer leaders transgressed school rules or did not live up to the peer leader pledge, they had to participate in a conference with other peer leaders and advisory personnel. It was rare that students were expelled from peer leadership because it was our goal, as much as possible, to have them continue, follow a plan for reparation, and learn from the experience. Probationary students would be led back to the Six Pillars of Character, developed by Character Counts and the Josephson Institute of Ethics in Los Angeles, California. These pillars defined the values that constituted the beginning and end points for students' reflection and became the focus in helping them to understand what was unacceptable and more importantly, why.

Our school motto of Respect, Responsibility, and Excellence was also an intrinsic part of the messaging and reinforcement that pervaded peer leader training and expectations.

Peer leadership without a doubt had an impact on behavior in our school. I even felt sorry, at times, for students whose behavior merited an after-school general detention. General detentions were monitored by the peer leader organization, and if your behavior was such that an administrator had to be involved, then you had to face the music with peer leadership after an assistant principal was finished with you.

One phenomenon that I noticed right away was how the peer leadership program became self-perpetuating. Consider how frightened new sixth graders grow in confidence and courage when they are not gobbled up, bullied, or shoved into lockers by the older middle school kids, the longstanding lore they hear when they are about to embark for the middle school from their smaller, close-knit elementary schools. Instead, seventh and eighth graders are showing them around, sharing a video they created for their transition, answering their questions and coming to do fun activities in homeroom every week. Younger students see the important and responsible roles peer leaders have in the school community, and they hear from their older siblings about all of the peer leader accomplishments, so they often can't wait to become peer leaders themselves.

In 2007, the professional education journal *Principal* published an article I wrote about peer leadership. The piece traced the program's humble beginnings, begotten with volunteers and no budget, to the present with nearly 400 students and stipends for 17 teacher advisors and 3 coordinators.

In addition to extracurricular funding provided by the district, the Millburn Municipal Alliance secured grants in support of peer leader efforts to teach students about the dangers of alcohol, tobacco, and drugs. The PTO generously contributed to peer leader events by funding refreshments, shirts, supplies and other special requests. The Student Assistance Counselor at the high school applied for Character Education grants on behalf of the peer leader organization. It takes a village to support an undertaking of this magnitude.

Student conflicts had declined since the peer leader program's inception. Our pupils were engaged in meaningful outreach to others, and in the process, they learned more about themselves. Middle schoolers grew up some, learned how to work together, and became responsible, not just for their actions and contributions, but to people who depended on them. The program advanced student leaders' executive functioning skills, such as planning, organization, and problem-solving, while also promoting a work ethic and reflective qualities. Without a doubt, our peer leadership mission lent itself to exploration of vocation and career by our students.

As principal, one of my most important messages to peer leaders, especially when I met with the newest crop at the end of the prior school year, was that they were the face of our school. Peer leaders would be ambassadors representing our school to the community and outside organizations. What and how they achieved in the realm of service reflected on our school. Their reputation was our reputation.

I could not have been more proud of our students and teachers.

In my speeches at peer leader induction ceremonies I have often expressed my sentiment that the peer leader program was the heart of Millburn Middle School because it taught values at a time when students were undergoing an important evolution toward understanding the world. I concluded my address with an invitation to our coming-of-age middle school students: "Peer leadership offers opportunities for you to come to the realization that it is time you took your place to make a difference."

This new view of leadership and our determination to see its potential in all students was a way of reinventing our school and, in my view, of deepening our commitment to the tenets of an inclusive and exceptional broader middle level curriculum.

---

# APPENDIX

## MILLBURN MIDDLE SCHOOL
## PEER LEADERSHIP ACTIVITIES 2016-2017

**BOLT (Bringing Our Lives Together)** supported a variety of school and community causes:

- Cheered on athletes with disabilities at *New Jersey Special Winter Olympics*
- Donated non-slip diabetic socks for senior citizens who lived at Daughters of Israel Nursing Home
- Distributed sandwiches at *House of Mercy Mission*
- Conducted readings and crafts *at Neighborhood House Nursery School*
- Provided blankets for veterans through *Soldiers' Angels*
- Sponsored *Light It Up Blue* tie-dye party to promote school awareness about autism
- Designed T-shirt for Autism Awareness Month
- Posted Autism Awareness monthly displays

**SPORT (Students Promoting Off-Road Training)** promoted a healthy middle school life:

- Produced video about the core qualities of a strong leader
- Planned a seminar with coaches and students on responsibilities of student athletes

- Sponsored Coin Wars Super Bowl Competition for *Global Sports* for athletes with cancer and ALS
- Coordinated *Expand Your Brain* healthy breakfast campaign
- Hosted a healthy bake sale

**SOAR (Students Of Art Respond)** used art/media to build bridges with the community:

- Constructed art projects for cafeteria wall
- Designed banners for Peer Leader Induction Ceremony
- Painted Minions and crafted a mock-up of Felonius Gru with the robotics club
- Painted chair art for the child study team office
- Recycled K-cups for art projects
- Partnered with English Language Learners for a fundraiser called "International Cultures and Art"
- Sent homemade Thanksgiving cards to Overlook Hospital patients
- Designed iPhone cases for holiday fundraiser in support of *Let Girls Learn*
- Collaborated with MASH, DECO and WISH to raise $3,200 from *Empty Bowls* for Community Food Bank of NJ and Millburn's *Down the Block* community non-profit
- Designed and painted stage sets for *The Little Mermaid*
- Crafted art with senior citizens
- Created 2nd annual Earth Day Mandala at the Cora Hartshorn Arboretum

**PLOP (Peer Leader Outreach Program)** ran school programs and sponsored global initiatives for people in need:

- Donated 2,500 pounds of groceries from Thanksgiving Food Drive to Community Food Bank of NJ

- Invited *Heifer* to speak about how donations of livestock make possible stable farming communities
- Sold Halloween candy grams in support of *Heifer*
- Sold Valentine's Day treats also in support of *Heifer*
- Presented *Heifer* with a check in the amount of $1,500
- Posted hallway signs to foster better etiquette and traffic flow
- Collected donations in homerooms for *UNICEF*
- Raised over $800 for *Operation Smile,* doubled by matching gifts, to fund cleft palate surgeries
- Collected toiletries for homeless persons through *Bridges Outreach*

**MASH (Machine and Software Helpers)** supported school functions/ performed tech training:

- Prepared New Jersey annual "Week of Respect" bulletin board displays
- Designed and printed Peer Leader Induction Night programs
- Produced Peer Leader Induction Night video presentation
- Surveyed teachers for after school 1:1 tech tutorials
- Taught Smart Boards/Google Apps workshops for teachers
- Trained students in Scratch and Minecraft in preparation for *Hour of Code*
- Preparation of programs/tickets/bowls for *Empty Bowls* event
- Produced a video shown at *Empty Bowls*
- Organized videos/tours/Q&A for fifth grade orientation
- Shuttled 400 fifth graders to 4 activities during a 90-minute orientation

- Planned the Peer Leader Award Ceremony
- Assembled the Move-Up Ceremony video montage

**PEN (Peers Enriching News)** Inaugural year for online newspaper, *The Millburn Penpoint*:

- Launched first edition
- Advertised website on bulletin board displays
- Delivered "commercials" over public address during morning announcements
- Published editorials on diversity and holiday conservation
- Initiated a "photo of the month" theme contest
- Produced podcast debate on permitting cell phones in classes
- Planned a game show based on newspaper topics for parent open house
- Wrote articles: middle school bucket list, split notes craze, the Millburn Film Festival, Earth Day, how sleeping later is bad for the local environment, and fidget cubes and spinners

**CORE 8** students were selected for training in mediation and facilitation skills in seventh grade. They represent the true essence of Peer Leadership, promoting understanding and compromise between students, and protecting the integrity of the peer leadership program by holding peer leaders accountable:

- Taught 6th grade leadership lessons about differences between HIB and conflict
- Performed skits that emphasized role of "upstander" over "bystander"
- Hosted Dialogue Night discussions/break-out sessions on risk-taking behaviors for 300 attendees

- Continued training in mediation
- Mediated student conflicts
- Developed 6th grade lessons on mediation/problem-solving
- Facilitated Career Day by guiding speakers to 15 classrooms and leading Q&A sessions
- Entered original scripts about substance-free lifestyles in *Partnership for a Drug-Free NJ* competition.
- Planned a culminating activity on character and tolerance themes for sixth grade novel *Wonder*

**DECO (Designs Educating Children & Others)** searched for opportunities for recycling and reusing art in an effort to save the environment while helping others:

- Recycled binders from locker clean-outs
- Fashioned new group banners for Peer Leader Induction Ceremony
- Created art as holiday gifts for children in foster care or who lived in impoverished areas of New Jersey
- Coordinated robotics display at Evening of Excellence
- Designed programs for Evening of Excellence
- Led opportunity to sketch submissions for the Honors Art program at the high school
- Created recycled wearable art clothing
- Fabricated dolls for a local children's hospital

**STEAM (Student Techs Educate and Mentor)** enriched the school using science, tech, engineering, art, and math:

- Hosted a STEMINAR that led students through a timed design challenge

**PALS (Peers Always Lending Service)** connected with sixth graders:

- Welcomed sixth graders and hosted Q&A session
- Visited sixth grade homerooms on Fridays

**PIPS (Personal Improvement Planners)** assisted peers with academics and planned special elementary programs:

- Tutored students after school and in study halls
- Cut out paper links to create a human chain connecting elementary school students during an assembly reading of Dr. King's "I Have a Dream" speech
- Read books in honor of Dr. Seuss's "Read Across America" month and helped elementary school children cut out Dr. Seuss letters to add words/phrases to extend theme of kindness

**WISH (What If Students Helped?)** worked toward an annual goal of raising $3,000 to grant a child's wish through the *Make-A-Wish Foundation*:

- Researched the *Make-A-Wish Foundation*
- Conducted two bake sales
- Sold button pins
- Raised $3,500 in student-faculty volleyball "play-in challenge" with over 225 participants
- Combined last year's funds to grant wishes for two New Jersey children with life-threatening illnesses

# SEVENTH GRADE PEER LEADER GROUPS

The Peer Leadership program included three seventh grade groups. Members of these groups were selected by Peer Leadership advisors and coordinators.

The **P2P REACH** group stood for "peer to peer" and educated elementary school students about the dangers of alcohol, drugs, and harmful substances:

- Made red ribbons with senior citizens and decorated the local area for *Red Ribbon Week*
- Planned five theme days for students to participate in a drug and alcohol awareness campaign
- Analyzed TV Superbowl commercials' focus on alcohol-related products and their target audience
- Studied the placement of cigarettes in stores
- Designed a scavenger hunt for students to find clues and solve challenges in keeping with the theme of staying substance-free

**SHOK7 (Students Helping Other Kids)** worked with students with special needs by eating with them at lunch. Peer leaders partnered with and encouraged special needs students in physical education or worked with students who had developmental disabilities in their classroom by assisting with activities and demonstrating life skills.

**TIGS (Teen Institute of the Garden State)** facilitated peer mediation sessions and assisted with school functions:

- Utilized their training to mediate conflicts that students faced in or outside of school.
- Served as ambassadors for visitors and new students
- Broadcast Black History Month and other special announcements
- Sponsored "Random Act of Kindness" Week

# 22. What You See Is What You Get

THE ULTIMATE REASON TO BECOME A PRINCIPAL SHOULD BE to have a greater impact on teaching and learning through leadership. To be sure, there are people who desire to move up the ladder of administration for reasons of ambition or income. Sometimes the end goal is to become an assistant superintendent or superintendent, and having experience as a building principal fortifies one's resume. But leadership, for me, like teaching, was also a calling, even if I wasn't sure I wanted to pick up the phone.

An elementary principal once contacted me to ask if I was tired of doing the same thing year after year. He had an ulterior motive, though. Since there was another administrative vacancy in the district, he suggested I apply for that job because he was eyeing my position in order for him to gain some secondary level experience with his future sights set on a superintendency. I liked being stuck in the middle, though, and I wasn't tired. In fact, part of what I discovered was that a principal keeps learning on the job and can never predict what will be coming around the next bend in the road.

The title of principal was shortened from "principal teacher." I continued to view myself as a teacher, which afforded me the ability to relate to the total school environment and view proposals and policies, mine and others, from the lens of a classroom teacher. Teachers do not want to think that as administrators we had forgotten what it was like to be a classroom teacher, and especially a classroom teacher in Millburn. One of my former teachers summarized it this way: "As a teacher I could see that our values were the same."

While I was working on this book, Dr. Goerss challenged me to reflect on what I believed about leadership by considering various facets of the job. The principal is the ...

- main teacher
- BOSS
- role model
- curriculum leader
- character authority
- political strategist
- public relations specialist
- evaluator

The principal is all of the above, but the term that uniquely captures me and my leadership style is "caretaker." It is compatible with my belief that administration is indeed a ministry.

I have indicated that I considered a school leadership position because of my belief in collegiality and collaboration. It is one thing to say that someone believes in a team approach, and quite another to live the creed. Every day I ate lunch with all or some of the other administrators, Assistant Principals Theresa Gonnella and Dan Brundage, and Program Chair Luisa Young. Often guidance counselors or the few remaining district supervisors would join us. Our conversations centered on our work as well as our personal lives. We found amusement in our various interactions with students. We shared the lessons we saw in our teacher observations. I took the opportunity to update everyone about the news from central office or Student Liaison or PTO meetings. We talked about our challenges and explored possible approaches.

It does not have to be lonely at the top.

We discussed upcoming events and articulated our specific roles. For years new sixth grade parents referred to the middle school as a "well-oiled machine," and I think this acknowledgement was owed to how we continually communicated to plan seamless transitions and experiences.

Always working within a team mindset, I knew my colleagues brought to the table their experience, training, perspective, and expertise. The process of reflecting, weighing, challenging, and debating expands thinking and aids decision-making. My administrative colleagues noted that this kind of partnership was not the way it was in other districts, and it is true that traditional leaders tend to be more unilateral in their thoughts and actions. John Rogers, in penning a retirement farewell in his final GUIDELINES column, wrote, "Their (our administrative team) welcome dialogue with the Guidance team has empowered us all; the "shared ownership" of middle school decisions has been a source of great professional satisfaction!"

The inner circle, in addition to assistant principals and program chair, included our school nurse, guidance counselors, and the child study team consisting of a school social worker, a school psychologist, and a learning disabilities teacher-consultant. This respective team of Linda Ariel, Linda Randazza, and Ronnie Thompson established a model of collaboration and shared expertise known throughout the district. In addition to case management, testing, writing reports, and meetings, each of them was a valuable resource for staff members and administrators regarding how to manage the multiple situations that arose with classroom learning and social interactions involving students with disabilities. They were the epitome of the expression, "If you want something done, ask a busy person." They almost never said no despite how overwhelming their workload or how much they were needed by kids, parents, and teachers.

The child study team kept me posted about developing situations and, though we tried to schedule regular formal meetings, there just did not seem to be time to do so. But, like with the guidance counselors, we had many impromptu conversations and check-ins. I considered them an important part of my administration; while we did not always agree on all matters, one would be hard-pressed to find such committed, competent and caring individuals who helped guide my decision-making and thinking, as well as learning on the job.

I trusted and depended on the people around me.

Detective Edward de la Fuente was a valued ad hoc member of our administrative team. Over the years Detective Ed dropped by often to check in and chat as we continually worked together on student incidents or developments regarding issues of child welfare, especially as we saw how technology was changing student behavior and opening doors to dangers that had not existed before. Our students knew him well from their days in the DARE program at the elementary level, and they greeted him like a movie star when he walked through the halls. This familiarity enabled him to play the role of a teacher or mentor in one-on-one situations with students, even if he had to assume a more serious posture at times. Detective Ed understood middle schoolers, and he really cared about kids.

The truth of the matter is that everyone in the building plays an important role in carrying out the mission of a school, including secretaries, custodians, cafeteria workers and paraprofessionals. Again, understanding and love for middle schoolers were key to their job roles and personalities. Our head custodian, Mr. Slawomir Dzieszko, known to us as "Suave," trained to become a teacher in his native Poland and was generous to a fault, as well as professional and kind to students and adults.

After working together for so long, it was true that members of the inner circle could predict what another was going to say, be able to finish someone else's sentence, or impishly await an anticipated reaction. After all of the deliberations, however, there was an endpoint, and the decision belonged to the principal.

Another way in which I tried to be a caretaker was to safeguard our staff's ability to do their jobs by protecting them from the broad unbaked ideas, rumor mill, criticisms or any other nonsense generated by parents, central office or the board. The exception to that rule, of course, was when there was an accusation or more serious criticism specific to a teacher who, in my opinion, had a right to know. In fact, depending on the nature of a complaint, I almost always asked parents if they had spoken directly with the teacher first. One would be surprised by how often teachers are not afforded a fair process, by parents or principals, to include the teacher's version of events or the context in which an interaction occurred.

I walked around the building at least a couple of times a day, to see and to be seen. I could tell a lot about what was happening by just observing. I ran into teachers prepping for class or on hall duty and had a chance to catch up. I would also, of course, meet students along the way, and one would be surprised at how many times I saw someone or something that later connected to an incident or a student under scrutiny. It felt like I was meant to be there, but the truth of the matter is that administrator visibility can prevent the opportunity for, or at least stem, the proliferation of unwanted behaviors.

Presence is important, but it is also challenging in a large school with many meetings, people, and ample administrivia to tether the principal to the office. I also learned that an "open door policy" meant the door was often closed!

In order to continue to have a finger on the pulse of the teachers' perspective, I dropped in on staff during their lunch gatherings, lunch duty, in their classrooms or offices, and sometimes at team meetings. I held round-table meetings after school with a teacher-driven open agenda, and teachers were also members of the School Leadership Team. I cherished my conversations with teachers about anything and everything, including topics from professional, social, spiritual or family realms.

Post-observation conferences provided opportunities to talk about teaching and learning, about greater instructional, programmatic, or even district initiatives and changes, and a chance for me to personally acknowledge teacher dedication and craft.

As an educational leader, I encouraged teachers to take a risk and try something new in their pedagogy. The surest way to create a positive teaching and learning environment is to be supportive and encouraging. I hated the idea that teachers looked at observations as a "gotcha" opportunity for administrators. Announced classroom observations created more stress because there was an expectation that because the teacher knew about it, the administrator would be looking for the perfect lesson replete with bells and whistles. In more recent years teachers would tell me that they would rather not know and I should visit anytime I wish.

Translation: Every lesson is worthy of being experienced.

While I was writing this book, my daughter asked me if I had ever taken the *Myers-Briggs Type Indicator Test*. I partook of this assessment in graduate school a long time ago, so I was game to do it again. It was determined my indicator type was "The Caregiver." Maybe it was coincidental that I had already written about how I characterized my perceived principal leadership style, but here was a form of validation within the context of something I think is extremely important to the success of a school leader: personality.

Some of the terms used to describe my type were "people person," "extremely good at reading others and understanding their points of view," "highly supportive of others," "takes responsibilities very seriously," "natural tendency to want to control their environment," "dominant function demands structure and organization," and "traditional." While there were more details, most of which I agree were reflective of my personality, not all of it was a match. What was also not surprising was that the list of possible career paths for my personality type included teacher, administrator, clergy, or counselor. Maybe "LT," the nun who hoped I would join the clergy, was onto something. It made sense that I could also see so many of the characteristics common to the helping professions in my administrative and teacher colleagues.

So many rituals revolve around food that it would not come as too much of a surprise that foods, mostly sweets, were a way of expressing our gratitude and celebrating personal milestones for our faculty. With an assistant principal like Theresa who loved to bake and feed the masses, the end result was a lot of happy people. Theresa would bake brownies, cookies, muffins and cupcakes for the entire staff (125 people) for the opening of school and again on Valentine's Day. Theresa would also host showers to celebrate upcoming weddings and babies, and she even baked for her department meetings and our monthly superintendent summits.

Some of us had our own specialties that we would share within the office, including Theresa's mountainous chocolate brownie birthday layer cake, Lisa's Flan, Roseann's Salami Pie, Ann Marie's Pignoli and Anisette cookies, Rene's Italian cheese pie, and my Irish soda bread. The trough of chocolate in my office gave people reasons to wander in "looking for something sweet" and some fellowship.

I would like to think we as administrators tried to create a family atmosphere at the middle school, one in which we valued our relationships with each other. And that did not necessarily mean everyone was happy all the time, or always liked everything that another person said or did, just like any other family.

Some musings about being the boss. Sometimes I forgot that I was the boss. Perhaps that was because I did not always have to be the boss in the traditional authoritarian sense that I eschewed early on. I had something of a history, connection, or relationship with just about everybody in the building. I was sometimes unaware how meaningful it was to others when I spoke to staff members about an upcoming event or proposal or invited them to participate on a committee or an interview panel or host a visitor. It meant a lot to be included, to be validated, and it was more powerful because it came from the principal. But I also learned that as principal I had to safeguard that personal relationships and approachability did not impede my responsibility to put kids and school first, or to have an honest conversation with staff about change or professionalism or some ineffective facet of job performance. My job as the school's leader was to keep everyone moving forward; I had little time or capacity for egos, games or prolonged grudges. And I quickly learned some leadership survival skills such as knowing how to pick my battles (early on I learned the expressions "not a hill to die on" and "legitimize what you can't control"), discovering the importance and benefits of being patient, and reserving the right to reflect on a response.

Other times I could not forget that I was the boss. Everybody needed me to do something, usually right away. Speak with a contractor. Return to the office because of an unexpected situation. An impromptu meeting with the fire marshall. Union grievances about classrooms being too hot or cold, bathroom cleanliness, and copiers, copiers and copiers. Unexpected visits from child protective services. Review or reconsider a decision about a placement. Read and sign time-sensitive HIB or special education documents. Find out more about new students before scheduling them. Sometimes I had to be the mediator for adult conflicts or intervene to stop parents from being disrespectful or attacking a member of the staff. Freedom of expression has to be tempered with civility and appropriate language.

When it came to making what I thought were the most difficult decisions, I realized that there were actually two parts. The first was to render a decision, and the second was to communicate it. The latter was more challenging because of its personal impact, such as conveying student placement decisions. Or informing a non-tenured staff member that his or her contract would not be renewed. Or reassigning a teacher to a different grade level or school building.

For several years in a row, a half dozen teachers had to leave their comfort zone grade level to teach a different grade that had a larger enrollment. While teachers are certified to teach all middle school grades, they often develop an expertise in the subject matter at a certain grade level or have a special connection to the developmental nature of a specific age. Looming grade level reassignment was another source of stress in what had become an overcrowded, underfunded school. Luckily, teachers oftentimes volunteered their service in response to my solicitation at a faculty meeting. It said a lot about their willingness to work together as a community and to expand their own professional learning.

I would like to think that another summary term for my leadership practice was "communicator." I always tried to connect the dots as I participated in meetings with the PTO, Student Liaison, faculty, administrative councils, and School Leadership Team. Legitimate concerns might come up at Student Liaison that needed to be addressed with the faculty. Questions or issues could arise with teachers or parents that required discussions with both. Cross pollination of groups and issues provided perspectives and shed light on what was a real problem and what was mere perception. Sometimes, communication, rationale or clarification is all that is required to calm the stormy sea, even if only for a little while.

Our School Leadership Team was an exchange between school personnel and parents. These meetings were led by me and included a guidance counselor, four teachers, and four parents, including a PTO co-president and a special education parent representative. Parents shared perceptions based on their observations of their children doing homework, eavesdropping on pupil conversations in the carpool, or talking with other moms. Teachers provided insights into the behind-the-scenes of what we did in school, enlightening parents who discovered there was more to an assignment or rule or practice or event than met the eye. I provided articles on leadership, middle level education, homework, and other contemporary topics.

We often did not get through the agenda because of our hearty discussions. Sometimes, we decided to seek more information or conduct a survey, such as about the amount of homework or school start times, or reach out to other districts or bring in a speaker who had expertise. The whole purpose was school improvement. It was a small venue conducive to debate and analysis, and it was a way for me to be collaborative, engaged and transparent.

Penning a PTO newsletter column every month was another way of communicating and threading the topics of conversation from various stakeholder groups. It was also a tool for me to educate parents about middle level learners and our school's mission or to share timely organizational messages or information about imminent school reforms.

I did not understand early on that the role of a public school principal is impacted by political decisions that sometimes thrust the school's leader into the middle of a maelstrom. I could not anticipate that there would be massive resistance to a standardized test that pitted me between parents and my mandate to administer the PARCC. Or that I would be vilified for having to conduct an HIB investigation if an allegation met the state criteria. Or that I would be considering unisex bathrooms to accommodate transgender children. Or that I would be criticized for a curriculum that included such topics as global warming or socialism or suicide prevention or sexuality.

On rare occasions, I had to deal with people who had personal political agendas. A central office administrator tried to convince me to change my recommendation about the best way to schedule excess students before construction of additional classrooms was completed. Two camps had emerged, and this person was aligned with some board members while other board members supported the superintendent's stance. This administrator explicitly charged that I would rather agree with the superintendent than do what was right for students in my care. I was furious at the accusation that I would hurt kids in order to be on the same page with the superintendent in a political tug-of-war. What the administrator failed to understand was that the superintendent, who valued my thinking, was supporting my position, not the other way around.

Anyone who really knew me understood that this was the case.

Other personal political machinations can test one's character with an unanticipated or uncomfortable question. A new board member approached me privately at a social event and asked me what I *really* thought about the superintendent, you know, just between the two of us. I did not know this individual. We had never met or spoken before. Said board member was obviously on a fishing expedition. On two other occasions, former board members put me on the spot with their prying questions and immediately and amusingly concluded that I did not have the ability to lie. I was raised to believe that was a good thing, although judging by their reaction it must have been a rare expectation in their circles.

I wanted nothing to do with any of this, which was why I never sought a central office position. Headhunters tried to recruit me to fill superintendent vacancies, and a board member of another upscale New Jersey community personally contacted me about applying for her district's top leadership post, but the most authentic setting in education for me was working with kids and teachers.

What you see is what you get. That did not change regardless of whether I was speaking at a faculty meeting, PTO meeting, principals' meeting or in a parent conference. My colleagues have also told me that my facial expression, body language, or even attention span communicated some response, judgment or decision long before I uttered a sound.

# 23. The State of the Union

IN THE TWILIGHT OF MY TIME AS PRINCIPAL, WITHOUT A doubt, a landslide of more enduring and revolutionary changes challenged principals and teachers to keep up, not just with the volume of revisions but also with the pace. During this 21st Century "reformation," other external developments occurred as well that exacted a greater toll, emotionally and financially, on all who called themselves educators. Ominous dark storm clouds had gathered over the Little Red Schoolhouse, threatening the livelihoods of professionals who dedicated their careers to working with children.

2011 will be remembered by teachers and all public school staff in New Jersey as the culmination of years of betrayal. It was the year that Democratic State Senate Leader Stephen Sweeney colluded with Republican Governor Chris Christie to broker a deal on how to salvage a state teacher pension system that probably would not have become insolvent had it not been for the neglect of this governor as well as his predecessors. Changes promulgated by new regulations forced educators to contribute a higher percentage of their salary into the pension fund, altered the age at which new tiers of state employees would become eligible for retirement, revised the formula for pension income, and suspended Cost-of-Living Adjustments (COLA) for present and future retirees. The most draconian reform compelled school personnel to contribute up to 35% of the cost of their health care premiums whereas until this time health benefits were included in the state benefits package for free. In return for these "givebacks," Christie promised to make full annual payments into the pension plans.

Wasn't he supposed to be doing that anyway?

This bipartisan collaboration was a sweet victory for a governor with Presidential aspirations. But Sweeney's pact with Christie came back to bite him, and all educators, when Christie later reneged on his promise to fully fund state contributions and vowed to veto any legislation that legally required the state to do so.

The New Jersey state teachers' pension fund was robust in the 1990's, but according to a *Star-Ledger* article (3/5/18) entitled "So How Did New Jersey Get Into This Crisis, Where the Giant Public Employee Pension Systems Are $46 Billion in the Hole?" Lisa Fleisher wrote, "Since 2004, the state has withheld $9.5 billion in recommended payments and municipalities have withheld $1.9 billion." Robert D. Klausner, who authored an op-ed for *njspot-light.com* (12/23/16) entitled "Christie Will Leave Taxpayers Huge Bill in Pension Payments," explained the compounding financial impact of skipping contributions: "But here is the reason taxpayers should be outraged by this financial mismanagement. By continuing to skip or reduce payments now, as has been over the past 15 budget cycles by both Democratic and Republican administrations, our pension bill is growing exponentially because it is not accruing investment returns on these missed payments."

A recession and an ill-advised decision to increase benefits further diminished the value of the pension fund.

Even in 2018, after all of the changes forged by the 2011 legislation, politicians recommended additional reforms as the pension crisis escalated, including cuts in health insurance. A *nj.com* article (5/24/18) by Samantha Marcus entitled "How Is New Jersey's Public Pension Fund Doing?" reported that "New Jersey's pension fund is considered the worst-funded of U.S. public retirement funds, with enough assets to cover just 62.4 percent of its $159 billion in liabilities." There were those who predicted that the day would come when the pension would fall short of its ability to meet its obligations - not the fault of those of us who did our part and held the expectation that, in order to honor its contract with state employees, the state would do its part, too.

The passage of the Health and Benefits Reform law, Chapter 78, P.L. 2011, a.k.a. "The Sweeney Bill," was a scary time for New Jersey educators, especially for those who were eligible to retire. Thousands of teachers retired out of fear that future pension benefits would erode before they were able to retire - thinking once retired, hopefully, politicians would not poke the retired bear. Retired educators did not have to pay for health benefits, though that, too, had become a proposal under consideration. It made sense for employees to retire and receive free health benefits instead of continuing to work for a paycheck significantly less than they were already bringing home.

So many people retired, in fact, that the state pension system was now more imperiled by the addition of thousands of retirements by panicked educators, many of whom would otherwise have remained on the job and continued to contribute to the pension fund. According to a *nj.com* article (2/28/11) entitled, "NJ Public Workers Are in a Hurry to Retire," by Jarrett Renshaw, 7,132 teachers retired in 2010, nearly doubling the number of teachers who retired in 2009. This exodus, driven in part by a governor who attacked teacher benefits and unions and was captured on video shouting and wagging his finger at teachers, was also accompanied by a significant brain drain of so many experienced and talented teachers.

Those who remained started to count the years.

On top of that, new legislation capped superintendent salaries based on district enrollments. This resulted in a migration of superintendents, including Millburn's, out of state. New Jersey superintendents could work in New York or Pennsylvania earning, as in our former superintendent's case, nearly $50,000 more than allowed by New Jersey law. The long-term effect was the hemorrhage of seasoned and often respected district leaders.

Now, several years later, an article written by Adam Clark for The *Star-Ledger* (12/16/18) titled "Christie's Cap on Superintendent Salaries Totally Backfired" explained the effect of this misguided attempt to save taxpayer money: "Minimal reductions in districts' overall spending, all likely offset by the loss of talented and experienced school leaders, according to a new study." Clark quotes Michael Hayes, an assistant professor of public policy and administration at Rutgers who conducted the study: "Restricting just one employee's wage, base salary, would not have a major impact on education's cost." His study also backed up anecdotal evidence of superintendent after superintendent either retiring or fleeing to nearby states for higher salaries. But what the article also does not say is that boards of education, like Millburn's, offered their new superintendents merit bonuses based on achievement of established goals, devising a roundabout though legal way to further compensate the district CEO. It did not seem like saving money was necessarily a district goal.

Overall, these new legislative acts demoralized teachers and administrators throughout New Jersey. That is not to say that our education colleagues in other states across the nation did not have their challenges as well. In her 2014 memoir *Breaking the Silence: My Final Forty Days as a Public School Teacher*, New York City teacher M. Shannon Hernandez wrote, "After fifteen years as a public school teacher, I knew my time was limited due to dealing with issues such as pay freezes, increased insurance rates, principals who forced me to work outside of my contract, and teacher evaluation systems that are neither logical nor fair. While I love teaching, I refuse to be someone else's whipping girl or stay in a job where my value is not recognized or appreciated."

In fact, in a *Wall Street Journal* article (12/28/2018) written by Michelle Hackman and Eric Morath entitled "Teachers Quit Jobs at Highest Rate on Record," it was reported that in the first 10 months of 2018 public educators quit at an average rate of 83 per 10,000 *per month*, according to the Labor Department, the highest rate for public educators since such records began in 2001. The writers suggested that "educators may be finding new jobs at other schools or leaving education altogether," linking this phenomenon to "six states where teachers in some cases shut down schools over tight budgets, poor raises and poor conditions."

Back in New Jersey the rough rhetoric between the governor and the New Jersey Education Association (NJEA), the state teachers' union, made rank-and-file members feel like they were being persecuted. Christie seemed to ignite greater resentment in people who begrudged the fact that educators received a state pension. Needless to say, there was little public sympathy for the new requirement that educators pay for health benefits "just like everybody else," especially after the recession of 2008. Others still insisted that educators were overpaid because teaching was not so hard a job and teachers were home by 3:30 and got vacations and summers off.

Where was the public outcry when I accepted my first teaching job for an annual salary of $15,000, also in an affluent New Jersey suburb? Even in 1983, New Jersey was not an inexpensive place in which to live. How would a fledgling teacher pay rent, college loans, car payments, and provide for the basic necessities of food and clothing on those pre-tax wages?

My parents had hoped that I would move on from my desire to become a teacher. In our conversations they talked about the lack of respect and poor compensation, but what I did not understand until many years later was the connection between the two. However, it was the promise of a pension and health care that would make up for the delta between the compensation of education majors and our peers in the business school after graduation from college.

New Jersey is a funny place. The very people - like some members of my extended family - who resented public workers' benefits were the same relatives who encouraged younger members of the clan to work for the state precisely to obtain those benefits. Today more and more people, including those who can afford to live among the wealthiest zip codes, are vocal about public worker pensions. It is ironic to me that teachers, cops, and firefighters are demonized, despite their essential public service, instead of the governors, their appointed cabinets, and legislators who sabotaged their pensions. While there are some outliers in public service whose contracts have had a bright spotlight shone on them for collecting outrageous sums of money for unused sick and vacation days upon retirement, the vast majority of public workers are not the recipients of these sometimes not-so-small fortunes.

Shortly after my retirement, my wife and I encountered a former school parent in a Millburn store who had heard I retired and commented, "At first I paid taxes to fund your salary and now I pay taxes to fund your pension, and I bet it's a good one." The store owner, my wife and I were frozen in disbelief. I was saddened by this treatment after 30 years of service to this community. Oddly, I understood that there was nothing personal in her thinking toward me; nonetheless, it was appalling treatment from anyone, but harder still from someone whose children were blessed to grow up in such an affluent community and attend reputable schools.

In this climate it seemed there would be no demand for accountability for what happened to the teachers' pension fund, that is, how payments to the future financial well-being of loyal state employees who perform one of the most important jobs in society could be skipped with impunity. It did not make sense to me that there effectively was no legal requirement for the state government to *fund* pensions despite a legal contract for the state to *provide* pensions for state employees.

Even if governors did not have a legal obligation to contribute to the pension on an annual basis, it did not mean there was no moral imperative. Teachers and taxpayers entrusted governors, state employees, and lawmakers with a fiduciary responsibility for the maintenance of state employee retirement plans. Ironically, the casualties of their dereliction of duty were expected to make up the difference. It is tantamount to our government leaders and their financial expert panels saying to educators, "It does not matter how we got here, we are here now, and it is your problem, and YOU have to fix it - and good luck with that."

Educators with fewer than twenty years in the pension system on the cut-off date saw their retirement postponed and their pensions and benefits decreased. For the first time I heard teachers talk about how they would not encourage young people to join the profession because of this rising culture of resentment and lack of respect for teachers in which they not only lost wages, but also a sense of security.

In a CNBC article (7/11/17) entitled "America's 10 Most Expensive States to Live In in 2017," Scott Cohn wrote that New Jersey was ranked #10, an explanation for why many New Jersey retirees head to financially friendlier places like Delaware, the Carolinas or Florida. But the teachers who lived and worked here not only had more money deducted from their salaries, they also had to hope that their local association could procure for them a new contract with a reasonable raise won through the negotiations process. Even with increments gained in successive contracts, they would never make up the cumulative out-of-pocket sum for the required portion of their health insurance premiums since the Sweeney Bill was enacted. And, if one's salary increased, so too could one's required share of the cost of the premium.

New Jersey residents live in one of the costliest states in the nation, but also attend schools in one of the best states for education in the country. In fact, on its website, *U.S. News and World Report* declared New Jersey "the top state for education" in the nation for 2021 (Brett Ziegler, *usnews.com*). The teachers who achieve this kind of "first place" success also need to be able to provide for themselves and their families.

The word "negotiations" is a misnomer when it comes to renewing a contract between a board of education and the teachers' union, or in my case, the administrators' association. While the NJEA supports its teachers through the negotiations process by providing skilled negotiators and the money and resources of a powerful lobby, it is not the same way with administrators. Both teacher and administrator associations, though, are subject to the hidden agendas and control of the local board of education, its superintendent, business administrator and attorney. If they don't want to meet with you, they don't. What are you going to do about it? Get your teachers to wear blue shirts on Mondays? Picket in front of the school on Wednesday mornings? Crowd a board meeting and pray to make your point early on so you can go to bed because you have to get up early and teach the next day? Educators are professionals who have no other recourse but to hope to influence the board and community for a fair settlement through their activism, but they feel degraded to have to fight for a decent wage.

For administrators, with our expansive managerial and leadership responsibilities, there is literally nothing one can do in protest that does not feel like it is a breach of post or professionalism.

In the September of my last school year in Millburn, the board of education published as one of its goals the settlement of personnel contracts. I was impressed that the board, who did not negotiate in earnest during the prior collective bargaining process, was going to get it done before the end of the school year, before the current contract expired, and before the president of the administrators' association, me, retired.

But it turned out to be another shell game. Even after I left the district, another entire year went by without a settlement. The resources of the district were spent on the reopening of another school.

According to *Oxford*, "negotiation" literally means "discussion aimed at reaching an agreement." Seems to imply two sets of people talking to each other. The reality of contract negotiations is something vastly different.

For that prior round of negotiations, our association representatives and several board members commenced the process with a cordial introduction before contract talks started where we dined on curry and other potluck foods while sharing our perspectives and ideas. So, imagine our surprise when, at the next negotiations meeting, those same board members made a fleeting appearance merely to inform us that the scheduled session for which we were already present was being canceled and henceforth they would not talk to us without the presence of the board attorney. At the subsequent gathering, the board attorney did all the talking. We were told that no consideration would be given to any of the items laid out in our handsome spreadsheet, and the take-it-or-leave-it increment was what it was. And if we did not agree tonight, we would risk losing our retroactive increment pay.

My negotiations team would tell you that we, and especially I, have been called names and yelled at in the pursuit of bullying us to accept what the board's representatives were offering. In the end most of our members, who constitute the district's so-called "leadership team" of administrators and supervisors, did not really have the stomach for this way of trying to improve our lot in life, and minimal increments were approved by our members, most happy to receive a raise. Some of my colleagues shrugged off the name calling and bullying, saying it was just a part of the game. But I have a hard time accepting that this process involving professionals on both sides of the table is unable to be conducted in a more respectful manner. It simply required the will to do so.

In an earlier round of negotiations, the board actually violated our contract by removing what was known as the "traditional" indemnity health benefits plan. This more expensive plan had been grandfathered only to employees like me who were hired before the late 1990's. The board's action precipitated a lawsuit from the teachers' association and also the administrators' union. But, in the end, even though a settlement was reached in which our members received a one-time payment to resolve the Unfair Labor

Practice complaint, this board of education tactic had the potential of yielding longer-term savings for the district at the financial and emotional expense of its employees. Teachers, administrators and staff depended on the board for their health benefits and compensation as well as for the board's fidelity to provisions of earlier negotiated contracts still in effect. It is an illustration of how boards and district officials bully and maneuver instead of negotiate, even in one of the most affluent and reputable school systems in the country. Unfortunately, it reinforced the idea that educators were not only vulnerable to what state politicians were doing, or not doing, but also to the brazen war games of the leadership in their very own district.

Ironically, all of this drama was moot because soon after came the Sweeney Bill, which would have required even more money deducted from the paychecks of district employees if they chose to continue enrollment in this more costly insurance option.

With regard to local district decisions about salaries, increments, and other expectations of fairness, there are two assertions I hold as true about all the supposed "negotiating." First, compensation, as people in most professions know, says something about what you are worth. Second, the way you are treated in the process says something about your employer.

At the beginning of this decade, after our association agreed to an increment and contract language, the board's negotiating team sent us to the superintendent to figure out how to put together an administrative salary framework. The new superintendent was surprised that our paltry administrator contract lacked any structure on starting salaries based on job descriptions, years of experience, or anything else. Those of us with longevity in the district joked that a former human resources director decided what new employees would earn based on how the Yankees performed the night before. Needless to say, salaries were all over the place, and this was another example of that infamous "Millburn Way," a mindset that Millburn is exempt from working within the normal conventions, requirements, processes or frameworks one would expect in most districts. This leaves room for flexibility, evolving preferences, broad interpretation or alternate universe.

Let's just say that creating a salary guide was a monumentally complicated task, but one I was relieved and pleased we could put together. While not everybody was happy with the end results, they never are.

However, over time administrative starting salaries in every district have to be adjusted to keep them attractive for teachers earning at the top of the teacher salary guide who aspire to become school leaders. Candidates also look to the market for competitive salaries when searching for jobs, which is why my association and I had been lobbying during the years between contract negotiations to raise the starting points, and adjust the salaries of some existing administrators, to avoid having a newly hired administrator earn more than someone who has been on the job for, say, eight years.

My administrative colleagues and I watched candidates walk away from offers of employment because they were already making as much or more in their current salary or because another district offered greater compensation. We arrived at two conclusions. The first was that people were not willing to come to Millburn just for the privilege of working in Millburn. The second was that the district was left to hire candidates that were not top notch matches for the job. You get what you pay for.

Upon my departure Millburn had to hire a replacement for me and also for another principal. When the time came to apply these starting salaries, our association was told that the salary grid was not a part of the contract.

Say what?

I was a part of the process, as were several of my colleagues. As leader of my association, I was consulted many times over a period of six years by two superintendents about those starting points, and as much as they or I wanted to digress from the grid to make it more attractive for someone to accept a position in Millburn, or to increase compensation for someone already working in the district, we always agreed to stay on point in order not to establish a new precedent and avoid conflict and more Millburn mishegoss. Those starting salaries were even affirmed in corrections approved on board personnel reports when new administrators had been hired at an incorrect wage.

The work was done, collegially and as fairly as it could be, yet the district was disingenuous by claiming a technicality to disregard our work in order to set different starting points, without our input, based on new criteria and without regard for the compensation of veteran employees. The Millburn Way was again alive and well, adding fuel to the perception of a lack of fidelity to agreements and the unfair treatment of long-serving administrators. These stories serve to illustrate the kinds of war games that erode trust between educators and district bureaucrats, calling into question the integrity of any decisions achieved through goodwill collaboration or the nebula of negotiations.

In my opinion, the collective bargaining process is rather archaic and a product of the home rule of which New Jersey seems so fond. The types of benefits available to professionals who do the same job around the state actually depend on the district in which one works. Salaries are not always representative of the total package of compensation as some districts offer monetary benefits that may not technically be categorized as salary, such as paying employee union membership fees or making deposits into employee retirement savings accounts, for example.

All of us who worked within the field of education were affected directly and indirectly by the actions, or inaction, of state leaders from the past twenty years to the present as New Jersey educators continue to hear about the vulnerability of our pension fund.

Everything was changing, not just on the inside with curriculum, instruction, assessment, and technology, but also simultaneously on the outside, specifically the jeopardization of a once certain future counted on after a life's career of dedication to one's students and for the greater good of society.

It did not take long to see the impact of these wrecking ball reforms on the future of our profession. A *Star-Ledger* article written by Amanda Hoover entitled "Fewer People Are Studying to Become Teachers in NJ. Could Higher Pay, Appreciation Reverse the Trend?" published on May 6, 2020, summarized findings from a New Jersey Policy Perspective report. According to the report, the number of students in teacher education programs in New Jersey has dropped by almost half over the last ten years. "Researchers attribute those losses to an onslaught of issues. They include low pay in comparison to other college graduates, benefits changes, high costs to become a teacher and several statewide policy changes that both added barriers to receiving a certification and made the job more difficult."

Other nearby states - New York, Pennsylvania, and Delaware - were also cited as experiencing similar precipitous drops in enrollments in teacher preparation programs.

Nobody enters the teaching profession thinking he or she is going to make a lot of money. Teachers around the nation moonlight or tutor to supplement their take-home pay, just like I did, in order to continue to do what they love and earn sufficient wages to support their families.

Our profession is not just a job, it is also a vocation, a noble calling at its best, I believe, in a culture of collaboration, support and appreciation. Most practitioners in the field of education would tell you that emotional currency is just as important as the monetary one.

In this 21st Century, the great COVID-19 pandemic has introduced us to virtual learning, a stopgap measure until it was safe once again for teachers and children to return to the classroom. It is tragically ironic that our profession is simultaneously plagued by political malfeasance and conditions that cause teachers, principals, and superintendents to leave and discourage college students from pursuing a career in education.

No vaccine can remedy what ails one of the most important occupations in society. It is not enough to simply hope that young people will once again aspire to our profession despite the diminished remuneration and benefits that once made it both attractive and possible for talented individuals to spend their lives teaching, encouraging and inspiring their students.

Time is of the essence for politicians and school boards to inject significant support for educators and enact bold legislation that attracts teacher candidates of all ages and from all walks of life. In short, the reformers have to reform their reforms. And the voices of educators have to be a part of any movement to restore the profession's integrity and to re-energize the teachers who labor every day in the classroom.

If not, we have already had a glimpse of a potentially more permanent virtual reality where a child's education happens in isolation at home on a device.

# 24. Game Changers

THE "SLIPPERY SLOPE" IS WHAT WE CALLED THE WEEKS remaining on the school calendar after spring break. Time seemed to accelerate as teachers hastened to cover their curriculum and administrators organized activities in anticipation of the end of the year, a feeling I liken to running in front of an airplane as it taxies on the tarmac for take-off.

On one of these slippery slope days I seized the opportunity, at last, to visit a classroom where a maternity leave substitute was instructing a math class. I had been wanting to see her teach because I was always interested in finding the next great candidate should I suddenly have an empty slot to fill. I also wanted to be able to speak from personal experience if the substitute applied for work in another district and the principal there sought feedback from me. It was the second week of June already and, despite a hectic time of year, I made it up to the third floor and into her classroom.

It was not long before I heard a public address page for an assistant principal. Then came a call for the head custodian. Of course, I wondered what was up. We tried to avoid public address announcements when classes were in session, though at times it was a losing battle, especially if the office staff could not locate a student, substitute or principal. It was inevitable that I would be summoned as well. I was frustrated, once again, not to be able to spend time in a class.

I never could have expected what I found when I returned to the main office. My office had been commandeered by an overflow crowd of serious-looking people, mostly men in uniforms, and I felt the color drain from my face.

What was wrong? What happened?

Our school was undergoing an unannounced observation of an emergency drill by law enforcement and New Jersey Department of Education personnel. Welcome to the principalship of the 21st Century.

My office was standing-room-only with officials from the State Department of Education, New Jersey State Troopers, Essex County Police, Millburn Police, including Detective Ed, and our district superintendent.

To their much appreciated credit, and after having witnessed what few strands left of my original dark brown hair instantly joined the white ones, the tone was one of encouragement and improvement.

We were directed to run a lockdown drill, after members of the assembled militia fanned out around the building. The purpose was to make sure that our students and teachers knew what to do as quickly as possible in the event of a school shooter scenario. The leader of the group intentionally changed the school point person who usually announced a lockdown, and once the announcement was broadcast over the public address system one could hear the sounds of students darting to classrooms, keys jingling, tumblers turning, and then silence.

School shootings have become the nightmare that is real. Schools are supposed to be a sacred place, a sanctuary for children and for learning. Nowhere in the realm of reason could I, or anyone else who prepared for a career as an educator, have anticipated back in the day that our lives could be endangered by working in a school. Now, in addition to fire drills, schools in New Jersey and elsewhere conduct crisis drills. As principal, especially after the Newtown massacre, I began to feel more intensely the weight of responsibility for the lives of all of the adults and children in my building.

The New Jersey Office of Homeland Security and Preparedness released findings that the number of reported school threats doubled during the 2017-2018 school year. In an article that appeared in The *Star-Ledger* (9/13/2018) entitled "Reported Threats Against N.J. Schools Doubled, Keep Being Vigilant, State Tells Students," Olivia Rizzo quoted New Jersey's Attorney General, Gurbir S. Grewal: "We can attribute part of that increase to greater vigilance on the part of students, parents, and the community as a whole." The article also implied something else that has been reported in the press and shared amongst school districts: the copycat syndrome. Reports of school shootings or bomb threats cause an escalation of threats in other schools.

The Pew Research Center posted an article written by Nikki Graff entitled, "A Majority of U.S. Teens Fear a Shooting Could Happen at Their School, and Most Parents Share Their Concern," on April 28, 2018, reporting findings from surveys conducted on students and parents. 87% of students surveyed between the ages of 13 and 17 were either "not too worried," "worried," or "very worried" about the possibility of a school shooting in their own school. Only 13% of respondents said that they were "not at all worried." This study followed the shootings at the Marjory Stoneman Douglas High School in Florida, and the results were released on the anniversary of the carnage at Columbine High School.

We had taken many measures over the years to ramp up security, such as changing the main entrance, hiring a security guard, installing cameras around the building, requiring lanyards with identification cards for staff and visitors, replacing outside glass doors with metal ones, and installing a doorbell with a video monitor. We spelled out all of the crisis response procedures in our faculty handbooks and reviewed them with the staff every year before school opened. We no longer permitted parents or any visitors into the building unless they had an appointment. We set up baskets for forgotten lunches (and instruments, clothing, homework, etc.) in the foyer to permit parents to drop the items off without entering the building.

Preparedness and anxiety about a school shooting can certainly be earmarked as a game changer for principals. It is one that has affected the conscious and subconscious thinking of building administrators. We all like to think it can't happen here, but deep down we know better. Sadly, the expression "getting out alive" acquired a more literal dimension in schools, even for principals, in the dawn of the 21st century.

The second major impact on the work of principals and assistant principals came from the updated New Jersey Anti-Bullying Bill of Rights, which mandated the appointment of an Anti-Bullying Specialist in every school. The new law required schools to deal with all issues surrounding allegations of bullying, even if the bullying did not happen on school premises. No longer just addressing the bully in the school yard, now school administrators found themselves between angry parents of victims and defensive parents of the accused in incidents alleged to have taken place in their own backyards, at bar mitzvahs, on the athletic field, at the park, on the way home from school, or while trick or treating. These investigations consumed considerable time to interview students, document allegations, and gather evidence, and they usually necessitated more than one meeting with all of the students involved as a victim, bully, or witness.

It did not stop there, however. Much of the student-on-student bullying today is carried out via technology (emails, texts) or on social media (Facebook, Instagram, Snapchat, Twitter) through comments that belittle, bash, threaten, or isolate. Some posts urge peers to kill themselves, and here in New Jersey and elsewhere, students have indeed been driven to take their own lives. Administrators now have to work with police to trace the origins of bullying on students' devices. Sometimes other student witnesses share screenshots that may make it easier to pinpoint the culprits, but often these messages and comments are posted using aliases, creating another hurdle in tracking their genesis.

This HIB (Harassment, Intimidation, Bullying) role was foisted on a building administrator who aspired to be an educational leader, but instead investigates, documents, researches, consults with an attorney, renders a verdict, assigns consequences, and communicates with all parties before submitting it to the board for review and possible appeal.

The time it takes to complete these tasks can carve out most of a building administrator's day, especially in middle school where a lack of social skills and immaturity result usually in conflict, but sometimes in the more defined act of bullying. In the eyes of kids, and often of their parents, nowadays every mean word, roll of eyes, glare, or rejection constitutes bullying.

As principal, it was my responsibility to ensure the process. I read all of the reports and signed the formal letters required to be sent to parents of both the alleged perpetrator and victim. Decisions regarding consequences and next steps were within my purview as principal and spelled out in our school policies. I was often involved in conversations with the superintendent and attorneys and parents. At times, more than one administrator was drafted to assist with interviewing all of the students involved in incidents or to handle new allegations if too many incidents occurred at the same time.

Schools have an obligation to provide a supportive, tolerant and safe environment for all children. In order to do that, sometimes an action plan determined the precise time an individual student had to leave a specific place in school and the particular route he or she would travel; occasionally, even a class schedule change was necessary. These measures were intended to provide distance and separation between parties involved in an HIB allegation. In essence these steps were a way that our school enforced what we came to call "restraining orders" as a result of an HIB investigation.

Every single incident was different. Parents did not want their child to have a record of bullying for fear it would derail future applications or admissions endeavors, so they were often aggressive or obstructive, or showed up with an attorney. Hardly anyone was happy with the outcome, not the parents of the perpetrator whose name was on a HIB incident report, and not the parents of the victim who expected a caning in the town square.

This transformation of educational leadership requiring principals to conjure skill sets of police officers, detectives, reporters, attorneys, and judges is another game changer of running schools today.

The third game changer was the result of another New Jersey law, this one having to do with teacher evaluations. From 2011 to 2014 the state rampantly instituted fundamental changes in content and instruction, the level of rigor and format of a new standardized test, and new protocols for measuring teacher effectiveness. It all struck like a meteor.

Naturally, the process of change is accompanied by stress and anxiety, so consider the level of stress when everything shifts at the same time. It is easy to see how this modern reformation has added to, and altered the dynamic of, what it means to lead a school. Being the caretaker, I tried to simplify, streamline, and caution people not to make it harder than it had to be. But it is our lot in life as teachers to want to do everything well.

For the first time, the teaching of curriculum was linked to teacher evaluations through student performance on the new PARCC test. It is also noteworthy that these changes in curriculum and testing, debated in a state political climate that is very different today under new state leadership, continue to be contentious topics in the current news cycle, appearing to be winning at least some support for yet another round of changes.

English/language arts and math teachers had an extra helping of stress heaped onto their plates because these content area teachers were the only ones, in reality, being held accountable for student progress on the PARCC. The average of their students' performance on the test was compared to a range of how all test-takers with the same starting points performed, culminating in an "mSGP score" included on the teacher's summative evaluation.

As we saw earlier, one reaction to the new testing and teacher evaluation process was the disinclination of teachers to want to do anything but teach to the new test. This left little room, in their worried view, to host college student teachers, plan field trips, or engage in memorable interdisciplinary or other time-consuming projects or any frilly or silly activity that humanizes a school day chock full of academic learning.

The new instrument for evaluating teachers in our district was selected by our district administration not for any lofty notion of instructional theory or compatibility with our educational vision, but because it was free of charge. And, unlike other teacher evaluation rubrics approved for sale by the state, the instrument Millburn selected was also free of complications such as a process to certify administrators to use the evaluation tool.

Invoking the Millburn Way, the District Evaluation Advisory Committee set about to revise the rubric in order to clarify, simplify, challenge or dilute the standards.

Our first order of business as an administrative team at the middle school was to interpret the document's domains line by line to engender common understandings among the four building principals about what it meant to earn one of the four performance levels. It was often challenging to use this tool because it attempted to distinguish Highly Effective (the highest rating of 4) from Effective (rating of 3). Our expectation was that teachers were effectively fulfilling the roles of their positions, but to earn a 4 meant that you had to go above and beyond what was already expected of a Millburn teacher. It is difficult to explain, and more challenging to implement. If a teacher demonstrated excellence in any aspect of a domain, then the instructor earned a 3, because that's what was expected. If you aspired to be a 4, the highest score, you had to walk on water.

What made earning the 4 so difficult was often the way it was worded. It seemed to require administrators to see evidence of that which was not always possible or easily accessible or measurable or discernible after 10 ten-minute classroom observations. During a spirited conversation in our district advisory committee, I was asked my interpretation of a level 4 description and I began by saying that I believed that the evaluation designer was looking for... when the teachers' union president, with whom I had a collegial working relationship, interrupted, "I didn't know that you were a mind reader!" And perhaps that sums up the problem: it is difficult for mere mortals to know exactly how to interpret, apply, measure, prove or, at times, even accept someone else's constructs and descriptors when it comes to parsing teacher effectiveness.

The new process pitted a teacher's self-assessment and an administrator's application of the rubric against each other, with the administrator having the final say. And, like I said, teachers strive for perfection.

While some teachers had the mindset that I was the evaluator and it was my responsibility to convey my professional assessment of their performance, there were others who lobbied for 100% or all 4's on their year end evaluation. From my standpoint, the criteria did not easily lend itself to helping teachers to improve, or to master walking on water. It was as though, in the opinions of my administrative colleagues, myself, and teachers, it created its own metric of "perfect" and then made it nearly impossible to achieve or at least to verify. Without a doubt, this teacher assessment tool was designed in a way that a score of 4 would be a rare accomplishment. Some teachers, though, concerned about how their students' test score results might affect their overall evaluation, lobbied for higher ratings on the rubric section in order to counterbalance the unknown. However, the teachers most affected by this evaluation methodology were those who could not abide that they could be viewed as anything less than perfect, even if they were highly competent teachers. And this cycle repeated itself annually.

Unfortunately, this new methodology of teacher evaluation cast a shadow on what I believe was otherwise a climate of cooperation and mutual respect between building administrators and teachers. One administrator even used the word "despise" to describe this new way of evaluating teachers because of the emotion, anger, and frustration it generated for both administrators and staff. It compelled teachers to gather information or provide examples to prove their own efficacy, forcing administrators into the role of judge to determine whether those hard-to-document claims were sufficient to grant the coveted rating of 4.

Three game changers for principals: unimaginable school shootings, heavy-handed anti-bullying protocols, and counterproductive teacher evaluations. These areas cast principals more in the respective roles of protector, prosecutor, and psychic.

What is the impact of all of these game changers on educational leadership? The principalship is a monumental job that comes with a bundle of stressors, so how does the educational leader assimilate these weighty tasks within the panorama of other roles and responsibilities?

I believe that perspective is key.

We controlled what we could with regard to preparedness for a possible school shooting. Steps had been taken to prevent and to minimize an incident. Teachers were oriented to better protect their students by wearing the lanyard with the classroom key, following the procedures, and viewing each drill as a way to practice if, God forbid, the real thing ever happened. Having a plan, and rehearsing it, was a way of having a measure of control in response to a crisis.

Vetting students at risk can only be accomplished by having manageable enrollments in classes and on teams, and reasonable caseloads for guidance counselors and child study team members. In this way, the professionals in the building can come to know and support *all* students and be able to identify, monitor, and service students deemed to be a possible danger to themselves or others. Our school could then apply what they preach at the

Department of Homeland Security about being proactive: "If you see something, say something."

Principals bear the awesome and awful burden of responsibility for the safety and welfare of everyone in the building. In the wake of school shootings across the nation, just about all districts have had to grapple with decisions, including funding, about ways to increase school security. All of the stakeholders - teachers and administrators, students and parents - must be engaged in the formulation of policies and their compliance in order to create a safe school environment. Unexpected proposals, such as arming teachers, have spurred heated exchanges around the nation.

Teaching the difference between bullying and conflict became a way to enlighten the staff and students about what could be credibly reported as HIB. This helped to alleviate the plight of the harried middle school administrator spending all of her days untangling spats between middle school kids. Many of the students in these conflicts were friends or wanted to be.

Sometimes the caveman emerges even in the 21st Century with the unintentionally primitive ways that preadolescent boys try to get the attention of a girl they like with some clumsy attempts at paying extra attention (staring), following around or leaving notes in lockers (stalking), poking fun (harassing), or attempting daredevil stunts for an audience of one (scaring).

The truth of the matter is that our school had always responded quickly to reports of any kind of negative interaction between pupils. We dealt with cases on the full continuum of misunderstandings, unrequited love, conflicts, outright bullying, and physical fighting without all of the newly required paperwork, procedures, documentation, and the official communications, reporting, and recording. We accomplished our goals of making these "teachable moments" with a focus more upon what was to be learned by our students, through the consequences and counseling and partnership with parents appropriate for middle level learners, without all of the bureaucracy and hysteria about the culminating official written record.

With regard to teacher evaluations, even the state broadly defined teacher effectiveness as scoring a 2.65 or better out of a possible perfect score of 4.0. Our teachers were excellent teachers, and scores of less than 4 did not change that fact. The reality is that this method of rating teachers was a better match for industry assembly line workers, not teachers. In this expanding business model as applied to education, one might be able to standardize the curriculum and the test, but it is far from possible to standardize the learners, their abilities, backgrounds and challenges, or the host of ways that teachers relate knowledge, connect with young people, or create meaning. Also, educators teach across the K-12 continuum in a multitude of specialties, and yet one standardized form is supposed to capture the unique work they all do.

Filling in the level of effectiveness on 60 rows of the molecular matter of teaching and instruction allows the district and state to collect evaluative data. This data and documentation, combined with self-reported performance scores from Student Growth Objectives and a PARCC-generated mSGP score, leads to a teacher's performance over a year spent with a hundred students, or sometimes hundreds of students, reduced to a number with a decimal.

From what I have read, it does not seem like all this hoopla about teacher evaluations has changed the number of teachers in New Jersey who make the grade as "effective" teachers. And if that is the case, why not empower teachers and administrators to design evaluation formats that, while rigorous, represent each district's unique population and reflect the diversity of staff positions in a template that offers individuals useful professional feedback?

In my opinion, Millburn had a better evaluation format prior to the state's mandate that districts had to select from the state's menu of options. Our former rubric did not distill a performance criterion into a continuum; rather, a teacher was assessed on a continuum of performance for each criterion. This approach, more generic and therefore applicable in most classroom settings, also offered greater clarity about teacher efficacy and could be supplemented by additional details and commentary. This protocol supplied feedback, promoted learning, offered recommendations, and validated all of the personal and professional attributes and contributions that did not seem to fit, or even matter, in a one-size-is-supposed-to-fit-all evaluation process that culminated in a grade point average.

More than ever, schools are in need of true leaders. The role of principal comes with increased demands and expanding responsibilities that require different skill sets and nerves of steel. Schools, and the people who staff them, are constantly subjected to what is happening in the real time real world.

Perspective is a critical attribute for principals to hone as they integrate new roles they will assume and changes they will lead. Parents, politicians, state departments of education, the legislature, test makers and book publishers - the change makers - are responsible for many of the reforms that have impacted teaching and learning, testing and technology, and leading a school over the last several years. The perspective of the "principal teacher" helps everyone to see the bigger picture. It finds the connections to vision, goals, and practicalities and attaches meaning and value. Perspective helps to guide reform and reassure those who implement change. Perspective also preserves and protects what we do not want to lose.

# 25. Climate Change

YOU HAVE TO HAVE A TOUGH SKIN IN ANY LEADERSHIP POSI-tion. My journey as a principal included many obstacles to overcome along the way, but even in times of struggle or sadness I experienced a feeling of rising up again, thanks to the synergy of working with supportive, like-minded people. I perceived that I was a part of something bigger than myself and meaningful, and the work I did every day for my building, our teachers and students, fed my soul.

Over the years people have said that I would know when it was time for a change. About four years before I retired, I sensed that time approaching. It became obvious to me in September 2016, although I had originally intended to stay for at least two more years, that a change for me, and for my school, was more imminent than even I had expected.

After sixteen years at the helm I had this epiphany that I had accom-plished what I was called to do, namely lead my school through a period of tremendous growth and expansion, promote a true middle school culture, and establish a stable, supportive, and inclusive working environment after some years of revolving leadership. It seemed to me that time was shifting again, after a period of radical changes in society, schools and children, simultaneously innovative and worrisome.

Let me also say that there were other reasons to move on, both profes-sional and personal. I experienced another realization as well: the Millburn that hired me was not the Millburn from which I retired.

After so much time in one place, it might sound naive to have expected otherwise. The overhaul of curriculum content and skills, pedagogy, assess-ments, and teacher evaluations affected every school in every district. In recent years in our district there were so many things that we had to do, and other goals that we wanted to work toward, but with less time and fewer opportunities for thoughtful conversations about what it all meant for teachers, learners, leaders, and the systemic continuum of instruction.

And maybe the following is true of other school systems as well, but there was a shift within this community that felt like the board and central office were running the district more like a business. I was not alone in this assessment as most of my administrative colleagues and the many teachers who selflessly volunteered for committee work shared the same perception. The climate of the district was, internally, less people-friendly, with a widening disconnect between district administrators and the buildings. It was a challenge to communicate with, or relate to, central office personnel, especially those who never served in the role of principal or who did not understand the working dynamics of a school building, the urgency of a situation, or the timeliness of a response that are part and parcel of running a school. Schools became satellites orbiting around a more isolated central office.

Dr. Richard Brodow, the aforementioned superintendent prior to 2010, had been a former principal and was an energetic "people person." For eight years he frequented our schools and came to know just about all the members of the staff by name. He was approachable and could relate to what principals had to deal with. His assistant superintendent, Maryann Doyle, was well known for engaging teachers and administrators in meaningful dialogue and for promoting thoughtful curriculum revisions. Maryann would arrange to have lunch with me a couple of times a year where the world was locked out for an hour so that we could have a deeper conversation about our work. She was personally interested in knowing how I was doing, and I always came away with a new perspective because of her insights. Both of these district leaders used their intellect, experience, and warmth to connect with, mentor, and encourage the district's educators, including supervisors and principals.

During this era, building principals and district supervisors played a more prominent and vital role in the district. The Board of Education's Program Committee invited individual principals to participate in at least one meeting every year for a check-in conversation about our respective schools, and at other times for issues, questions, concerns or projects that required our attention. We were also consulted about formulating or updating policies. Board members knew who we were and addressed us by our first names. We felt both included and valued for our contributions, expertise, and commitment.

The winds of change swept across the political-educational landscape in Millburn in the latter part of the first decade of the new century, ushering in a more hierarchical era concerning how policy evolved and decisions were made. Principals and the few remaining district supervisors no longer spoke with board members and often only learned about new policies or revisions after they were approved and forwarded in an email by a secretary, usually with nary a word about the substance, the change, the rationale, the implementation or any implications.

As one teacher, someone in particular who had been very involved in many aspects of school life, said to me, "It feels like we have become a top down place," echoing more of that traditional command-control-comply style.

It was at times downright painful at our district leadership team meetings to listen to the dialogue that followed any proposal for change from district administrators regarding school operations. Within minutes, principals flooded the airwaves with so many practical questions and concerns that the idea was inevitably tabled for more research or pondering. It might have been perceived as resistance by school administrators, but for me it seemed more like gaps in understanding school building realities. Communication and implementation challenges could have been preempted if principals were included early on in the formation phase of a shift in procedure or a new initiative.

Prior to 2010, the Board of Education had maintained a Board-Staff Committee, a direct channel of communication between board members and district teachers and administrators on topics of concern that encompassed working conditions, facilities, and programs. But now all formal and informal communication between board members and school personnel had come to a screeching halt.

After a hiatus of more than almost five years, Board-Staff was finally reconvened a year prior to my retirement so that teachers could offer a counterpoint to the growing calls by parents and board members to eliminate qualifying exams for high school AP coursework. It appeared that the board, and our second new superintendent in that same time frame, might now allow Board-Staff meetings to continue, at least on an as-needed basis. There was no other official avenue for district personnel to converse with board members, leaving district staff as the only group denied access. Parents had an open invitation to speak publicly at any board meeting, and even students conversed directly with board members in their Student Liaison Committee meetings.

These were steps backwards from the more inclusive leadership model already in place. In a people-centered profession like ours, collaboration, trust, and appreciation are drivers of the culture, whether in a single building or in a district as a whole.

Many of the professionals within the district now saw procedures relating to instruction, professional development, teacher evaluation, and especially curriculum writing as more of an assembly-line driven process to meet compliance requirements - with drastically reduced compensation for which some teachers and even supervisors refused to participate - than a meaningful and authentic exercise of their professional practice. I was not the only one who felt the seismic shift from the importance of people, substance and relationships to an emphasis on efficiencies, technology, data, and optics.

No, this was not the Millburn I knew.

I have heard teachers talk about the lost joy of teaching, a pervasive sentiment around the state, too. It is no wonder why. Requirements, regulations, documentation and deadlines infiltrated everything teachers did. All of this on top of trying to conjure creative ways to present lessons that promoted higher level thinking for preadolescents with varying abilities, fleeting attention spans, and raging hormones.

The demoralizing effect on district employees was compounded by shifts inside and outside of the school system, all happening at the same time. On top of the changes experienced within the culture of the district and the daily hurdles of teaching were the state-imposed payroll deductions for health care premiums and higher pension contributions. The lack of will on the part of the board to provide a timely and fair compensation offer and contract disturbed and distracted teachers who had an important job to do.

Because just about everybody has attended school, some people think teaching children looks easy. Individuals and entities outside of education criticize, demonize, and call for change without a fundamental understanding of the everyday work of teachers, which can vary by school, community, and region. Even individuals like me who aspired to the profession experienced an on-the-job learning curve in discovering the complexities and challenges of teaching.

In the past decade the job of a teacher has changed drastically. It was more like a hostile takeover than a gradual evolution of content and practice, though. All schools will continue to need great teachers, and it would behoove district leaders to consider how schools can lighten the teacher load, support their efforts, include their ideas and expertise, and validate and appreciate teacher commitment to the diverse learners of the community, if they want to attract and keep good teachers.

Standardized testing has always been a component of the school year, but the adoption of PARCC by the State of New Jersey plunked principals into the political crosshairs of opposition by local communities. Parents around New Jersey did not want the federal government to dictate what should be taught and assessed in New Jersey public schools. Hordes of parents, in Millburn and elsewhere, refused to allow their children to take the test. Millburn parents were requested by the district administration to come to the main office of their children's schools to sign an official letter of refusal. They often wanted to be heard, or to debate the merits of the PARCC, but in the end my job was to administer the assessment.

Some parents openly hinted that I, too, should protest the test. One even suggested in writing that I myself might be a part of a "communist common core conspiracy."

To say that parents in affluent and educated suburbs like Millburn have always been involved is an understatement. These are the people who inspired terms like "bulldozer parents." Unfortunately, public and private discourse has been characterized by less civility in recent years. Parallel to the experience of educators in New Jersey and in many other places in our nation, teachers and administrators have become punching bags and scapegoats.

We called it "adult mean." It surfaced in day-to-day scenarios, especially when parents attempted to control conditions, consequences, or outcomes for their child. Deadlines, such as for yearbook order forms or field trip permission slips, despite mailings and multiple reminders, became a trigger for nastiness. Lack of compliance with vaccination requirements, even if long overdue, led to being called "heartless" for having to exclude children from school. A dress code violation precipitated accusatory career-ending questions like, "Why are you looking at my daughter?" Though parents had ample time to submit a "Not Request," an opportunity for a younger sibling to avoid a teacher who taught an older child, their procrastination would result in deflecting responsibility back on me, as in "You mean to tell me that you are going to punish my child for her parent's negligence?" In schools today, student and parent accountability and natural consequences are old-fashioned notions.

I have also had considerable interactions with parents on the topics of teacher assignment, level placement and HIB investigations or incidents that have raised my alarm about their angry reactions, character attacks, threats (including lawsuits), physical intimidation, and use of profanity. Parents dropping "f-bombs" in an exchange about a child with his or her entire team of teachers added to these new and toxic norms. Just a few years ago even our board of education adopted a policy on civility at board meetings, further evidence of climate change in the educational environment.

I know I speak for countless other administrators, teachers, nurses, child study team members and especially coaches who have also experienced more aggressive parent interactions. While this does not describe the majority of parents, my experience, as well as that of my colleagues, is that it is enough to be of concern and growing.

I have been a speaker at public meetings where conversations turned into demands and the rhetoric turned hostile. Even though the negative people were few, they had a louder presence, enabled by others who remained quiet because they did not want to enter into a public fray. When the meetings were over, however, I received calls or emails from parents who said, "After what happened at the meeting this morning I just had to call you to say that not everybody feels that way" or "I was so embarrassed for the way some people spoke to you."

It is impossible to please everyone. And often parents who publicly demanded that immediate changes be made had no clue about how a school, especially an overcrowded building like ours, was scheduled and staffed. They waved away the explanations or rationale because, in the end, they just wanted what they wanted. During my last two years there were parents who either criticized or demanded changes be made at the middle school before their child even arrived for sixth grade and before they understood the program, procedures or realities. Their angst dissipated once they learned more about our school; indeed, the feedback over the years has been that the overwhelming majority of our sixth graders happily crossed over the abyss and actually liked middle school.

Homework has been a volatile topic in Millburn, and elsewhere, but the only ones who have spoken of it publicly, including petition signers, complained about too much homework and teachers not posting the assignment or the necessary materials in a timely manner. The parents who wrote to me privately, however, said the reason they moved to Millburn was so their children would be challenged and it is not too much homework if kids are placed correctly. And they contended that their kids still had time to ride horses, practice piano, and participate in after-school activities, enrichment programs and competitions.

For more than a decade the topic of a too-short lunch time has haunted our building like the auditorium ghost. I explained that we incorporated a request for an auxiliary lunchroom in the 2005 referendum, but parents voted it down and I had no other options. One parent retorted that that was "ancient history" and accused me of being a "wall" with regard to other options such as block scheduling that would allow more time for eating. I explained that block scheduling comes with other programming trade-offs, but that they - the community of parents - would have to make that decision. Over the years, when questions arose about a possible need for modifying our schedule or altering our program of instruction, my guiding principle was always that we had to make decisions that continually opened doors for our students, providing every pupil access to all of the curricular, instructional support, and extracurricular offerings. It just did not make sense to me to move to a model that would deprive our diverse learners of opportunities already in their wheelhouse.

Parents questioned why we did not do things a certain way in school because it made sense to them - and maybe it even made sense to us - but there were often complex puzzle pieces, more appropriately called "constraints," that had to fit together including time, personnel, budget, space and safety, necessitating the intervention of powers greater than the principal.

They were often unaware of the issues with which schools had to contend. For example, some parents lobbied for recess at the middle school. They suggested that we convert lunch time spent in the auditorium into what parents called "unstructured free time." Preferably outdoors. For two hundred preadolescents at a time. Unstructured time in middle school is almost as scary as a health epidemic. It is the breeding ground of impulsive behavior that often results in injury, negative interactions and allegations of bullying. As a school we were already increasingly dealing with "restraining orders" for specific pupils to be separated in the auditorium, cafeteria, locker rooms and gyms as a result of past incidents of bullying or as a preventative measure. It was our responsibility, indeed liability, to keep a growing number of students apart and to limit the occasions that could ferment inappropriate interactions.

Today's parents often use technology as a venue to vent their grievances, debate issues, further their personal agenda, or formally present demands. It is a different world, one that fractures the community and the school system and promotes an "us versus them" mentality. There seems to be less inclination, maybe less capacity, as we all can see on the national political level, to have actual conversations. Parents sometimes serve up their vitriol, opinions, and judgmental comments on ratings websites for schools and educators, email servers, and blogs. An event, course, school, or entire career of a teacher or administrator can be summed up in an anonymously opined negative one-liner.

The 21st Century became an era in which those of us who worked in the field of education felt as though we were under constant attack. Indeed, I know I was not the only administrator who received phone calls in the evenings or on weekends at home thanks to parents being able to look up on the internet what used to be confidential contact information for school personnel. Like the parent who tried to talk to me while I was having dinner with my family in a restaurant, this was crossing the line big time.

The tone of a district is set by the superintendent whose ability to lead is hampered by an ineligibility for tenure protection. Parents should not be running a school district, but they are in fact doing so if the board of education, composed of parents, evaluates the performance of the superintendent and makes determinations regarding the superintendent's contract. People who are not certified in education and who have personal agendas are exercising powerful controls in what I consider to be a conflict of interest regarding district decisions and practices, for example, extracurricular activities, AP qualifying exams, scheduling, and the placement process.

The stresses generated by the "game changers" and the cultural decline of the district undeniably influenced my decision to move on as I saw how these debilitating developments impacted the health of administrative colleagues in my district and elsewhere. And the Millburn milieu seemed so unfamiliar that it felt like I was working in a different place.

During the years that passed since I had become an administrator, a different generation of kids and parents enrolled, among them more families just passing through the school system hoping to get on the "right track" to a top tier college. It was obvious that they did not know me, or the ways I was able to shepherd our school through some difficult times, or regard me in the same way as a generation of families whose grown children, former students of mine, returned to Millburn to make a home for themselves and whose children I referred to as my "grandstudents."

With this new clientele and lack of genuine connection to district governance, there no longer existed a regard for educators who spent much, or most, of their working life in one school or district, accruing the institutional history and wisdom that comes with experience and longevity. At the same time, central office became a revolving door for key positions, for various reasons, disrupting the continuity, stability, and synergy of the district. It was like starting over, again and again.

It was more apparent than ever that it was time for a new generation of leadership. Every era has its own peculiar set of new realities and challenges, and perhaps this new one even more so.

I don't belong here.

For me, leadership was personal. I took myself with me on this journey. If it happened in my school, to my school, or for my school, then it happened to me. The story of my school and me, hopefully, highlighted our outstanding middle level programs and staff while also exposing the challenges and stresses that came with the territory and the times. My time as principal was the realization of both my call to collaborative leadership and my vision for what our middle school could be. I take pride in what we all created together.

I met so many wonderful people, parents, students, teachers, and administrative colleagues who helped me and provided opportunities for fulfillment and friendship over the span of three decades. I learned so much and loved going to work, until I didn't anymore.

I could not have asked for a better cohort of professionals who were committed to kids and always wanted to do everything as well as it could be done, and then some. The dwindling time I could spend in classrooms or with students was the best part of my day, and I am forever indebted to teachers for their passion for their subject and love for middle schoolers; indeed, they were the reason our school had an excellent reputation.

I have saved every heartfelt note that a student, teacher or parent ever sent to me. I am grateful to the Millburn district for the opportunity to have played a leadership role in its evolution and expansion. Without a doubt, these experiences fueled this street urchin's own transformation and growth in a place I could only have dreamed of working, and in a role I thought I never wanted, so that I could learn my lessons and hopefully teach a few along the way, too.